THE BATTLE FOR BREEZY POINT

THE BATTLE FOR BREEZY POINT

Sebastian Danese

The Battle for Breezy Point
Copyright © 2014 by Sebastian Danese

All rights reserved. This book or any portion thereof may not be reproduced or used in any manner whatsoever without the express written permission of the author except for the use of brief quotations in a book review or scholarly journal.

First Printing: 2014

ISBN: 978-1-304-90321-1

Printed in the United States of America

Published in association with Tarrif.net

FOR THE VOLUNTEERS

None of the accomplishments within this work would have been possible without your support. If any words of gratitude or admiration are conveyed as a result of the telling of this story, they are ours to share equally.

God bless you all.

CONTENTS

PROLOGUE	MY HOME TOWN	1
CHAPTER 1	A LAST FIRST DATE	3
CHAPTER 2	STORM WARNINGS	9
CHAPTER 3	PREPARATIONS	11
CHAPTER 4	LANDFALL	17
CHAPTER 5	HELL BOUND	59
CHAPTER 6	AFTERMATH	79
CHAPTER 7	CAMP DUFF	91
CHAPTER 8	ALL SAINTS	103
CHAPTER 9	THE RECOVERY BEGINS	113
CHAPTER 10	REUNION	123
CHAPTER 11	OPERATION PORT-A-POTTY	129
CHAPTER 12	ESCAPE	139
CHAPTER 13	THE FUEL CRISIS	145
CHAPTER 14	NOR'EASTER	149
CHAPTER 15	SEMPER FIDELIS	155
CHAPTER 16	BUILDING MOMENTUM	169
CHAPTER 17	REBUILDING BREEZY POINT	179
CHAPTER 18	BREAKING POINTS	191
CHAPTER 19	CHANGING OF THE GUARD	199
CHAPTER 20	THANKSGIVING	207
CHAPTER 21	TURNING POINTS	215
CHAPTER 22	FRIENDS FROM AFAR	225
CHAPTER 23	NOLA TIL YA DIE	231
CHAPTER 24	STANDING DOWN	245
CHAPTER 25	A NIGHT AT THE GARDEN	249
EPILOGUE	NO HOLLYWOOD ENDING	253

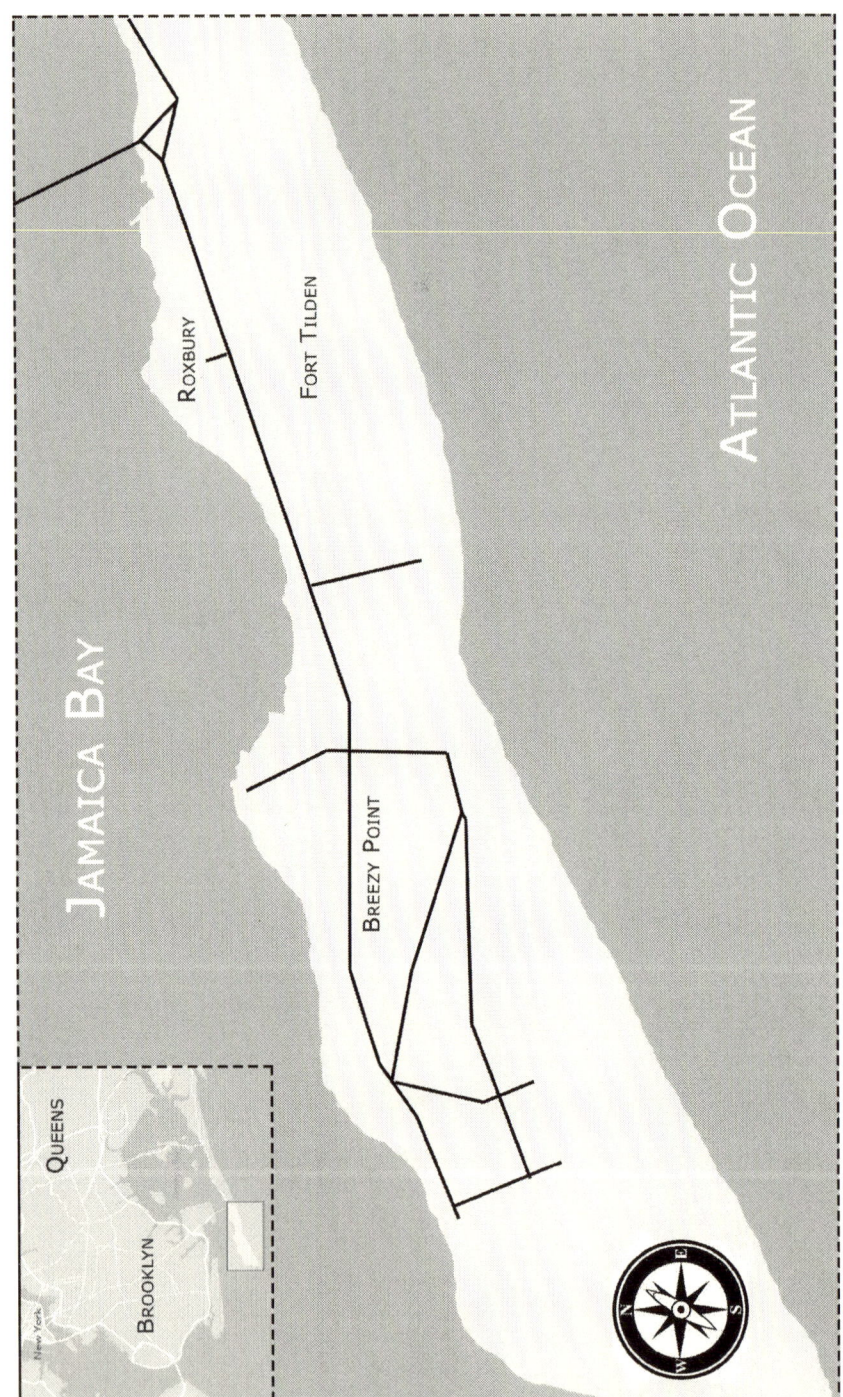

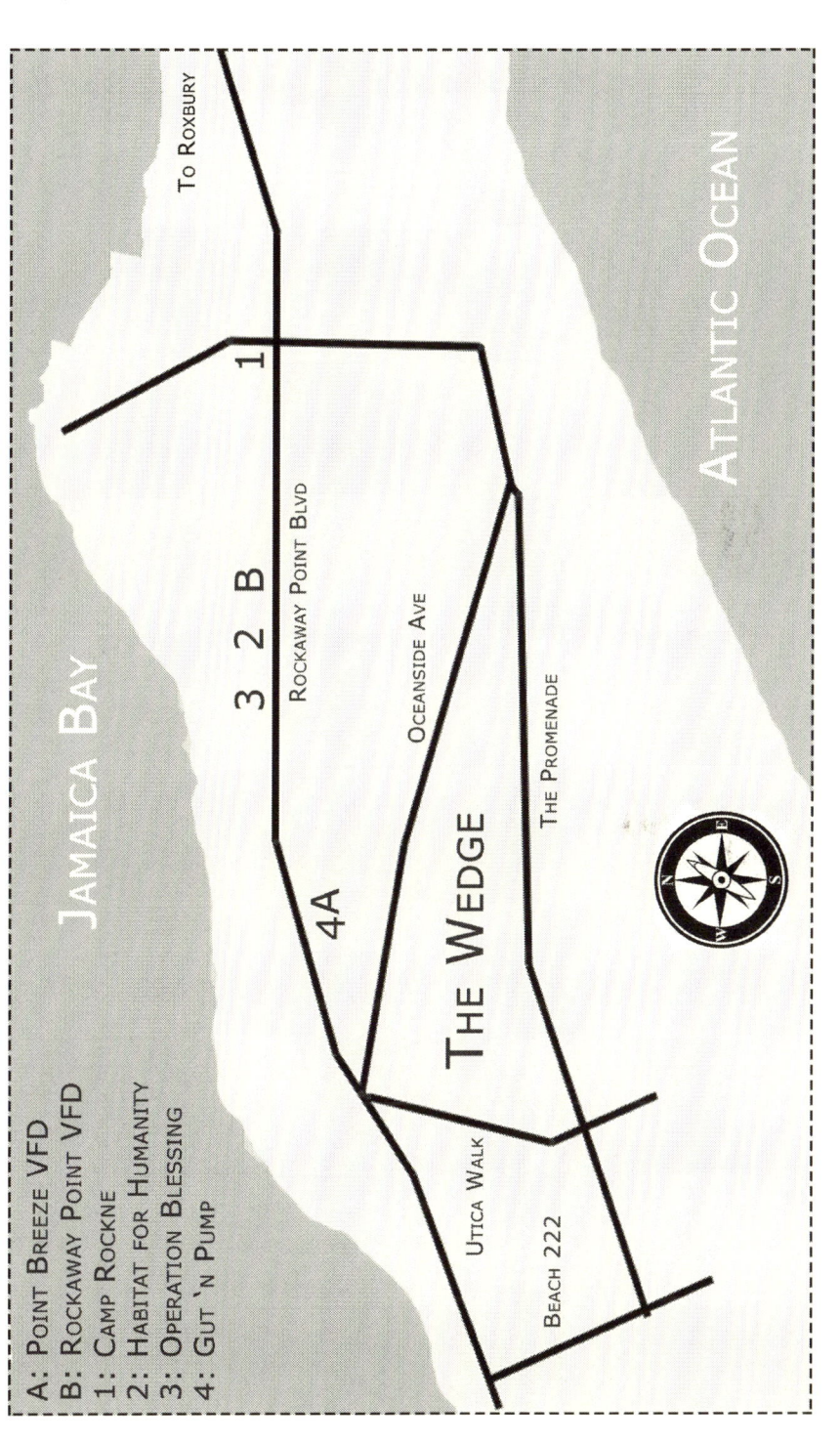

PREFACE

This work is by no means intended to be a complete portrayal of the period immediately before, during, and after Hurricane Sandy in Breezy Point and the Rockaways in New York City. My intention is to provide an accurate firsthand account within a scope that occasionally extends beyond my own personal observations. Nothing has been embellished for the sake of entertainment. Names have been changed upon request or when it was deemed prudent, but the contributions of those individuals remain unaltered. During the preparations for this book I heard many stories worth retelling which did not make the final version because of time and editing considerations. They remain in my records for possible future projects.

After the storm, as the recovery progressed, I assumed an increasing amount of responsibility which exposed me to the highest levels of local decision making, and I am eternally grateful to the powers that be for allowing me such exposure. Fortunately I had the foresight to save every email, text message, voicemail, picture, and phone call received during this time which formed the nucleus around which this story developed. Through Facebook and other social media I was able to recreate a very accurate timeline of events and remain in contact with the volunteers and organizers who rushed to our aid during our time of need. A year of research and over one hundred of hours of interviews were conducted in order to provide the most genuine depiction of events. That being said, I acknowledge the fallibility of any work no matter how thoroughly prepared. I take full responsibility and apologize for any errors therein.

In conclusion, though some portions of the following story may sound fantastic, everything you're about to read—including the miracles, the risks, and the relationships—is absolutely true

FOREWORD

In the final hours before the full force of Hurricane Sandy hit our shorefront community, my staff and I worked tirelessly to prepare for the uncertainty which lay ahead. My responsibilities carried me to every neighborhood in southern Queens, including Rockaway. My final visit, on October 29th at about 4:00P.M., before heading to my own home, was to visit my good friend Chief Marty Ingram at the Point Breeze Volunteer Fire Department. Sleeping bags and air mattresses were spread throughout the firehouse. Dozens of weary volunteers were back from the front lines for a momentary respite before heading out again.

After a short conversation and reassuring words to the many firefighters and civilians seeking shelter from the storm, I left the firehouse and travelled home. While driving along Beach Channel Drive, I looked out my window at Jamaica Bay and watched in horror as the water was already tipping over the seawall. In my heart, I knew what was about to take place would exceed our worst fears, and prayed for the safety of the volunteers and families in harm's way.

The rising sun on the morning after Sandy did not bring much comfort. Dawn's early light revealed the destruction of our entire community. We were shocked by the unimaginable destruction and chaos all around us. Through the kindness of strangers and neighbors helping neighbors we survived. In what seemed like a tunnel with no end in sight, days turned into weeks, then months, and with each passing moment we recognized the slow progress of our recovery.

Sandy blew in as an inexorable force of destruction the likes of which we had never experienced before, but what followed in Breezy Point and Rockaway was even more unexpected. We came together as a community, gaining strength through unity that no storm can wash away. With each passing day, as we continue our journey of recovery, our hearts mourn the many reminders of the mass destruction Hurricane Sandy inflicted upon us: the destroyed boardwalk, hundreds of missing homes, neighbors and friends who have not returned, and stench of drying mold.

As a resident of Breezy Point, a New York City police officer, and a volunteer firefighter in the Point Breeze Volunteer Fire Department, Sebastian Danese's experiences during the storm offer a unique insight on the challenges our community faced in the aftermath of Sandy. He and his fellow volunteers have served as a beacon of hope and strength for so many families drowning in grief. Their fearless dedication to our community before, during, and especially after the storm is truly remarkable.

This narrative will serve as a symbol of our resilience and testament to our faith as we build back our homes, community, and lives. What you're about to read is a true story of Hurricane Sandy—one which deserves to be told and forever remembered.

Assemblyman Phil Goldfeder

23rd District, Breezy Point

ACKNOWLEDGMENTS

I first considered writing a book about the events of Hurricane Sandy and the recovery which followed in Breezy Point when the grass roots volunteer organizations Camp Rockne and Operation Gut 'n Pump ended in December of 2012. What we, as a collective effort, accomplished was staggering. The volunteer firefighters in Breezy Point stayed on duty throughout the worst hurricane to hit our region in decades, rescued our neighbors from the flood, and fought one of the largest residential fires in New York City history. Despite a growing physical and psychological cost, the community held together. With the help of thousands of volunteers we began to rebuild our neighborhood—a process that is still ongoing and will be for years to come.

I would like to thank the dozens of people who took the time to speak with me after the storm, especially: Kevin Adams, Phil Pillet, Erin Concoran-Daly, Jason Fernald, Karen Donnelly, Troy Murray, David Shouse, Ann J. Lewis, Chris Williams, Becky Gray, Jeff Winn, Kathleen McCall, Robert Fogarty, Dana Daniels, William West, Nancy Carbone, Nick Pappas, Tim O'Brien Sr., Tim O'Brien Jr., Meredith Erickson, Michael Schramm, Christine & John Paolillo, and especially Marty Ingram as well as all the other volunteers who shared their experiences with me. A special thanks to the members of the FDNY and NYPD who gave invaluable insight from their perspective the night of Hurricane Sandy in Breezy Point.

Writing is no easy task. If it weren't for a handful of editors who took the time to correct my grammar and spelling mistakes I probably would be too embarrassed to put this work into print. The following people spent far too much of their own personal time listening to me obsess over fonts, layout, and paragraph spacing: Becky Gray, Kathleen McCall, Michelle Higgins, and Gary Urbanowicz. Without them, this book might as well have been printed in crayon.

ONLINE

More pictures and information concerning this book, Hurricane Sandy, the Rockaway and Breezy Point community and the people and organizations mentioned herein are available online.

www.battleforbreezypoint.com

THE BATTLE FOR BREEZY POINT

PROLOGUE

MY HOME TOWN

Thursday, April 11, 2013

Denise Neibel's voice echoed throughout my house from the answering machine in the living room, "Good morning Breezy Point, Rockaway Point, and Roxbury. This is an Alert Now message from the Breezy Point Co-op…"

I was too enthralled by the scene in front of me to pick up the phone. Heavy construction machinery was busy at the end of Essex Walk tearing down the wrecked houses with red tags in the windows. The ground shook as foundations were ripped from the sand by giant mechanical claws. Their roofs were already removed and the interiors gutted of anything which would pose a danger to the demolition. We're a small block located on the eastern end of a triangle of homes known locally as 'the Wedge'. One hundred yards to the west of my front porch are the charred remains of 126 homes burned down to their foundations. My girlfriend stood next to me, holding my hand while we watched in morbid fascination as the machines tore apart six of the eighteen houses on our block.

I thought to myself, "How did we get to this point?"

And then I remembered…

CHAPTER 1

A LAST FIRST DATE

Saturday, October 13, 2012

I love my job. When I was 29 years old I decided to join the NYPD like my father, uncles, brother, friends, and neighbors before me. It can be hard at times, but I finally found a job I'm passionate about for all the right reasons. After graduating the Academy and a brief stint in Operation Impact, I was sent to the 63rd Precinct which covers Marine Park and Mill Basin. I can't complain about my ten minute commute across the Marine Parkway Bridge, which connects Brooklyn to the Rockaways and Breezy Point. Day tours are a special treat for police officers like me who normally work the late shift. I have steady Sundays and Mondays off so ending the week early Saturday evening is the closest I could get to a three day weekend without using a vacation day. It doesn't happen very often and I planned on making the best of it.

I told her I would pick her up around seven o'clock. We met the month before, on my birthday, but thanks to my fat fingers, the number she gave me at the end of the night didn't match the one I entered into my iPhone. It was she who found me on Facebook weeks later and chided me for not calling, but after a little charm on my part she was gracious enough to give me another chance.

After getting myself ready, I walked down the sidewalk to my truck parked in the sand near the end of my block. Breezy Point is made up primarily of bungalows linked together by sidewalks and sand alleys. Towards the western edge of the neighborhood are some streets, but for the most part the residents must park in lots located throughout the property and walk to their homes. During the off-season we are allowed to park our vehicles on the beach area near our homes, which is as close to a driveway as I could hope for.

There was a chill in the air. As summer gave way to fall, most of my neighbors went back to wherever they lived during the rest of the year. Aside from myself and a few others, the rest of our block was vacant houses, though I didn't mind the peace and quiet the cold weather brings to our community. I grew up spending my summers here, living in a bungalow from late June to early September. My parents bought that house after they were married and lived there all year round before we moved to Staten Island when I was still a child. I had only moved back to Breezy Point a few years ago; the bungalow giving way to a proper house. I have a lot of great memories of Breezy Point, and feel a strong connection to this place and its history.

Sometime in the early 1900's, the first residents started building homes along the beach on the western end of the Rockaway Peninsula separating Jamaica Bay to the north and the Atlantic Ocean to the south. Many were servicemen from nearby Floyd Bennett Field and Fort Tilden looking for a place to get away. During the 1960's, the residents combined their money and founded the Breezy Point Cooperative, or "Co-op" as we refer to it, which purchased 500 acres of land from the Atlantic Improvement State Corporation. Originally intended as a summertime beach community, today more than 4000 residents live in Breezy Point year round, myself included. Those of us of Irish descent make up 60% of the population, with another 38% from other western European countries. For the most part, we're a generational, family-orientated, blue collar community.

Because of our unique firefighting needs, three of the ten volunteer firehouses in New York City are located in Breezy Point. Working in conjunction with the Fire Department, City of New York (FDNY) the volunteers exist to provide firefighting coverage in the beach areas where most FDNY apparatus cannot get to. All of our fire trucks and ambulances are four-wheel-drive (4WD) in order to operate on the sand, and are custom built to specific dimensions so they can traverse the tight corners and narrow alleys throughout the community. They are lighter, more compact, and more maneuverable than the City's larger engine and ladder apparatus which must stay on paved roads.

The job of volunteer firefighters in Breezy Point is to make first contact and extinguish or contain any fires until the FDNY arrives. Combined, the three firehouses operate three ambulances, five trucks, and three 4WD beach rescue trucks. Active membership in all three firehouses numbers approximately one hundred. These firefighters are unpaid volunteers, although many are professional police officers, firefighters, paramedics, and other first responders for New York City. Hundreds of jobs are handled annually. The summer is the busiest time of year, but with an increasing number of residents living in the community full time, each off-season is more active than the last.

The Roxbury Volunteer Fire Department is the first firehouse along Rockaway Point Boulevard when traveling to Breezy Point. This station primarily serves the Roxbury community with one fire engine (Engine 202) and an ambulance (Roxbury Rescue). The Rockaway Point Volunteer Fire Department is between the Roxbury and Point Breeze firehouses along the main road across from St. Thomas Moore Catholic Church. One fast- attack ladder truck (Ladder 4), one fire engine (Engine 5), and two ambulances (Rescue 1 & 2) are complimented by a water rescue squad complete with motorboats and dry suits. The Point Breeze Volunteer Fire Department is the last firehouse, inset from the main road across from Kennedy's restaurant. Two fire trucks (Engine 7 & Ladder 8) operate from this station with no ambulance service, although many of the members are emergency medical technicians (EMTs).

The closest FDNY firehouse to Breezy Point is Engine 329, adjacent to Fort Tilden at the base of the Queens side of the Marine Park Bridge. A heavily modified 2007 Ford F-550, known as an All Terrain Response Vehicle (ATRV), is paired with Engine 329 for support. The ATRV has no rig or booster pump and is used to reduce the amount of manpower needed to run hundreds of feet of hose from the engine to the fire. Standard procedure calls for the engine to hook up to a hydrant along the road and use the ATRV to stretch a 3.5" supply line wherever needed. From there, several 2.5" hoses can attach to the ATRV to put water on the fire.

* * *

My truck bounced as I drove westward along the sand track running parallel to the oceanfront promenade and then onto the streets. One road, Rockaway Point Boulevard, bisects the entire Co-op and connects Breezy Point to the rest of the city. Along this route I passed the Point Breeze Volunteer Fire Department of which I was a member, although not a very active one back in those days. A mile to my left I pulled into our market area which includes a bar, the Co-op offices, a grocery store, hardware store, liquor store, restaurant, and bank.

After a quick trip to the ATM, I made my way back along Rockaway Point Boulevard towards Roxbury. While still a part of the Breezy Point Co-op, the Roxbury community is geographically separated from us by a mile of scrub brush and dunes. The residents of Roxbury also have their own grocery store, restaurant, church, and the Roxbury Volunteer Fire Department. Though we're all part of the same neighborhood, I could count on one hand the number of times I had actually been in Roxbury.

I parked my truck in the lot behind her house and went to her door. She's a Rockaway girl who had just bought her home in Roxbury a few months prior. Despite my inauspicious performance to this point I was determined to make up for it with a fun night of dinner and drinks at a local favorite, the Harbor Light Pub. We had a fantastic evening. When it came time to say goodnight I was already certain I'd like to see her again and was confident she felt the same. I returned to my house and found a text message waiting for me.

"I had a great time tonight," she wrote. "Hope to see you again soon!"

The connection which developed between us happened swiftly and unexpectedly. Neither of us was waiting for lightning to strike. I believe God puts people in our lives for a reason, and although we didn't know it at the time, the deep emotional bond which was forming between us would play a major role in surviving the tribulations and hardships of Hurricane Sandy. We would be there for each other, love each other, and support each other in ways most new couples usually do not have to. Although this isn't a love story, I couldn't imagine telling this story without including our relationship. Without her by my side, taking care of me when I was too busy to take care of myself, I don't believe I would have been able to endure the things I did.

"Me too," I replied. Metaphorical walls were crumbling, and I couldn't be happier.

CHAPTER 2

STORM WARNINGS

Tuesday, October 23, 2012

God bless my parents. I can always count on my mom and dad calling about whatever random thing is going on in the world and why I need to know about it. Don't get me wrong, they're the best parents a guy could ask for, and I'm usually too busy to pick up the phone otherwise. News and weather headlines are some of our common topics of conversation, and since moving to Florida they have become hurricane savvy. It was under this guise that I first learned about a storm named Sandy.

"John?" My parents call me John. It's a long story.

"What's up?"

"I'm just checking in. I wanted to see how you're doing. How's Mister Jiggs?" asked my dad, always concerned about my sister Marie's 28 pound behemoth of a cat. She got him while attending college from a townie when he was just a kitten. Seven years later, Jiggs is an oversized mass of shiny black fur with a belly that sways back and forth beneath him as he walks. Somehow I get stuck taking care of him from time to time.

"He's fine. Still fat. I fed him today," I replied.

"You hear anything about this monster storm they say might hit New York?"

"What? No. I haven't been told anything at work and if it were as big as Hurricane Irene last year we would have known about it already." That was the truth. Last year when Hurricane Irene was on the horizon, we were a frenzy of activity. Documents in the basement were moved upstairs to prevent water damage, boats at Floyd Bennett Field were readied to pick up stranded residents if needed, and vehicles were evacuated further inland. This supposed storm was less than a week away and this was the first I was hearing of it.

The next day I was in the office of the Special Operations lieutenant. We were reviewing the details of a very successful anti-graffiti initiative the conditions team had been working on through the summer and into the fall. Before I left his office I asked if he knew anything about a serious storm like Irene coming to New York this weekend. Like me the day before, it was the first he was hearing about it too.

I assumed my dad was probably just over-reacting. Hurricanes don't make their way to New York very often, and two of them less than one year apart seemed like a long shot. The weather outside was sunny but cold as expected in late October, not like the torrential rainfall which had accompanied Irene the August before. I turned on The Weather Channel and the meteorologists made some comments about a tropical storm in the Caribbean, but nothing on our local weather report indicated impending doom. From my perspective, if the NYPD wasn't worried about it, then neither was I. After all, we have specially trained units to predict these things and alarm bells weren't ringing. It was business as usual.

✶ ✶ ✶

Hours later, in Jamaica, 1,577 miles to the south, Hurricane Sandy made her first landfall.

CHAPTER 3

PREPARATIONS

Saturday, October 27, 2012

I should be focusing on work but all I can think about are the preparations I need to make to my house. Last year, during Hurricane Irene, I managed to get back to Breezy Point for a half day to secure my home before the job called me back in for the next three days. I spent those twelve hours at home digging trenches, filling sandbags, boarding up and taping windows, and waterproofing my house the best I could. The end result was two inches of water in the basement. My hard work paid off, and I planned to do it again.

My boss at the time of Hurricane Irene appreciated my work ethic but wasn't exactly sympathetic about my or anyone else's concerns of home. As cops we are first responders, and if the job wanted us it trumps any personal needs during an emergency. We knew this when we were sworn in as police officers, but it's a hard pill to swallow sometimes. He knew I was a volunteer firefighter and had some extra training most other police officers didn't, and he planned on utilizing that. The day after Hurricane Irene struck New York City we worked together to provide a little extra personal service for certain people.

"I heard Breezy Point got hit pretty hard," he observed, as I packed up my equipment. A tree had fallen down in front of a home with an elderly woman inside and I cleared a path so she could get out.

"Yeah, Dempsey told me my house is still standing." Pat Dempsey was my old partner and fellow Breezy Point resident. We traded shifts so he could be at home and take care of his dad during the storm.

"I hope you don't plan on applying for any of that FEMA money."

"Well, I hope I don't have to."

"They shouldn't give you a dime. You were stupid enough to build your house on a sandbar. You get what you deserve." And with that happy exchange we drove to the next crisis.

Although I have a new boss who seems like a really nice guy, that memory concerned me as this new storm approached. I didn't want to spend another three days away from home wondering if I had a house when I returned. While riding in the Conditions Auto, a police car assigned to address issues specific to our precinct, I made a mental inventory of all the things I needed to have before the storm arrived.

Flashlights?

Check.

Batteries?

Check.

Canned food and bottled water?

Check and check!

Based on prior experience, my assumption was I had 24 hours to get home and make my house ready before work called me back in. The only consolation I would have is the knowledge that my house was prepared as best it could be.

The various city agencies were busy with storm preparations, but it didn't have the urgency like last year. I guess the way Irene fizzled out made skeptics of us. There are only so many times forecasters can throw around the 'storm of the century' label before you stop believing. At the end of my tour, I stopped at the 63rd Precinct Desk Officer before leaving fully expecting a notification ordering me in for Regular Day Off (RDO) overtime on Sunday and Monday, however there was nothing. I was shocked, albeit pleasantly so.

* * *

In Breezy Point at the Point Breeze Volunteer Fire Department, a meeting was called by our Chief, Marty Ingram. He's a retired Air Force Colonel and former executive for the Federal Aviation Administration

(FAA), and a clean cut natural leader who inspires confidence in the people around him. To the best of my knowledge his only vice is using old, sometimes corny truisms. With the hurricane two days away a decision had to be made in regard to the firehouse staying open during the storm.

"Why do you guys want to stay?" asked Robert Johnson, our resident mechanical genius and retired FDNY firefighter. He was concerned we might get washed out and suffer fatalities. Like many veteran first responders, he had lost friends and wasn't eager to go through that again.

"The coastline is right next to the road and that could breach and this could easily become an island," Marty replied. "Nobody's being ordered to stay. It's strictly volunteer, but we need to man the firehouse. The city is leaving and going back across the bridge into Brooklyn. If there's a fire someone needs to be here to put it out."

A discussion ensued, and although a mandatory evacuation order from the Mayor's Office was in effect, two dozen members volunteered to stay behind. With that issue out of the way, the next order of business was making sure that enough food and water was stockpiled and the equipment was in good working order. The trucks were fueled and serviced, gasoline powered tools tested, and anything electric was checked and charged. Items which needed to be fixed or replaced were taken care of.

* * *

On my way home from work I picked up an extra inverter and made sure my MiFi (a portable device which converts cellular service to a Wi-Fi signal) was fully charged. I topped off my truck's fuel tank at the Hess gas station on Flatbush Avenue, just in case. If Hurricane Sandy was going to be like Hurricane Irene, my plan was to make sure my house was water-tight and to run the pumps off my car if need be. Since I didn't have to go to work, I saw no reason to suffer another two inches of water like the previous year.

That night, after a rigorous few hours of taping windows and buying last minute supplies, I picked my girlfriend up in Roxbury and went to Daltons Seaside Grill on Beach 108th Street to enjoy a few drinks before the day of labor I intended for tomorrow. It was Halloween weekend but I was tired and didn't have the energy to put a costume together. Still, storm or no storm, like any man I wasn't gonna pass up the chance to watch women strut around in skin tight cat suits, Wonder Woman costumes, and naughty school girl outfits. Despite all the eye candy though, the topic of conversation was Sandy.

"Do you think it'll hit us?" asked Kathleen, a girl we knew from Roxbury. Even the TV at the bar was tuned to The Weather Channel.

"I think it'll be worse than Irene but nothing we can't handle. Weathermen blow these things way out of proportion for ratings. We'll get some water and lose power for a few days, but we'll get by. I bought an inverter for my car and a MiFi device so I can play video games and watch Netflix on my laptop." At no point did I imagine waves would be crashing against my house and seawater surging down my block.

We got in after closing time at Healy's Bar, across from Dalton's, and started our storm preparations later than I expected on Sunday afternoon. My plan was the same as the year before: tarps on the outside face of the basement windows, reinforced by bricks, then pile on enough sand to completely cover the window. On top of that, I placed a tarp over the sand pile to prevent erosion, then more bricks to keep the tarp in place, and more sand on top because…well…you can never have enough sand. It held back the waters of Irene as the ocean swirled and pooled around my house. The only water which penetrated my storm defenses came up from the basement floor and should have been handled by the pumps if there was any power. I was confident in the integrity of the poured concrete foundation of my house which was only a few years old. My porch is already five feet off the ground, and I figured if the water made it that high then I would be screwed anyway and a flooded basement would be the least of my concerns.

Five hours of digging later and my outside preparations were complete. As a precaution, I moved as much as I could out of my basement and up to the first floor. Anything that couldn't be moved was placed three feet off the ground whenever possible. I taped the last of the windows, secured anything that might be blown away, and helped my neighbors as best I could. By sunset my girlfriend and I were exhausted. The rest of the night was spent watching The Weather Channel together, hoping against hope that the forecasters were wrong.

CHAPTER 4

LANDFALL

Monday, October 29, 2012

I woke up to the wind howling and occasional raindrops pelting against my bedroom windows. The weather, as expected, had gotten worse overnight. The first high tide that day was at 8:03 A.M. and the water had advanced beyond the Promenade along the oceanfront and into the sand alleys. It was then, looking out my window, I finally accepted this was not going to be another Irene. A decision had to be made: to stay or to go. We had been under orders by the Mayor's Office for a mandatory evacuation since yesterday, but a quick look at the houses around me suggested most of my neighbors hadn't taken the order seriously. As they started to wake and realize how far the waters had advanced overnight, plans were changing.

I took some pictures of Essex Walk and posted them on Facebook for the people following along from safer ground. I remembered what it was like the year before when I was stuck at work, wondering what was going on in Breezy Point, so I figured the least I could do for my friends and neighbors was to keep them in the loop as long as possible. After that I went down into my basement and brought up a few more things since it seemed likely there would be substantial flooding. I packed a travel bag with supplies enough to last me a week in the event I had to evacuate my house in an emergency.

In my bag I had a Mossberg shotgun, a Glock pistol, hand tools, three flashlights, two lanterns, twelve cans of Campbell's soup, some dry goods, four Sterno cans, several matches and lighters, a portable radio, and three complete changes of clothes for cold weather. In my car I had more food, batteries, ammunition, and fire starters. I also had my MiFi device and my laptop. The guns were an issue since, as police officers, we're responsible for safeguarding our weapons. If I left them at home in the safe in the basement, they would probably be destroyed by the flood and I didn't want to leave them in the house unsecured. The best bet, I figured, was taking them with me so at least I could keep an eye on them.

A view from my bedroom window at 9:42A.M. during the low tide. The ocean had already passed the Promenade and was advancing up the alley behind Essex Walk.

At 8:43A.M. I sent a text to my friends, Christine and John Paolillo. Both are retired NYPD police officers now working for Breezy Point security. I wrote, "Water is up to the Promenade. You guys still staying? I'm for it, but I don't want to be the last idiot here." John called me back shortly thereafter and told me Christine went to Brooklyn but he and Dan Donahue, another Breezy Point security guard and Point Breeze firefighter, had volunteered to remain behind until 4:00P.M. and help the residents evacuate.

My dad called, and after dodging his calls all morning I figured it was time to have the inevitable argument…

"John, listen to me…" my dad always talks slowly and in a deep voice when he's trying to make a point, "…it isn't safe in Breezy Point. I want you to leave. I want you to leave right now!"

"No, I think I'm gonna stay," I replied.

"Listen to me you little son of a bitch you don't understand what's coming…"

The line went dead. It wasn't the storm; I just couldn't go on with that conversation at the moment. My mind wasn't made up yet, and it needed to be. Getting out of Breezy Point and heading inland was the much safer choice, but leaving my community behind didn't sit well with me. I knew the risks and understood the destructive power of Mother Nature. I suppose everyone had to make the same decision, and every individual had their own particular reasons. For me, it was a matter of pride. I wasn't comfortable backing down when I knew I could be of help to those who needed it.

Eleven years, one month, and 18 days before Hurricane Sandy I found myself in a similar position. I was on my way to work at Solomon Smith Barney when some jackasses flew a plane into the building I was supposed to be in that day, and another into the one next to it. As fate would have it, I never made it inside, and although I had a chance to leave with everyone else, I didn't. The experience of working on the 'bucket brigade' over the next week, sifting through the rubble at Ground Zero, would change my life forever. It also made me realize a few things about myself which I would never have known otherwise, and I am proud I stayed to lend a hand.

You see, like most seasoned first responders I'm okay with not being the smartest, or the strongest, or the fastest guy in the world. I am, however, competent and consistent, and being consistent when things around you are falling apart is what people need most in a crisis. Being the best means nothing if you're in a panic and running away when it counts. It's a quality which helped me through the horrors of September 11th and the recovery afterwards. It's why I chose to leave my desk job and become a cop. Now, here I am, a decade later, faced with another disaster and I have to choose: stay or to go.

Go? I would regret it for the rest of my life if I did.

Just then my father called back, "Listen to me you little…"

I didn't give him a chance to finish his sentence, "Let me cut you off right there. I'm staying. I know you don't like it, but that's what I'm gonna do. The house is as secure as it'll ever be. I'm gonna help evacuate Mr. McGowan next door then I'm going to the Point Breeze Fire Department where I belong. I'll let you know how that turns out tomorrow. I love you. Goodbye."

I didn't wait for a response. It wouldn't have been anything productive anyway and time was wasting. My dad is a retired NYPD lieutenant, a Marine, and a disabled Vietnam veteran with two AK-47 rounds still embedded in his calves. He told me and my brother if we became cops or joined the military he would break our legs, so naturally we did exactly that. I think deep down inside he knew how I felt. The apple doesn't fall far from the tree I guess.

At 11:06 A.M., I sent several text messages with a picture of me with a fishing pole in one hand and a Bud Light in another, sitting on my neighbor's porch at the end of the walk. The accompanying caption I posted on Facebook read, "They keep talking about Sandy. And I'm like 'It's always sandy on the beach! It's my day off. I'm going fishing!" I thought I was funny. When I turned and walked back down Essex Walk I had no way of knowing I was the last person who would ever set foot on that deck again.

Minutes later I sent a text to Pat Dempsey, "What are you up to? Everything good so far?"

He replied, "Wish I was there. I'm working." It was a role reversal from Irene. I knew how he felt being stuck at work while wondering what was happening to his home, or if he would have a home to come back to. It's nerve wracking.

At noon I kissed my girlfriend goodbye so she could help her family in Belle Harbor. As she left I wondered when we would see each other again, and was immediately tempted to drop everything and chase after her. I met with John Paollilo to help the security detail left behind. They were only staying a few more hours to make last minute preparations and assist those who were still trying to evacuate. Rain was pouring down on us and the wind howled as I climbed into his blue Breezy Point Security pickup truck.

"What's up handsome?" said John, in his usual greeting.

"Not much. The house is as ready as it'll ever be. My sister evacuated yesterday with the cat."

"You gonna stay tonight?" he asked.

"Yeah, I'm gonna head over to Point Breeze after this and see if they need a hand. What are you up to?"

"It's just me and Dan right now. We're heading back over the bridge at 4 o'clock. All the other guys are already gone."

"Do you mind if I ride with you for a bit? I did everything I could at home and on my block," I asked.

"No problem. There are still some people looking to leave. Just making sure no one gets stuck," he said as we watched a mini-van packed to the gills make its way down the main road and towards the Marine Parkway Bridge. We entered the easternmost parking lot in Roxbury at 2:00 P.M. to take a look at the playground and check on cars left behind to be sure no one was stranded. Our line of sight to the bridge, 600 yards to the east of us was obscured by fog, sea spray, and rain so thick it was as if the bridge had vanished entirely.

John drove us along the road westbound towards the security booth, stopping into every parking lot and service road along the way. Our patrol took us to the Sugar Shack in the main Roxbury parking lot near the volunteer firehouse, then the ball field. They were already flooded. Some houses still had lights on, with people running back and forth on their decks trying to secure loose items against the wind.

Ten minutes later we were back in Breezy Point and turned right at the main gate into the Reid Avenue parking lot. We parked on the bayside near The Bay House, a popular restaurant and bar. The waters of Jamaica Bay were higher than at any point during Hurricane Irene that I could remember, and it was still low tide.

"Holy shit, take a look at the Henny's dock!" I said, not sure if he got the reference. John's relatively new to Breezy Point, so he probably didn't know years ago The Bay House used to be Henny's, a candy store and bait shop for the kids on the bay side. That's how I knew it.

"It's moving back and forth with the waves like a snake," he observed.

"That shit's not gonna be there in the morning I bet. Let's get the fuck out of here," I replied. For the next hour we drove from one place to the next, looking for neighbors who might need our assistance. Traffic along the main road increased as more and more people decided to evacuate while they still could. By 3:30P.M., I was reunited with my Honda Pilot, wished John good luck, and headed to the Point Breeze Volunteer Fire Department.

The dock in front of The Bay House, pictured just prior to its destruction. It remains a wreck almost two years later.

It had been awhile since I was at the firehouse, and I wasn't much of a firefighter to begin with. I knew the basics, and if you told me to run into a fire I would do it, but when people ask for specific stuff my eyes start to gloss over and I develop a blank look on my face because I don't know what a Halligan tool is (that's the long silver pole with the hook at the end, right?)

"Seabass!" rang out a chorus of voices. My family calls me John and my friends call me Seabass. Even the NYPD has me down as Sebastia because there's not enough room for the 'n' at the end. The only time I hear my entire real name is when I'm in trouble.

"What's going on?" I asked rhetorically.

Eddie Wolfe, nicknamed "The Godfather", and a long time member of the firehouse brought me up to speed. "This hurricane is gonna be a real pain in the ass. A crane is dangling off a building in Manhattan. The news says most residents in the mandatory evacuation zone haven't left yet. How's your house?"

"Good. Did as much as I could so I figured I'd come up here and help out. So what's our plan?"

"I don't know, we'll have to wait and see if this storm is gonna be as bad as they say or another Irene."

Most members were milling around the giant flat screen television hanging behind the bar. Mike Schramm was making a turkey dinner while the younger guys were in the office setting up air mattresses. Tables and chairs were still set up and the general opinion seemed to be that the water wouldn't breach the firehouse. Even the rain had stopped. Maybe the meteorologists were wrong. My gut told me otherwise, and my instincts are pretty good.

"What's going on Seabass?" asked John Fahy, a big man we ironically call "Tiny."

"Nothing much. Came up here for the hurricane. What's with all the stuff lying around? I thought we're gonna get flooded?"

"I thought so too. Marty went up to the Co-op office to see about getting into the Clubhouse, but we haven't heard back from him yet." The Point Breeze Clubhouse is directly behind our firehouse but had three or four more feet of elevation. If there was going to be flooding, it was the ideal place to base our operations out of. Tiny shared my concerns, and we discussed plans for moving gear and water to the Clubhouse just in case.

In the office were Captain Kevin Hernandez, Lieutenant Mike Scotko, Firefighters Kieran Carley, Gerard Carney, Joe Drenan, and Mike Scannell. Computers and desks filled with paperwork were still in place and air mattresses covered the floor. I asked the guys about the expected flooding during the tidal surge, but they didn't believe the waters would get into the firehouse. We cautioned them about moving the TV and X-Box to higher ground, but the concerns of Tiny and me mostly fell on deaf ears. The firehouse didn't flood during Hurricane Irene, and it was expected that during Sandy it would not be different.

Members of the Point Breeze Volunteer Fire Department at the Rockaway St. Patrick's Day parade. Standing left to right: Mike Scotko, Kevin Hernandez, Kieran Carley, Mike Ulrich, Kevin Madden, Colin Brosnan. Also pictured is Nick Pappas (kneeling), a firefighter from Streamwood, Illinois.

Taking the initiative, Tiny and I went behind the firehouse to the Clubhouse. As expected the doors were locked, but the front lawn still had spots available for vehicles. Since the Clubhouse sits on some of the highest land in Breezy Point, I prudently decided to move my truck right up to the front doors. I thought we might need the supplies I brought including the inverter I installed in my truck to recharge our phones and radios. We still didn't have a key, but a 12 gauge sabot slug through the door's locking mechanism and hinges would probably do the trick if it came down to it. If not, we had axes handy.

It was nearly 5:30P.M. when the Chief returned from his meeting with the Co-op. He had secured the key to the Clubhouse, but was still reluctant to move our base of operations. As a compromise, Tiny and I received permission to move some flashlights, water, and food just to the Clubhouse in case. Marty called the first of many group huddles that night and told us the latest news. Not long afterwards we received a phone call from FDNY operations reminding us that all FDNY units based in the Rockaways would be pulling back to Brooklyn at 6:00P.M. Following that somber news was an announcement from the Mayor's Office, on television, informing us an estimated 75% of the Rockaways had not been evacuated despite the mandatory orders to do so. We also learned the Marine Parkway Bridge, our only lifeline to the rest of the city, would be closing at 7:00P.M.

Schramm's amazing looking turkey was just about ready to serve when Pat Dempsey showed up with his dad and two dogs. They had let him out of work early. "You wanna take a ride?" he asked, "I gotta pick up Billy at his house." Bill is Pat's older brother. He lives between Bedford and Reid Avenues on the beach side of the community. We had heard reports from the people trickling into the firehouse about waves crashing over the homes nearest the beach, but so far the flooding in the parking lot near the firehouse was only a few inches. We got in Pat's pickup, turned right onto Rockaway Point Boulevard and started the one mile journey to Billy's house.

"Jesus Christ! Pat, the water is getting deep really fast!" I said.

"I know, I see it!" he replied as we watched floodwater, that was only inches over the pavement moments ago, start to bubble and swirl. The surge we were told to expect by the meteorologists had begun. Seawater was rushing into the street. As we neared Bill's house a minute later, the water was already nearly a foot deep and we dared not go too far off the road and into the sand alley. The truck's headlights shone down the sand alley, which runs behind the houses, and my heart nearly stopped.

"Dude, those are fucking waves. That's the ocean!" I yelled as he tried to keep the truck in motion. Frothing seawater was crashing down the alley, sweeping aside garbage cans and anything else in its wake. Just ahead of it was Bill Dempsey, running for his life.

"Open the door! Open the door, Seabass!" he yelled as Pat turned the truck around. I opened the door and he jumped inside. "Son of a bitch! I never ran that fast in my entire life!" he gasped, nearly out of breath. Pat gunned the engine and the pickup began to push its way back down Rockaway Point Boulevard towards the firehouse. We were in big trouble. The water had risen nearly two feet since we started this trip only five minutes ago. The truck was starting to struggle as we made our way along the flooded street.

Pat let out a yell as he pushed the accelerator all the way down to the floor. The engine roared, but something wasn't right: seawater had reached the air intake and was suffocating the combustion process. The truck gave us the last of whatever life it had left in it and we used that momentum to reach the quickly flooding firehouse parking lot. The tidal surge was raising the water levels dramatically and now the firehouse began to flood.

"The water came out of nowhere!" I said as we burst through the firehouse door, stating the obvious and with just a little 'I told you so' attitude in my voice. I noted the return of Kevin and Timmy O'Brien, two brothers who are police officers in the NYPD like Pat, Billy, and I. They had just come back from rescuing their father, also named Tim, who is a retired NYPD detective. Kevin, the youngest of the O'Brien men with us that night, is a Captain in Point Breeze Fire Department, while Tim Sr. and Timmy Jr. are both very experienced firefighters. Between all three, the O'Brien men have over fifty years of volunteer firefighting experience, and nearly the same as police officers. Like many in Breezy Point, they are a blue collar family with a legacy of volunteer and city service.

Tim O'Brien Sr. spoke to me after the storm about his rescue, "It happened very quickly. A friend of mine called me and said I better batten down the hatches because the water is coming up over the bay. I looked down the block and sure enough the water is rushing down Ocean Avenue. Kevin came by and asked if I wanted a ride out, but I told him I would be okay. We had been through this before. I figured the water would be a couple of feet but no more. So he left with the fire truck. Not ten minutes went by when I looked out the door again and knew I was in real trouble. The water was coming up much faster than I thought possible. So I called Kevin back and put Timmy's bunker gear on, which was at the house for some reason, turned out the lights in the house, and jumped onto the fire truck.

Kevin couldn't stop the fire truck for fear of it stalling in the quickly rising waters, so his father had to jump aboard while it was still moving. The storm surge which had surprised Pat and me during our rescue of Billy nearly clobbered them as well. Like most of our harrowing moments during Hurricane Sandy, timing was everything. Had we waited five minutes longer, the fate of Bill Dempsey and Tim O'Brien Sr. could have been very different, and we could have lost irreplaceable men and equipment in the process.

"Okay, everyone get whatever you can carry and we're gonna evacuate to the Clubhouse. Everyone find a buddy and stick with him!" shouted Marty Ingram, our Chief.

We used rope and extension cords to link each other together. Pat and Billy escorted their father and carried the family dogs. Tiny and I helped prepare some of our older residents who had sought shelter from the storm in the firehouse. Six of us made our way into the office to try and save the records in the bottom drawers of the desks, but they were already soaked. Inflated air mattresses were floating in the three-foot deep water and getting in the way. Schramm's turkey sat on the bar, having already been picked over before I got a chance to try it.

Eddie Wolfe hadn't left yet and was having trouble moving around in the deepening water so I asked if he was okay. "I'm fine, Seabass. Just leave me here. I'll be alright." There was no chance I was going to leave him behind, so I grabbed him, tied an extension cord between the two of us, and moved out the side door of the firehouse. The wind was pushing against us with tremendous force while the ice-cold water created a freezing, swirling current that sapped the energy from our bodies as we trudged through it. Several times Ed nearly fell down, and to be honest, I'm not sure if we could have gotten him up if he went all the way underwater. I grabbed the back of his bunker jacket as tight as I could and pushed him forward until we made it to the front door of the Point Breeze Clubhouse.

Ed joined three dozen civilians, which had come to the firehouse or we had rescued along the way, on the stage in the Clubhouse. Water was already flooding the Clubhouse, bubbling up through the seams in the floor. The Dempseys' dogs were up on a table just high enough to keep them out of the water. Billy and Pat were trying to keep them calm while their dad stayed up on the stage and out of the water. Other people brought their pets along too. A cat anxiously pressed its face against the chrome gate of a purple plastic cage. Several small dogs sat silently on their owner's laps.

On the stage, a table was set up with an electric lantern which, aside from a few flashlights, was the only source of illumination separating us from the cold, dark desperation of our current predicament. Some people had barely escaped their homes before the water trapped them and a few nearly drowned. I walked onto the stage to check on the people sheltered there. A bottle of Jameson's Irish Whisky had been found and passed around to steady the nerves.

One of our members wrote on his Facebook page: "Trapped in the Clubhouse with 37 people. Water rising…"

Civilians and firefighters alike grew more concerned with the rising seawater. We marked off water levels on the cinderblock wall to measure the ocean's progress. Directly in front of the building was my truck. I watched through the windows as the water crept higher; first at the base of the hubcaps, then the running boards, and eventually past the lower door frame. My truck was at the highest part of the hill leading up to the front doors, but all the other vehicles in sight weren't as fortunate.

I walked around the Clubhouse and surveyed the varying reactions of both the civilians and firemen trapped inside. The purpose wasn't to shame or judge anyone, but to determine who might need a little extra fortitude from us on this terrible night. Some cried, some prayed and others sat quietly with a stoic look on their faces, accepting whatever fate befall us. One of our firefighters sat on the stage, unresponsive and in a catatonic state. Another one found an orange life vest and rocked back and forth talking to himself. He had hit his proverbial brick wall; the limit when your mind says enough is enough and you just can't go any further without some time to heal. We all have it. It's something we would see a lot of in the coming weeks.

After I passed by, he stood up, walked over to Marty and told him, "We gotta get out of this building. We're all going to drown in here." In his panic he became convinced the water was going to keep rising and we were going to be trapped inside and drown. To be fair, it was a perfectly reasonable concern given the circumstances and how quickly the water drove us from the firehouse, but there was no place left to go and he offered no alternatives. This was the high ground. Only one more desperate option remained, and it was a decision the Chief was already wrestling with.

Across from the Clubhouse was a home of one of our members who decided to shelter in place on his second floor. The temptation to move everyone to that location weighed heavily on Marty's mind. If the water kept rising at this rate, in an hour or two we might regret not moving while there was still a chance. On the other hand, we had a difficult enough time moving the fifty yards from the firehouse to the Clubhouse. The distance from the Clubhouse to this next refuge was ninety yards; almost double. It would mean walking through rushing water filled with debris and up to our necks for nearly the length of a football field. The fact that we seriously considered it was a testament to how dire our situation was at the time.

"Okay, let's get a plan together. Break into the storage closet and see if there's anything we can use," said Marty. Mike Scotko, Gerard Carney, and Tiny took turns on the lock, eventually breaching the door. Twine and short pieces of rope were discovered, along with Christmas lights and extension cords.

While we were taking stock of our new equipment, one of our Captains, Kevin "Brillo" Hernandez, pulled Marty aside and convinced him of the foolishness of even considering this option. During their conversation, Kevin asked, "What if the house is off its foundation?" Marty hadn't considered that.

Kevin continued, "And what are we going to do with all these people? You want to cram sixty of us onto the second floor? It's going to collapse. Half these people are old and would never make it."

Brillo was right, and Marty knew it. The civilians were in no shape to travel and might not survive the attempt. Even the younger firefighters were exhausted from the last trek, and marinating in the frigid Clubhouse floodwaters hadn't allowed them to regain much of their strength. Most importantly his guess about the foundation was correct. After the storm we discovered the house was off its foundation and the deck was askew. Adding a few thousand extra pounds to the second floor would have collapsed the house entirely and probably killed those of us who survived the trip and made it inside.

"Okay guys," said Marty, "let's scrap this idea. It's too dangerous."

Our debate was not lost on the civilians; some of who looked truly dejected once we concluded there were no alternatives but to shelter in place within the flooding Clubhouse. Marty took notice. The last thing any leader wants is for the people under his command or in his care to start thinking there isn't a plan. He decided to address the situation before it got out of control.

"Some of you are worried about what's next. We're going to stay here. It's the safest place for all of us. We are all wet and cold, but think about this: This is a beach community. We stand in three feet of water on the weekends for fun, so we can do it now."

That got a few laughs and calmed some nerves. People started talking again and the Jameson's made another round. Eddie Wolfe, however, was starting to show signs of diabetic shock and was becoming a real concern. We talked to him to keep him awake and alert. There was no chance for a medical evacuation and no medicine available to treat him on the scene. If he gave up and slipped away, there wasn't anything we could do. Eddie is a tough guy though, and he hung in there, although barely at times.

I found myself looking out the windows on the south side of the building facing the parking lot next to the Clubhouse. We could see cars bobbing in the water with windows down, headlights on, and hazard lights flashing. The debris and sea spray whipped up by the high winds made it hard for us to see clearly, but a few guys said they could see things floating in the water. Word spread that people might be stranded in the parking lot and signaling us for help.

"We gotta get out there and help them!" We pleaded with Marty, "We can tie the extension cords and Christmas lights around someone so we don't lose him in the water. We'll form a human chain as far as we can until he can reach the parking lot."

Several firefighters stepped forward to volunteer. The plan required someone strong enough to fight against the wind and the swirling water currents which we barely escaped when we evacuated the firehouse. That volunteer would have to be able to reach the parking lot, and still have enough endurance left in him to bring back any survivors. A debate carried on as to who was most qualified.

I pulled Marty aside: "I know I'm not the best firefighter in the world but I know a thing or two. Did anyone actually see any survivors out in the lot? All of those flashing lights we are seeing may be the result of the cars being submerged. The department sent me to Auto Crime School a few years ago. Every new car has a feature in the event a vehicle drives into a lake or something. The windows automatically go down and the trunk pops open so people can escape and the lights flash so rescue divers can find the vehicle. I think what we're seeing out there is a car's automatic response to the flood, not people signaling for help. If we see someone out there I'll be the first one to go for them, but right now we're planning an extremely risky rescue based on bad information."

Marty considered my advice, but knew I had presented him with only a theory and couldn't say for certain if my hypothesis was correct.

However, if I was wrong, and people were in those cars signaling for help, ignoring them would have fatal consequences. He had to weigh the possibility of leaving our neighbors out to drown versus risking the lives of our own guys because of some flashing lights. "You're right Seabass. Let's hold off unless we actually see someone signaling for help. Has anyone actually seen a person out there?"

No one had. In the excitement everyone assumed it was someone else who saw something. We walked back over to the windows and looked for survivors in the water. After a few minutes, we realized there were dozens of cars with rhythmic flashing lights. One or two was understandable if it was a signal for help, but clearly my information was correct. We nearly sent our guys out on an extremely risky rescue mission for nothing. It could have been a disaster.

"Besides," I thought, "anyone still out there in that parking lot had drowned already. I barely made it from the firehouse to the Clubhouse. Those cars are under water. We'll know by tomorrow when the ocean recedes." The notion sent shivers down my spine.

Marty shared the same concerns. During an interview after the storm I asked him about the decision to call off the sortie into the parking lot. He said to me: "I didn't know if I signed the death warrants for the people in those cars. That was a tough decision. Those were our neighbors and people I grew up with, or people I most likely would have known."

Another huddle was called so the Chief could share his thoughts with us and get our input. He's always willing to listen and not afraid to admit when he's wrong. These are two of the qualities which made him such an effective leader for our firehouse. Assignments were given to every firefighter. Some were mere busy work, but it was good to keep people active instead of standing around and letting their minds wander. There really wasn't much we could do though, and I think we had a half-dozen guys checking water levels. Marty was also concerned about the morale of the civilians.

"You might think this is unusual," said Marty to the people on the stage, "but I'd like you to join me in prayer. I'd like everyone to hold hands and join me in the Our Father."

Breezy Point is an Irish Catholic community with a strong emphasis on faith. The folks you see partying at one of the local bars, The Blarney, starting on Saturday night and continuing until 4 o'clock in the morning on Sunday will still make it to religious services a few hours later. Some of the younger guys rolled their eyes, but it gave the people huddled on the stage a way to contribute and something to do. Besides, we could use the help. We bowed our heads and prayed, "Our Father, who art in Heaven, hallowed be Thy name…"

The prayer ended, and for a moment we stood in the water, lost in quiet reflection. A few were still visibly upset, hoping in vain the hurricane would just go away. It didn't, but what happened next was just as surprising.

A beam of light from a high powered flashlight sliced through the haze in the direction of the summer stores 100 yards to the east on the opposite side of the parking lot! Then another! There *were* people out there, but the lights were moving too fast. My first thought was that the people were being swept away, but they were moving against the wind and the current.

"There's a boat out there!" shouted one firefighter.

"It's Rockaway Point! Grab a light and signal them!" said another.

Our own flashlights were quickly brought to the windows facing the east and soon several beams of light lanced out in the direction of the boats. The men in the boats saw this, and made their way towards the Clubhouse. They pulled up to the front of the building and tied their two boats to the pole supporting the overhang next to my truck. We opened a window, pushed out a small ladder so they could climb through, and helped them inside.

"Do you think they're here to rescue us?" said Marty.

"I think we're rescuing them," I mused. "We'll see soon enough."

Hugs and handshakes were exchanged as the boat crew opened up their yellow neoprene "dry suits" to cool off. They looked like they had been through hell. We gave them bottles of water and provided some folding chairs to rest on, then pressed them for information about what they had witnessed during their sortie. Marty approached Jim Morton, a Lieutenant from Rockaway Point, and asked, "Are you here to rescue us, or are we here to rescue you?"

* * *

Earlier in the evening, at approximately 7:00P.M., five members of the Rockaway Point Volunteer Fire Department donned their survival gear and headed out into the raging waters of Hurricane Sandy which had enveloped the community. Capt. Michael Valentine, Lt. James Morton, Lt. Brandon Reilly, and firefighters Mike Kahlau and Brian Doyle deployed in two boats—one an inflatable Mercury and the other a green flat-bottomed aluminum whaler—in an attempt to rescue residents of Breezy Point forced from their homes by the floodwaters.

The water was deep enough to use their outboard motors and still rising. Cars floated just below the surface of the water and presented a real danger. A disabled motor on either of the boats from a collision with underwater debris, or entanglement, could have fatal consequences in these weather conditions. The five Rockaway Point firefighters knew this before they departed and, considering the needs of their neighbors over their own safety, went out into the raging storm anyway. Captain Valentine and his crew had endured the worst Sandy had to throw at them for over an hour before they arrived at our refuge in the Point Breeze Clubhouse.

* * *

Sometime around 8:30P.M., a yell came from the windows where several firefighters were keeping lookout. They had spotted a fire to the east in the Wedge. The Wedge is a triangle shaped cluster of a thousand houses, with Oceanside Avenue as the northern border and the Promenade running along the oceanfront to the south. The point of the triangle is near Arcadia Walk where both borders join at a local beach bar, The Sugar Bowl. From this point they continue west, separating more and more until the Wedge is closed by Utica Walk. Blocks within the Wedge, are named alphabetically, except for Atlantic Walk and Ocean Avenue which are sandwiched between Essex and Fulton Walks. Arcadia Walk, where the Wedge is most narrow, has seven houses, while Tioga Walk, where the Wedge is widest, has eighty-six.

The faint smell of smoke was in the air and we could observe the occasional lick of flames as they danced above the rooftops of houses which were obstructing our view. The wind was blowing northwest at over eighty miles per hour, spreading the flames from one house to another, and bringing an increasing amount of smoke and flaming debris directly towards us. We watched helplessly.

"Let's huddle up and have another meeting," said Marty. "Now that the Rockaway guys are here we can bring them up to speed and get a better idea of what's going on out there. We have 25 firefighters and 41 civilians with us, not counting the guys from Rockaway Point. Our primary responsibility is to keep the civilians safe, but there's nothing we can do until the water stops rising. It looks like we also have a fire to deal with in the Wedge."

Suddenly more lights appeared by the summer stores across the parking lot to the south. There were people fleeing the fire at the Wedge. The smoke and oncoming flames forced them out of their homes and into the chest-deep floodwaters in a desperate bid to reach the firehouse. They had made it as far as the parking lot before the water currents became too strong. Everyone looked at the Rockaway Point boat crew.

"Can you guys make it to them?" asked Marty.

"Yeah, we can do it."

They buttoned up their "dry suits" and climbed back out the window. All we could do was watch as they boarded the Mercury and raced to the south, dodging debris and floating cars along the way. I held my breath as one boat seemed to get stuck for a moment, then worked itself free and continued on towards the stores. For several long minutes they were out of view, although we can see beams of light flickering along the houses nearby. Finally, the boat crew reappeared, and was on the way back to the Clubhouse, laden with additional passengers: Jack O'Meara and his wife Aileen, their two children, and two cats.

I looked over at Pat standing next to me as we watched the rescue from the Clubhouse windows, "Those guys are fucking crazy."

"Yeah," he replied, "I'm not sure you could get me to do that. I think I would, but you never really know."

Tim O'Brien Jr. was behind us and said, "Let's help them back in."

The boats were secured and both the rescued and rescuers were hauled back into the Clubhouse. My words can't do justice to the admiration and professional respect we have for the firefighters of Rockaway Point, not just for going out into the storm in the first place, but to go back out again to rescue our neighbors and friends. In a night full of heroics their actions truly stand out among the boldest and bravest. It was in these selfless acts of bravery by all the volunteers that night in which Chief Marty Ingram finally got his answer to the question posed to Jim Mortin earlier. We weren't here to rescue them, and they weren't here to rescue us. We were here for each other.

The water was already up to our knees and still rising. If it kept advancing at this rate we would be in real trouble. Several ideas were suggested including one that involved using the Christmas lights and extension cords to strap ourselves to the roof of the Clubhouse, if need be. It was madness. The fact was that we had no more places to fall back to. If the water didn't stop, we were doomed and that was that. High tide was at 8:43P.M. and we were still a half an hour away. We needed a miracle.

"We need to get out there!" fumed one frustrated firefighter.

"No, you can't," ordered Marty. "You will go at the right time; not a second sooner or a second later."

Our two trucks, Engine 7 and Ladder 8, were parked in their berths at the firehouse which was almost completely submerged in seawater. With the floodwaters still advancing and hurricane force winds howling around us, it would be suicide to try and reach the firehouse only fifty yards away. Even if we could reach the firehouse, the trucks wouldn't likely start because of the damage to their engines and electrical systems by the salt water. We also couldn't just leave the three dozen civilians behind. Even if, by some miracle, the trucks did start, we needed to get them out of harm's way first.

Among the evacuees on the stage was a retired FDNY chauffer; a firefighter whose job it is to drive the truck. Marty pulled him aside to get an expert opinion. "Tell me, how deep can these trucks operate?"

He was vague, since our trucks were custom built and he didn't know the specifications. He guessed, "Four feet. Going through a flood will create a bow wave, so you might get another foot from that if you keep moving. But four feet is my best answer."

"Thanks. We'll wait until the water goes down to four feet before we launch." Nobody wanted to wait, but Marty was right. There was no sense driving our trucks into a water level they couldn't handle and lose them before we reached our objective. We needed to be patient until the time was right, but it was easier said than done.

Our friends and families who stayed behind were in those houses and faced with the possibilities of burning to death, asphyxiation from smoke inhalation, or drowning. Some cellular phones were still working and received frantic text messages and posts on Facebook from people trapped near the fire begging for help. We knew it would be hours before the FDNY could get back into the Rockaways, and when they did their trucks still didn't have the four-wheel-drive capability or the ground clearance to maneuver through the sand. Their mechanical limitations are the reason our three volunteer firehouses in Breezy Point exist.

My phone still had sporadic service, so my girlfriend and I traded texts. "My parent's house is flooded into the first floor and there is a huge fire a few blocks away," she said at 8:45 P.M. Fifteen minutes later I replied, "Do you know where exactly? I'll be honest. We're fucked. Gotham Walk is burning. Water is rising. We're trapped." The idea of another massive fire in Rockaway was a troubling thought which I shared with Marty.

More texts started to flood in. My sister asked if I was alive, to which I replied, "Breezy Point is under 5 to 7 feet of water. Houses are on fire. Any car still here is done. Just done. We are expecting many dead. I'm okay. Just gonna be a long week."

I shut my phone off and returned to dealing with our own immediate problems. If the wave action, which had pulverized the beachfront, made its way to the Clubhouse we were doomed. If the water levels rose another few feet many of us would drown. The surge arrived three hours before the expected high tide. Would it take three hours for the water to recede? Smoke was starting to fill the Clubhouse in increasing density—would it overwhelm us before we could evacuate? Nervously we watched the minutes tick by. I thought back to all the time she and I spent in front of the TV watching The Weather Channel before the storm hit.

The experts say tonight was an astronomical high tide because of the full moon, which meant the water would be at its highest for the 28 day lunar cycle. There was also the storm surge, which would raise the water level past the normal tidal increase due to the storm's low atmospheric pressure and hurricane force winds pushing water onshore. The worst-case scenario was for the surge to coincide with an astronomical high tide while the storm maintains a counter-clockwise rotation as it approached land. This was exactly what was happening.

The high tide was expected at 8:43P.M. The eye of the storm was passing through southern New Jersey near Brigantine just north of Atlantic City, which put the violent northeastern edges of the swirling maelstrom over lower New York. The high tide, which usually brought a 5-foot increase in water level, surged to 14-feet in Battery Park. In Breezy Point the surge was even higher. The coastlines of New Jersey and Long Island join to create a right angle and form a natural funnel to maximize the force of all the wind and surge waters. At the meeting of these two shorelines, in the center of the funnel where the weather is at its worst, are Breezy Point and the Rockaway peninsula.

Once again Marty called us all together and lead us in prayer, offering a second Our Father and asking God to stop the rising waters so we can escape the smoke filled Clubhouse. We were trapped like rats in a flooding cage with the air becoming less breathable by the minute, rendering us powerless to stop the fire burning down our homes and dooming our neighbors to an awful fate. All we could do was pray for deliverance. Standing in the freezing water with smoke starting to burn our lungs, things began to seem very hopeless.

Then we got our first miracle.

* * *

On Liberty Lane, John Norton was sheltering in his home with his wife, Stephanie, and their three month old son, Trevor. He put plywood up to cover all the windows of his two story house. A rope was used to secure one of the wooden boards so he could push it aside for a quick peek outside from time to time to check the water levels rising around them. The howling wind was blowing so strongly he feared the roof would rip off. Before joining his wife in an upstairs closet, John peeked out the window facing the Wedge, "The field department put on the lights by the ball field!"

"That's impossible," his wife replied.

"Well, it's all lit up. It's hard to see but there's definitely an orange glow coming from that direction."

"Did it ever occur to you that might be a fire?"

"Fuck…"

* * *

By 9:00P.M., the water levels, carefully measured on the cinderblock walls of the Clubhouse, showed a noticeable decrease for the first time since we arrived. Another check of my car's front tires confirmed the water was indeed receding. We had gotten the miracle we needed.

Although slow at first, the flood progressively subsided and soon the water levels outside the Clubhouse were lower than inside!

"Open the front doors! Let's drain some of this water out of here!" said Marty. The doors were opened and the water trapped within the Clubhouse poured out, but thick smoke from the fire bellowed in. Softball-size chunks of flaming embers rained down all around those of us who stepped outside to watch the conflagration. We might not drown in the Clubhouse, but we were suffocating nonetheless.

I went outside to try and get some air since the smoke was thicker in the Clubhouse and getting worse. The devastation all around us was heartbreaking. I turned my attention east to gaze at the fire and prayed to God for the people trapped in the Wedge. At 9:05P.M., I recorded several videos on my iPhone. The glow of the fire could be seen just beyond the summer stores, while the smoke belched higher and higher into the night sky. "That's fucking Gotham Walk in flames..." I said, "son of a bitch."

Behind me, someone vented, "Where is the rain? How the hell do you have a hurricane with no rain? If it were pouring rain like Irene last year there would be no fires!"

"You have a point," I said, "but on the other hand, if the rain raised the water level even a little bit, we would probably be drowning right now. But yeah, that's weird. I never heard of a hurricane with no rain."

After a few minutes we all went back inside. The hail of fiery debris was making things interesting to say the least and we didn't want anyone to get hurt. Even though the Clubhouse is located on the highest ground in Breezy Point the water was still up to our shins. A few steps off the concrete pathway leading up to the Clubhouse the floodwaters became waist-deep. We would continue to be trapped here for a little while, but for how much longer? That was the question on everyone's mind.

Would the water levels recede fast enough for us to make our escape before the smoke overtook us or the embers set the Clubhouse roof on fire? What about the trucks? If they didn't start we would have to fight the fire on foot, dragging whatever serviceable equipment was left along with us. Also there was the issue of evacuating the dozens of civilians in our care. They were already wet, freezing, and slowly suffocating. We had to relocate them out of the path of the smoke and flaming debris. Getting them out of harm's way was our top priority.

A picture taken from my iPhone of the glow created by the fire developing in the Wedge. The time was 9:03p.m.

Marty called for another group meeting to discuss our firefighting options when an argument at the front door got his attention. Tim O'Brien Sr. was trying to commandeer one of the boats when the guys from Rockaway Point stopped him. Marty looked up at one of our firemen on the stage, Steve Glavey, and told him to take over and get another group prayer going. The other two had worked for us, so why not try again? Then he marched to the front of the Clubhouse to settle this new problem.

Tim O'Brien Sr. had gotten word from his wife that one of his lifelong friends, Mary Lapera, and her family were trapped inside her home near the fire and needed help. The youngest Lapera sister, Joeanne, works with Tim's wife who relayed the distress call by voicemail. My sister is good friends with the oldest daughter, also named Mary, and sent me a text message at 9:09P.M., "Last I checked, Mary and her family are in the attic on Oceanside." These two corroborating pieces of information confirmed our worst fears: there were still people trapped near the fire with no way to escape.

"I'm taking this boat. I'm gonna save Mary!"

Marty pulled him aside, "No, you're not. We need you here. I just re-activated you tonight and I need everyone I can get to fight this fire. Besides, you'd never make it in these winds. You'd wind up on some suicide mission and that wouldn't be very useful to anyone."

"Marty, we gotta get one of these boats over there. They're still in the house and it's flooded and starting to catch fire!" he yelled, clearly frustrated.

"It's too windy! Even the Rockaway Point guys are afraid to take that boat out right now. It'll flip over." replied Marty.

"There are people in that house who need us. We gotta at least try. I'm not leaving them to die," said Tim, as he looked into the face of his friend for over fifty years. Marty and Tim have known each other since grade school and worked together as volunteer firefighters as far back as the 1970's. But Marty is the Chief, and it was his call.

"It's great what you want do for Mary, but you have to believe she'll be okay." Tim Sr. didn't like Marty's answer. We were all frustrated to the point of tears knowing there was nothing we could do for the Lapera family right now. It was one thing to assume your neighbors may need help, however the situation is very different when you know for certain and are unable to act, not for a lack of bravery, but because of circumstance. Times like these are when our trust in the Chief is crucial, and our faith in Marty was unwavering. He gave an order and the issue was settled.

The Chief returned just as Steve Glavey was finishing up the Hail Mary. Later Marty told me his nerves were so on edge a little thing like substituting the Hail Mary for the Our Father got under his skin. Months after the storm, he questioned Steve about the change of prayers, "Tell me, how come you did the Hail Mary when I did two Our Fathers before? That was working pretty good for us."

"Marty, when I was in the 4th grade the nun had me stand up in front of the class and say the Our Father. I botched it so bad that the nun yelled at me. I knew I couldn't say the Our Father up on that stage without screwing it up. But I could do the Hail Mary!"

No matter which prayer was spoken, the same result was needed. We were downwind of the fire and the smoke was overwhelming us. The people on the stage were starting to panic. We needed to get out of the Clubhouse

"Listen up!" Marty shouted. "Get your things together because we're going to evacuate this shelter very soon. We have a detailed plan and need you to be ready to go."

Brillo steered Marty away from the stage and to the firefighters standing in the corner. He said, "Let's go check on the trucks. A few of us will go back to the engine deck and see if one of them will start."

"Okay," Marty agreed. "I want a life chain set up. See if you can get into the firehouse. We left the bay doors open. Get to the trucks and check if they'll start. They shouldn't, but at least we can rule that out as a possibility."

A detachment of firefighters was sent over to the firehouse in the waist-deep water deep. The chauffeurs picked their way through the debris and into the cabs of Engine 7, "Big Jack," and Ladder 8, "Sand Flea." Fingers were crossed and silent prayers were whispered. With the fate of dozens of lives on the line, the chauffeurs, in defiance of all mechanical reason and expectations, tested their ignitions.

The older engine on Sand Flea roared to life first, followed by Big Jack. Blue smoke sputtered from their exhausts and for a moment the engines sounded like they would seize as they suffocated from a lack of oxygen and too much seawater in the intakes below. The lights on Big Jack were flickering on and off from damage to the electrical system. But inexplicably, the engines kept going and their transmissions could be put into gear.

Big Jack and Sand Flea.

The rumble of diesel engines and the hiss of air brakes, as the trucks rolled down the shallow ramp of the engine deck and splashed into the flooded street, surprised all of us back at the Clubhouse. It was mechanically impossible. When we brought our trucks back to their manufacturer to be repaired months later, the mechanics didn't believe our story. To this day no one can explain why they started and kept going other than some sort of divine intervention. We didn't have time to dwell on it. All that mattered to us was the ability to evacuate the civilians and then take on the fire. We were in business.

The Hail Mary worked.

★ ★ ★

A half mile down the road, our brothers in the Rockaway Point Volunteer Fire Department weren't so lucky. The men who had bravely gone out into the thick of the storm in their rescue boats to pull people from the water were hampered by the mechanical realities of what seawater and silt will do to a submerged engine. Both of their fire trucks, Ladder 4 and Engine 5, as well as their two ambulances, Rescue 1 and Rescue 2, were inoperable. The loss of two of the five fire trucks stationed throughout Breezy Point was a severe blow to our firefighting capability at a time when we needed it most. Undeterred, the men and women of Rockaway Point stayed in the fight, helping Roxbury and Point Breeze volunteers in our struggle against the raging inferno at the Wedge.

✷ ✷ ✷

The smoke became too thick to breathe inside the Clubhouse and we simply could not wait any longer. Despite hurricane force winds, flaming embers, and floodwaters still rushing around us, we were forced to evacuate the Point Breeze Clubhouse and go back into the Point Breeze Firehouse. In a reversal of events, it was the lower stature of the firehouse which fared better against the smoke since it was shielded by the taller Clubhouse next door. The waters were still too high on the street, so we ushered the civilians out the back door of the Clubhouse and along an elevated pathway which lead to the side door of the firehouse.

This route kept us a few feet higher off the ground and so no one would be swept away by the flood's current, but it exposed us to the debris and smoke since it ran along the side facing the fire. Slowly we shuffled the twenty yards from door to door, keeping a steady hand on the civilians we were escorting. Marty, a retired Air Force officer always mindful of military tradition was the last to leave. Chunks of flaming embers rained down on the conga line as we made our way into the firehouse, and more than one person was hit.

"God damn what the fuck was that? That hurt!" A flaming piece of wood the size of a baseball crashed into my head, but my fireman's helmet saved me from any serious harm. As I escorted an elderly man through the side door of the firehouse I turned to look at the fire behind me. "Oh my God," I said to Tim O'Brien Sr. "It looks like tracer bullets from one of those World War II movies. The whole fucking Wedge must be on fire." I watched mesmerized as glowing embers arced up out of the fire hundreds of feet into the air, then continued along their downward trajectories toward those of us in the path of the wind. You could hear the sizzle of the ones which landed in the water nearby. My house is in the Wedge. I found it ironic and sad that the piece of debris which smacked me in the head could have been a piece of my own home.

"We better get inside, Seabass," said Tim O'Brien Sr. For a man in his sixties he sure as hell could keep up with the rest of us. "Let's check in with Marty and see what's going on."

Inside we found the firehouse was a shambles. Water had risen almost to the ceiling and scattered debris everywhere. The floor and just about everything else was covered by thick brown silt from the sea floor. Chairs, tables, vending machines, and inflatable mattresses were strewn about. More importantly our electronic equipment such as radios, flashlights, and various detectors were destroyed or missing. The only light came from a handful of flashlights taken with us when we evacuated, and the malfunctioning lights of Big Jack outside.

We checked in with Marty as Big Jack drove away with the first load of civilians and the Rockaway Point boat crew hitching a ride on top of the hose bed. He was happy to see us. "Great, you made it out alive. I need you to go back into the Clubhouse and do a final sweep to make sure we didn't leave anyone behind while we get these people evacuated to the church."

I looked over at the senior O'Brien, "You interested in doing something stupid with me?" He just laughed. By re-tracing our steps of the initial evacuation through the parking lot, we avoided the bulk of the smoke and embers thanks to the Clubhouse as our shield. Unfortunately, it meant we had to trudge our way through waist-deep water for part of the way, falling several times in the muck because life wasn't miserable enough. It was exhausting. My wingman, Tim O'Brien Sr., needed help because he had so much muddy water in his boots he couldn't lift his leg over the three-foot wooden fence separating our parking lot from the Clubhouse.

As we got closer to the Clubhouse, walking became easier but the smoke became unbearable. With wet sleeves we covered our mouths as we made our way to the front door, barely able to see more than a few feet in front of us. Waiting for us was a family of six who had struggled through waist-deep water in order to flee the fire in the Wedge. They were on the verge of collapse when we found them and escorted them back to the firehouse, and then into one of the trucks shuttling evacuees to the church. Tim and I went back looking for more survivors and did a thorough search but found no one else. The only two people left in the Clubhouse were us.

"I need to sit down. Just can't go any more," said O'Brien Sr. as he sat on a step on the stage. We were wiped out and barely able to move.

"Dude, if we don't get up right now we're gonna die in here," I said. We looked at each other in agreement, and somehow got the strength to stand up and stumble our way out the back door toward the firehouse. We took the same path facing the fire, and although embers rained down on us, it just didn't matter anymore. I held the door for him as we made our way back into the firehouse, found a bottle of water on the floor, wiped off the muck around the cap, and we split it.

"The Clubhouse is empty," we reported to Marty. "Don't send anyone back in there. It's a death trap. O'Brien and I nearly called it quits. If we had to wait ten more minutes for the water to go down we'd all be dead. We got lucky." It was true. The fire was growing at an exponential rate as more and more buildings became engulfed. Likewise, the smoke and debris were getting proportionally worse as well. Had the water not gone down as fast as it did, we would have definitely lost people from smoke inhalation.

The Chief looked at us with concern. We were having too many close calls for comfort. "Seabass, why don't you guys get on Ladder 8 with Dempsey and the Duffman. Truck 7 is loading the last of the civilians now. I'll join you in a minute." Before that I needed to use the bathroom which had no running water and, therefore, no option to flush. This didn't stop someone from wrecking the ladies room, which wasn't cleaned up for weeks afterwards. I'm looking at you Godfather.

Mike Schramm stopped me on the way to the rig and asked if I could help him find his dogs which were still trapped in his house across the street. Once again I found myself wading through floodwaters. When we entered Schramm's home the first thing I noticed was that the first floor was an absolute wreck. It made me think of my own home and how if it wasn't burned to the ground by now, surely it must be flooded. Into my arms went Bailey, who Mike assured me was the nice one. Nice or not, the dog was upset, and I had the scratches on my neck to prove it. We loaded both dogs into Sand Flea.

"Where's the FDNY?" someone asked as we watched Big Jack pull out of the parking lot with a dozen of our guys.

"They're still on the other side of the bay in Brooklyn. The bridge is closed because of the wind. A few trucks have made it across but most of them are getting stuck in the flood on the main road. It's too deep to drive through. We're on our own for now," replied Marty. It was a sobering thought. The forty or so volunteer firefighters who stayed behind were all that stood in the way of the raging inferno threatening to engulf the entire community. The Battle for Breezy Point was going to be won or lost by these men in the next few hours before the city units were able to cross the Marine Parkway Bridge.

* * *

Roxbury was flooded by the surge, but fortunate geography protected them from the ocean's waves which had pulverized Breezy Point. The hills and scrub brush in Fort Tilden created a half-mile wide barrier protecting them from the Atlantic Ocean which even Hurricane Sandy couldn't breach. A dozen firefighters sheltered from the rising floodwaters in the attic above the firehouse, and from that vantage point an ominous orange glow was first seen on the horizon to the southwest in Breezy Point. They watched helplessly as the blaze belched pillars of smoke and flaming debris, which were carried by northwesterly winds across the end of the peninsula.

When the tide receded enough they sprung into action to assist their neighbors to the west. Unencumbered by evacuees, Roxbury Volunteer Fire Department raced along Rockaway Point Boulevard in Engine 202 and reached the fire first. Their Chief, Richard 'Dickie' Colleran, deployed his men and equipment on the north end of the burning section of the Wedge on 7th Avenue, between Beach 208th and 209th Streets. They immediately started pouring water onto the fire by drafting seawater from the flooded streets surrounding them. Drafting is a method by which a pump is used to suck up water from the area around the fire truck. For instance, if a hydrant isn't available a drafting hose can suck water out of a pool, run it through the truck to build water pressure, and feed it to the hose and onto the fire. Unfortunately drafting is vulnerable to clogs from silt and other small debris, even with a filter, and can ruin a fire engine's pump.

Despite the risks, Chief Colleran and his men sprayed seawater onto burning houses in the Wedge, hoping to contain the fire until the FDNY could arrive. Soon Roxbury was joined by Rockaway Point firefighters who arrived on foot since their own vehicles stubbornly refused to start, and a dozen of Point Breeze's volunteers on our injured engine, Big Jack. Hoses from both apparatus snaked through the streets and down the narrow sidewalks towards the front lines. Water hissed as it struck the flames reaching out from windows and doors to the adjacent untouched homes. The fire had become a living breathing entity, hungry for fuel and desperate to expand. The firefighters from Roxbury, Rockaway Point, and Point Breeze stood in the way.

The battle had begun.

* * *

I found Tim O'Brien Sr. and we made our way to Sand Flea where we found the rest of our company. Tim "Duffman" Dufficy was our chauffer, with Mike Schramm and his dogs ready to operate the pumps. I found my old partner, Pat, who was ready to show me a thing or two about fighting fires. The brothers, Tim and Kevin O'Brien, were reunited with their father. Chief Marty Ingram hopped in the front passenger seat. Also on board was Danny Sullivan, an off-duty FDNY firefighter. He had flagged down Sand Flea during the last trip to the church to drop off evacuees. His father, a retired NYPD detective, and mother were trapped in a house on Clinton Walk right behind Duffman's. We had a new mission.

"You guys ready?" Marty asked over the thud of embers hitting the roof of the truck. We all looked at each other and nodded our heads. "Let's get out of here and check on Mr. Sullivan then come up 219th Street. Maybe we can fight this thing from the other end."

As events would prove, our mission to find Mr. Sullivan on the other end of Breezy Point was a fateful one. We didn't know it at the time, but other fires caused by the flaming embers had broken out in the community and threatened to create a second massive firestorm on the bayside. With most of our manpower and two of our three trucks committed at the northeast corner of the Wedge, we would never have discovered this new threat until it was too late.

Sand Flea proceeded west along the main road. We passed the firehouse on the left and drove back into the cloud of smoke the wind blew in our direction. The fire was glowing in the distance behind us, but the wind carried the smoke along our route, choking us. All of us peered through watery eyes into the dark, watching for debris on the road or people in need of help. We were passing Bath Walk when I looked to the north and spotted a house ablaze.

"Stop, stop, stop!" several of us shouted at once. "Did you see that? Duff that's right next to your house!"

"It looks like we have a house fire on the bayside. I'll call it in," said Marty as he attempted to make contact with FDNY over one of our few remaining radios. Dufficy maneuvered Sand Flea into the parking lot at 12th Avenue and Bayway Walk and, with the help of Schramm, got to work prepping the hydrant and hose. Mike had dragged an entire length of hose to a nearby hydrant only to find out that he had the wrong end and had to manhandle it all the way back to the rig. A detachment went to Clinton Walk to find the Sullivans, and after a brief search we were able to locate and rescue them.

In a letter to Deputy Inspector Roy Richter of the NYPD, who also lives in Breezy Point and lost his home the night of Hurricane Sandy, John and Ursula Sullivan wrote the following:

On October 29, 2012 not anticipating the drastic results of Hurricane Sandy, we decided to remain in our home right on the beach on the Bay in Breezy Point. Late in the evening, after the surge, not being able to get out of our home safely, the following members of the Point Breeze Fire Department voluntarily came to our door to assist us to safe ground:

Timothy J. O'Brien

Kevin E. O'Brien

Patrick Dempsey

Sebastian Danese

Timothy W. O'Brien Sr.

We are both 78 years old; my husband being handicapped with Parkinson's disease was carried out bodily by these young men, cheerfully with great care and concern to safer ground. My husband John R. Sullivan retired Detective 70 Squad has always had a great love and respect for The NYPD and we were never more proud and thankful as on that night.

Note: The letter's intent was for recognition by the NYPD for our actions that night, and therefore only includes the names of police officers. Other volunteers and neighbors joined us in the search and deserve just as much credit as we do for the rescue.

We returned from our search with hoses ready but pressure from the hydrants was low due to cracked water mains. This was a serious obstacle we'd face that night and in the months following Hurricane Sandy. Normally, we would expect 50 pounds of pressure per square inch (PSI) but that night we were lucky to get ten. It meant we would have to get in close since our effective range would be reduced to a few yards. It also meant the spray would be erratic since the rig would have to pause and let pressure build before channeling it out through the hose.

Pressure or not, Dufficy and Schramm are old hands in this business and kept the water flowing, even if it was only a trickle at times. Fortunately, we received some unexpected, albeit much appreciated, help from three of our neighbors who saw the fire and came to assist us. As luck would have it, two were retired FDNY firefighters, Ray Hendry Sr. and Mo Jackson, and their help fighting the fire at 5 Bayway Walk is immeasurable.

The O'Briens stretched and managed the hose while Pat and I got our tools together and prepared to enter the burning house to look for survivors. Before we could go in, however, the fire needed to be knocked back a bit and our two retired FDNY helpers were more than happy to work the nozzle. While working the hose with no bunker gear or safety equipment of any kind, the fire was fought at point-blank range by the retired city smoke eaters. What I was witness to next can only be described as an amazing display of bravery laced with an impressive dose of profanity. I loved it.

"Come get it you fucking mother fucker. That's right you bitch. Yeah, take it. Take it you fucking son of a whore. Yeah…you like that? I got more of that for you!" shouted Hendry as he advanced towards the fire, disregarding the flames as they angrily lashed out at him, singeing the hairs on his face and arms, "More water! I need more fucking water God dammit! Tell Dufficy to give me everything he's got. Stay on my ass. Brace me. I'm gonna shove it right down this motherfucker's throat…"

It took a few minutes and an untold amount of profanity for Hendry, Jackson, and Tim Sr. to clear a path for Tim Jr., Pat, and me to get into the house. The door was breached, resulting in a large mirror falling on Ray Hendry Sr.'s head, though he was unfazed by the resulting lacerations. With the door ajar we could see a stairway on the right leading up to the second floor with electrical wires and other debris hanging from the ceiling. It was a two story house with both levels on fire, but only the front facing us was burning. It was possible there were occupants trapped on the second floor in the rear where the fire hadn't yet reached.

We looked at the Chief, "Can we go inside yet? There might be people still inside."

Marty considered the risks, "Go for it!"

* * *

Now is a good time to pause and remind the reader that, in my own opinion, I was not a very experienced firefighter at the time. Most of the guys at the firehouse have been volunteering since they were in their late teens, while I joined after my 30th birthday. Consequently I lacked their experience and training, but I make up for it in spirit. I was carrying tools I couldn't name but they were big and heavy and one looked like it was a crowbar. That's the kind of firefighter I was at the time, an enthusiastic novice among seasoned experts.

* * *

With water still spraying on the doorway, I rushed past Pat and Tim, ran right under the electrical wires, and started to make my way up the stairs to the smoke-filled second floor. I had no Scott pack or mask on to supply me with oxygen, and although I had a bunker jacket and helmet my lower half was unprotected, clad only in blue jeans and hiking boots. I had shed my bunker pants and boots because they slowed me down and were tiring me out. I needed to be more cautious, but with the adrenaline rushing and the thoughts of people upstairs counting on us to rescue them I just couldn't help myself.

Summoning all the wisdom and skill I had acquired from watching *Backdraft* and *Ladder 49*, I took my big heavy crowbar (I later learned it's called a Halligan tool.) and smashed in the bedroom door near the rear of the house. It was clear. Another door burst open and another room was clear. Bathroom? Clear. Proud of myself I turned to go back from where I had come and noticed there was a lot more fire and a lot more smoke than I remembered. Suddenly it dawned on me by opening those doors I was feeding the fire fresh oxygen. Now I was in trouble.

"Seabass, where are you? Are you alright?" I heard Pat's voice from the stairway. He was holding a fire hose and spraying the first level, using his foothold on the top step for elevation. Tim O'Brien Jr. was on the second floor as well, at the front of the house looking for survivors, and probably me. He had on an oxygen mask and looked like an actual firefighter.

"I'm up here. The second floor is clear. I'm coming down," I replied.

Pat laughed and said "You're a fucking retard. Don't do that again." With one hand gripping the lever on the nozzle which controls the flow of water and the other on the nozzle's pistol grip, he briefly shut the water off to let the pressure build. Then my partner on the job for four years and best friend turned the business end of the hose towards me and let loose a fusillade of water as I walked down the steps. I totally deserved it.

We stayed in the house, fighting the fire from the inside and when it was safe the rest of Sand Flea's compliment joined us. The walls were opened, and the second floor was cleared again, however this time it was done properly. We determined the homeowners had evacuated before the hurricane, and hot embers from the firestorm in the Wedge had broken the windows on the north side of the house and probably lit the curtains on fire. With the fire contained we collected our gear and packed up the rig.

Sand Flea had a few new faces on board who requested our assistance to escape the smoke as we headed to the makeshift evacuee center at St. Thomas Moore Church. Included in this trip were a cat and a parakeet in a bird cage, as well as Schramm's two dogs, Maggie and Bailey. Rockaway Point Boulevard was empty on our last trip, but now the sides of the road were filled with residents from the western end of Breezy Point trying to escape the smoke and embers.

Minutes later we arrived at the church and helped the civilians inside. There were already dozens of people strewn about the pews. Many of them had barely escaped the flood and fire, and sobbing could be heard echoing throughout. The younger ones handed out water, blankets, and what little food they could find. We finished our business there quickly then headed across the street to the Catholic Club, where Rockaway Point had set up a triage center, to check on Eddy Wolf. He was in bad shape and first in line to be evacuated to the nearest hospital. He was incoherent from diabetic shock as it slowly overwhelmed him.

Mike Schramm took this opportunity to find shelter for his dogs who were cowering under the passenger bench in the cab of Sand Flea. Although suffering from badly cramped legs, he went into the church looking for anyone who might be able to watch his dogs, Maggie and Bailey, while he went with us to fight the fire. Finally, a neighbor, Nancy Jackson, agreed to take the dogs. He went back out to the rig to get them and found us waiting inside. Bailey left without a fight, but Maggie nipped me a few times as I tried to dig her out and hand her to Schramm.

"Go ahead without me," he said. "I'll meet you at the fire."

He led the two dogs into the church and handed them over to Nancy's care, but Maggie followed him out the front door as he began his trek through the flood. As he waded in water up to his waist she couldn't follow any longer, so he left her on a deck and planned to come back to pick her up later. Mike missed the rendezvous with Point Breeze and assisted FDNY units unfamiliar with Breezy Point. Hours later he returned to where he last saw Maggie, but the deck was empty.

He went back to the church hoping to find her there, but found Bailey miserable and alone. There was no time to search for Maggie. Large NYPD barrier trucks arrived in front of the church to evacuate people through the flooded streets to the Marine Parkway Bridge where MTA city buses were waiting to transport evacuees further inland. With a heavy heart, he joined the Dempsey family, who had two dogs of their own, and rode to Hillside High School in Brooklyn, leaving Maggie behind and praying she would be alright.

With his departure, Sand Flea was reduced to Marty Ingram, our Chief, Tim Dufficy, our chauffeur, Tim O'Brien junior and senior, Kevin O'Brien, Pat Dempsey and me. The fire at 5 Bayway was discussed in detail, especially how quickly we were able to extinguish it. We acknowledged how lucky we were to stop it before it spread. A second multi-dwelling fire on opposite ends of the community would have been disastrous.

"Duff, lets hook a right and see if we can get into the 208th Street parking lot to check on our guys." Sand Flea lurched forward as we began our trip towards the parking lot closest to the fire. The sights that greeted us were out of a nightmare. Several entire blocks consisting of more than 100 houses were ablaze. How many of our neighbors were unable to get out in time? It was Hell on Earth.

"Jesus Christ the whole Wedge looks like it's on fire. Which walk is that? Gotham?" asked one of the O'Briens.

"Looks like Fulton and Ocean too," replied Duffman. As the driver he had the better view.

"Can anyone see Essex?" I was desperate to know if my house was still standing. Since we were still on the north side of the fire the wind was blowing heat and smoke right at us. Cars in the parking lot were ablaze, while propane tanks and other combustibles exploded intermittently. The gasoline pumps used by the security trucks and other Co-op vehicles lay directly in the path of the blaze. For now this area was far too dangerous to begin firefighting operations. FDNY and NYPD units were just starting to arrive at the scene.

"Can't see that far, Seabass. This isn't going to work, let's keep going. Maybe we can find a spot to set up on 207th Street," ordered Marty as we rolled past the vehicle shed. We found the Roxbury Volunteer Fire Department at 207th Street and 8th Avenue feeding a FDNY tower ladder with their drafting pump. Aside from the two engineers needed to run the pumps, Roxbury's members were at the front, guiding the arriving FDNY units to the fire and fighting alongside them.

With their trucks out of action, Rockaway Point operated on foot to assist Roxbury and Point Breeze. Our own engine, Big Jack, was set up only a few yards from where Roxbury was drafting. Marty checked in with his Captains to assess the situation while the rest of us dismounted briefly to lend a hand. As more city units arrived on the scene it became apparent that our primary mission as a fast attack unit could be better utilized elsewhere. Taking up hydrants along paved roads, which the city units could put to better use, was counter-productive.

Captain Kevin O'Brien left Sand Flea to help lead the men on Big Jack. It was a bittersweet moment for Tim O'Brien Sr., who looked on with both pride and concern as his son stepped off the back step of the rig. Tim Sr. was the only firefighter in Point Breeze that night fighting alongside his children. His oldest, Tim, is not only his namesake but also the father of his grandchildren. He would have preferred Kevin, the youngest, to remain at his side but he understood Kevin was an officer and had a duty to perform. All Tim Sr. could do was pray for Kevin's safety and hope they would be united when this was over.

While the men on Big Jack trained hoses on the burning houses in front of them and helped the incoming FDNY get set up, Sand Flea looked for a new spot to deploy. Our high ground clearance and off-road capability gave us some interesting options. Everyone on board was either a seasoned firefighter, police officer, or both. Our youngest, Tim Dufficy, was also our best. We had more combined experience in Sand Flea than all of Big Jack, which had twice the number of personnel. Marty considered that, and was developing a plan to attack the fire from another location. One the city units couldn't reach.

* * *

Every firefighter, except the volunteers on Sand Flea, was at the northeast corner of the Wedge trying to contain the fire on its eastern side along Ocean Avenue. We decided to try and attack the blaze from the west near Hudson Walk. As we made our way westward along the main road, a woman towing a tube behind her waved at us frantically and we stopped to assist her.

"Are you okay?"

"Oh thank God you stopped! Here," she pushed a small dog towards me, "take my dog someplace safe. I can walk but I can't pull him behind me any longer." I'm not a pet owner, but I understand people who treat their dogs and cats like they're part of the family. My new love interest has two dogs and they mean the world to her, plus my sister has an oversized cat she refers to as her son. But this was too much.

"Lady, are you crazy? We're not going to safety. This truck is headed back to the fire. We can't take your dog."

"Well, go fuck yourselves then!" She was upset.

I checked my phone during the ride. At 11:13 P.M. I received a few texts from my girlfriend. "Since I'm about to die," she wrote, "I just wanted you to know I had a great weekend." It was the last thing I read before my phone's battery finally gave out. I had no chance to write her back and let her know I was alive, or to receive any more updates from her. We only knew each other for two weeks and it was a whirlwind romance. It broke my heart to think that I might never see her again.

As Sand Flea lumbered westward on Rockaway Point Boulevard, I volunteered to stand outside the driver's compartment, gripping the handholds and searching for debris on the road which might damage the truck. The smoke was thick, but I was able to see hundreds of glowing orange embers streaking across the night sky, carried by the northwesterly wind from the conflagration in the Wedge to our south. The embers rained down upon us like fiery hail, pelting Sand Flea and landing among the homes downwind of the fire. I wondered how many other fires might be out there which we didn't even know about.

CHAPTER 5

HELL BOUND

Tuesday, October 30, 2012

Just after midnight, Sand Flea came to a halt at the intersection of Rockaway Point Boulevard, Utica Walk, and Oceanside Avenue. Our original plan was to enter here at the westernmost corner of the Wedge and follow Oceanside as far as we could. This would allow us to attack the fire from the west and contain it until FDNY could arrive in force. The latest we heard through our few working radios was that they were on the way, but there was some confusion about which units were going to the fires in Rockaway and which would come here to assist us.

Unfortunately, Oceanside Avenue was inaccessible because of a large amount of debris blocking the entrance. Derelict cars and flotsam were strewn everywhere and couldn't be moved without heavy equipment. We were left with two options: go back to Beach 207th Street and join the other volunteers or continue west and probe the other entrances, hoping Sand Flea could navigate around the debris we assumed was there.

By going back to 207th Street, we could re-group with our guys and concentrate our efforts. We would also be with Roxbury and Rockaway Point volunteer fire departments, fighting the fire alongside each other from the north. However most of the incoming FDNY apparatus could only get to the fire from paved roads, and there was no sense deploying in the one area they could get to. All things being equal, they had better equipment and training than we could ever hope for. Our little Sand Flea would just get in the way and take up premium hydrant connections. The fire would also consequently be left uncontained on the west side, free to jump to the next block and consume more homes.

Our second option was to weave our way along Rockaway Point Boulevard to Beach 219th or Beach 222nd Street and from there make our way onto the Promenade.

Blocks within the Wedge, like much of Breezy Point, are sidewalks. The Promenade itself is only a double wide sidewalk and not capable of supporting heavy equipment, especially when it's been undermined as it was the night of Hurricane Sandy. Any large truck attempting to drive on the Promenade was likely to cause the sidewalk to cave in and become stuck. Days after the storm, we were told 26 FDNY vehicles became stranded by the sand and caved in portions of the Promenade while attempting to reach the fire in Breezy Point.

Marty turned his head from the front passenger seat and looked at us, "What do you guys think? Go up 219th and see what the story is out there?"

"Sure, we might even find another house fire on the way to the Wedge."

"Okay Duff," ordered Marty, "carefully now. Let's not run into anything and get stuck."

Sand Flea crept along the main road, smoke enveloping us and reducing visibility to only a few feet. Duffman expertly navigated us around debris strewn all over the road. We passed a fallen tree, a flooded car with its lights nearly out of battery power but still blinking its distress signal, and all sorts of maritime flotsam washed ashore by Sandy. At 219th Street, we found the street blocked by dozens of cars which had floated from their driveways, carried along by the surge. It was impassable so Duffman's horsed the truck to the next block where we found a similar situation. Our next chance was Beach 221st Street, which is one block from the western edge of the Breezy Point Co-op. Thankfully it was clear enough for us to pass.

We were quiet as ghosts. The turn south brought us out of the smoke and now we were listening for the sounds of neighbors calling for help. All that could be heard was the sound of Sand Flea's diesel engine and water splashing as we plodded along the flooded street.

Abandoned cars were everywhere; most of them turned around and pushed onto yards and into homes like children's toys after a tantrum. Entire front decks were torn away from houses and lying in the street. They were especially dangerous because of the nails and other sharp edges. We couldn't afford to lose a tire.

Occasionally we would see someone come out of their battered home and stare at us. They looked haggard and worn, but thankful to be alive. One older gentleman calmly walked out onto his porch which had somehow survived the storm, cigar in hand, and gave us a salute. He was taking in the devastation around him in stride. I saw him bend over and right a potted plant which had fallen over on his porch. He shrugged and looked back at us with this stoic look on his face that conveyed the notion, "you gotta start somewhere." I watched him until he was out of sight and thought out loud, "I don't know who he is, but that man is unbreakable."

More people came out and we would stop and ask if they needed assistance, but everyone declined help whether they needed it or not. They knew we were on the way to the fire, and no one wanted to hold us up. As we got closer to the oceanfront houses, the damage was clearly worse. Sand Flea turned left onto Breezy Point Boulevard, which eventually continues as the Promenade. We were greeted by the sight of more shattered homes and an obstacle course of debris. We passed 215th Street and all heads turned to the right.

Tim Jr. said, "Holy shit! Look at that. There's a house in the middle of the street!"

"The hurricane must've knocked it right off the foundation," observed Marty.

Duffman brought us back to the mission at hand, "You can see the fire up ahead. We're almost there."

"Pull us up to the gate but don't go onto the Promenade until we've had a chance to check it out," ordered Marty. "What do you guys think?"

* * *

When Marty asked us what we thought he was not only asking for our opinion, but also giving us a moment to consider what we were about to do. If anyone had objections or wanted to back out, now was the time.

The Atlantic Ocean to the south was still crashing over the Promenade, thanks to the high winds, although it was doing little to put out the blaze. The firestorm in the Wedge was to the north of the Promenade and at its most severe. The plan called for Sand Flea to make its way onto the Promenade and find a working hydrant close to the fire in order for us to put water on it. We would have to drive along a path only a few yards wide, possibly undermined, and could cave in at any time. We hoped the water main was still supplying enough pressure to make the risk worthwhile. Due to the narrow width of the Promenade and deep water on either side, once we started there was no turning around.

It was extremely dangerous.

The only solid ground, if you could call it that, was the Promenade and the sidewalks branching off it. Stepping off either of those would land a firefighter in chest-deep water if he managed to stay upright. Getting one's self out of a situation like that would be nearly impossible while wearing twenty pounds of bunker gear. The buddy system was crucial. The power was off and we had few working flashlights, so the only illumination was provided by the fire. In the shadows we had to be very careful where we stepped. Breezy Point doesn't have a sewer system so we rely on cesspools, which were overflowing and exposed. Each house has one or two cesspools, so there are thousands in the Wedge alone. One of us could be instantly swallowed up by a hole in the sand with but a brief moment to scream for help. The chances of rescuing one of us in that scenario were slim. It's like fighting a fire in a mine field.

There was also Mother Nature to worry about. The waves and sea spray were close enough to crash into our already battered truck which could be knocked out of action. If the hurricane force winds changed again and blew the fire and smoke towards us, we would have little hope for survival considering how close we were to the blaze. Even a strong gust of wind could push a firefighter off balance into the murky water around us. Our only chance to fight this fire on our terms and make it out unscathed was if wind continued blowing to the north so it would be at our backs, the waves would dissipate with the looming low tide, and the wind would die down as the storm passed. If our luck ran out, especially with the wind, there was a good chance of failing our mission and getting hurt, or worse.

Marty's question gave us the pause we needed to really think about what we were getting into. We had pressed our luck thus far and made out okay, but this was pushing it. On the other hand, we were here for a reason. The FDNY couldn't reach this side of the fire, and Mother Nature had presented us with a unique strategic opportunity to prevent the fire from spreading to other houses. No one knew how many of our neighbors were trapped in their homes in the Wedge counting on us to save them.

* * *

"I'm good," replied Pat.

Tim Jr. offered, "I think we're all good."

For any of us to say we weren't scared would be a lie. As we crossed onto the Promenade from Breezy Point Boulevard and inched closer to the fire, the men inside Sand Flea were quiet for a moment of personal reflection. We thought about our families, our friends, our wives or girlfriends, and for some of us, our children. This time there were no group prayers or hand-holding, only our own individual hopes we would make it through the night.

Moments like that, as they tend to do in a crisis, pass quickly. No sooner had we entered the Promenade than we saw the true destructive power of Hurricane Sandy's surge. All eyes were focused to the left where the houses at the beachfront should have been. Entire homes were washed away and those remaining barely stood. Some houses were smashed together into their neighbors, while others simply collapsed in on themselves. The blocks were choked with debris. Utility poles fell onto rooftops, while decks as far as we could see were twisted and mangled. It was something out of a nightmare.

"It's going to take us years to rebuild all of this," I muttered. Everyone was thinking the same. I thought back to the man with the cigar straightening his flower pot. Where do you begin to fix a mess like this? Could it be done? I thought of my own home and wondered if it looked like these houses, if it wasn't burned down already. The Chief snapped me out of it.

"We got a hydrant coming up. I think it's at the end of Gotham. I can't be sure. I think its Gotham," said Marty. "Yeah, I know that house. It belongs to Sheila Scandole. She's a 9/11 widow."

Tim Jr. echoed all of our thoughts with, "It's as good a place as any to make a stand."

"Where do we even start?" I asked.

"The same way you eat an elephant, Seabass," replied Marty, "one bite at a time."

The scene before us was horrific. Homes were ablaze as far as the eye could see, with flames as high as fifty feet. Most of the homes near the oceanfront of Fulton Walk and Ocean Avenue were burned down to their foundations. The framing and rooftops had long since collapsed on top of the furniture and personal belongings within. Through the shimmering light we could see the houses on Atlantic Walk were not yet alight, but the western sides facing the fire were starting to melt and burn. My home is on Essex Walk, one block over.

Tim Dufficy brought Sand Flea to a halt before the hydrant and went to work attaching a large red feeder hose from the hydrant to the rig. The rest of us went around to the back of the truck and started to pull down lengths of fire hose from the hose bed, located on top of Sand Flea, and dragged them into position. The work was slow going as we fought against the wind and had to test every step. Our boots were still filling with water which gave us the feeling of working in cement shoes. Every few minutes we would hold onto someone or something for support and lift our leg behind us, one foot at a time, in order to let the water spill out.

Despite Sand Flea being a mere twenty yards from the fire, we were quite cold. The high winds blew the heat and smoke away from us as planned, though creating an odd situation in which we could walk right up to the fire and barely feel any warmth. We could see at least one big FDNY ladder apparatus unit trying to put water on the blaze, probably the same one being fed by Roxbury's drafting. The wind was blowing the heat and smoke towards them like a blast furnace.

"It sucks to be those guys," observed one of the O'Briens. "They must be roasting alive up there. Look at the water coming from their hose. It's barely reaching the fire." Reduced water pressure hampered firefighting efforts of both professionals and volunteers alike.

We stretched three fifty foot lengths of hose from Sand Flea and snaked it down Gotham Walk. Pat was first up as the nozzle man while I braced myself behind him for support. It takes a lot of strength to manage a fire hose, and the bigger the hose, the more effort is needed to keep it under control. The O'Briens were behind me while Marty and Dufficy kept an eye on the water levels coursing through the rig.

We yelled, "Charge the line!"

Water rushed through the hose and made the previously slack line stiff and heavy. Pat had one hand on the pistol grip under the nozzle and another on the lever above, ready to engage. With the wind at our backs pushing the heat and smoke away from us, we were ready to advance into the fire and fight the blaze at point range. The irony of four off-duty police officers attacking the fire while FDNY struggled across the conflagration was not lost on us.

Pat looked back at me, "You ready?"

"Ready!" I replied. Tim Jr. gave me the thumbs up.

Pat brought the nozzle up and aimed towards the north wall of the nearest home on our left. The house only a few yards next to it was already fully ablaze and seeking a new source of fuel. We could see that the siding on our target was already alight, but the interior hadn't caught fire yet. This one could be saved if we could prevent the fire from getting a foothold and jumping.

"Hit it!"

* * *

On the other side of the Wedge, Big Jack and the bulk of our volunteer firefighters were working alongside Rockaway Point and Roxbury to contain the blaze on their end. The conditions in which they fought the fire were different than our own. By risking a deployment along the Promenade, the Sand Flea firefighters had the hurricane force wind at our backs, blowing the heat, smoke, and embers away from us – and directly into the faces of the other volunteers. Low water pressure meant the fire would have to be fought at point-blank range, but the searing heat and clouds of smoke threatened to suffocate the firefighters and drive them away. Flaming embers, lofted into the sky along high parabolic arcs and which struck from above at long range, came at them head-on at this distance. It was Hell on Earth.

Undeterred, the firefighters relentlessly continued their efforts to contain the conflagration, dodging flaming missiles and choking on waves of superheated smoke-filled air with every step. A steady stream of firefighters was pouring into Breezy Point and the Rockaways, summoned from firehouses across New York City. Earlier this night, in Howard Beach, the FDNY Queens Borough Commander, Deputy Assistant Chief Robert Maynes, conferred with Assistant Chief Joseph Pfeifer. They agreed Chief Maynes would lead the operation in Belle Harbor (a neighborhood in Rockaway where my girlfriend's parents live and the scene of another large fire) while Chief Pfeifer would take command in Breezy Point.

As a Breezy Point resident himself, Chief Pfeifer knew the lay of the land. He understood how the community was situated, where his assets could and could not go, and the role local volunteer firefighters could play with our specialized vehicles and equipment. His strategy was to halt the spread of the fire without jeopardizing the lives of the firefighters under his command. To accomplish this, the fire had to be methodically contained. The eastern and northern flanks, because of their proximity to roads on which the FDNY apparatus could operate, were secure. Chief Pfeifer then deployed four tower ladders (Tower Ladders 159, 12, 142, and 115) near the northwest edge of the fire in an attempt to impede the flames from advancing further west. Although the crews on those towers fought bravely, their capability was diminished due to low water pressure and the hurricane force winds blowing against them.

Firefighters advance along the northern flank near Ocean Avenue.

The southern flank along the Promenade remained exposed. Several FDNY units had probed south along the debris clogged roads and parking lots but were turned back or became stuck in the sand. If the wind were to shift to a more westerly direction, hundreds more houses would burn while the fire swept unopposed through that part of the community. The southern flank of the fire was in jeopardy, and only one unit with a handful of men stood between the fire and the southernmost homes in the Wedge…

Sand Flea.

* * *

Water burst from the nozzle in Pat's hands and cascaded down the walls of the houses still standing on Gotham Walk. The fire sizzled and hissed at us as we sprayed the flames. With the low water pressure, we advanced up onto the deck and drenched the side of the house as best we could. When it looked like we had stopped the flames from jumping, water was poured onto their source. This house was a total loss, burning inside and out.

"This is bad Seabass," lamented Pat, "Did you ever think we'd see something like this?"

"I know what you mean, but this isn't the worst part. Tomorrow when we're pulling the bodies out…that'll be the worst." The look on his face told me he hadn't really considered that. Memories of New Orleans during Hurricane Katrina came to mind. "Save your strength dude. We have a long night ahead of us. Let me take over."

One by one we splashed water onto the flaming houses around us. I took over for Pat on the nozzle and another 50-foot length of hose was stretched so we could advance further into the fire. Sometimes we would have to double back and fight a fire which had sprung up behind us. The last thing we wanted was to get trapped. Soon we were at houses which were merely foundations, but still fiercely burning with blue and purple flames spouting into the air.

"What is that? Gas? They didn't turn the fucking gas off?"

"Yeah, has to be," Pat agreed. "We put water on it, but it just lights up again."

"You gotta be kidding me," was all I could say. Someone screwed up, big time. The story we heard afterwards was the gas company wasn't ready for the rapid pace of the storm surge, and most cut-offs were underwater before they realized it was too late. The problem couldn't be fixed until the water receded. All we could do was keep an eye out for blue flames relighting fires behind us.

Back at the rig, Tim Dufficy was running another feeder line from the hydrant at the end of Ocean Avenue a hundred yards away. Marty, frustrated at the limited response from the city thus far, got on the radio. "I want back up. Get me back up right now."

"Roger that," replied Brillo on Big Jack, "we're pulling out of here. FDNY is taking over here now."

"We have good pressure on the Promenade. Come around on 219th street and join us at Gotham." Before a reply could be heard, Marty stepped into a sink hole and was submerged up to his chest, destroying his radio. The O'Brien men quickly pulled him out but he was soaked in freezing water.

"Pressure is dropping. Shut off the nozzle and let it build up for a minute," advised Pat as he taught me how to properly fight a fire. As we stood and waited for the water pressure to build, I noticed we had advanced further into the blaze than I thought. Working the nozzle gives you a sort of tunnel vision, so I was genuinely surprised to see us nearly a third of the way down Gotham Walk. We had stopped the fire from spreading to the cluster of homes at the end of this block, but the rest was burned to the ground. Across the Wedge we could see more FDNY units had arrived and were battling the blaze on their end.

A few yards ahead of us a utility pole was turned to cinders and looked like it could fall at any moment. I looked over at Pat and we both had the same thought, "Let's pull back a little. This could get real bad, real fast." We backed off to where the houses were still standing and sprayed them down again for good measure. It felt good knowing we were able to stop the fire from spreading on this end. With FDNY on the scene, we could shift focus from containment to extinguishing this blaze.

A short, tough looking man wearing an FNDY uniform marched up to us and introduced himself as the Chief of the 33rd Battalion based out of East 14th Street in Brooklyn. He had walked all the way around the eastern perimeter of the Wedge and saw us deploy at the end of Gotham Walk. "Don't worry about hosing down the debris field," he suggested, "Those houses are done. Focus on the ones that haven't burned yet."

"That's our plan," we replied.

"Good. You're doing a great job. City units can't get out here yet but we've been trying, so be real careful. You're on your own if something goes haywire. Don't worry though, we're gonna beat this thing."

He walked away westward on the Promenade as we happily handed over the nozzle to the O'Brien men and took up their former position managing the hoses. Several times we heaved the lines forward as the O'Brien men advanced further into the fire. They needed more slack, so I pulled and tugged but the line was snagged on something near the house at the end of the walk. In my exhausted state, I ambled over to where the hose was caught and tried to get into a better position to free it. Before my brain could catch up to my body, I had stepped off the sidewalk.

My right leg immediately sunk three feet below the pavement level while the rest of my body fell forward. The fact that I didn't snap my leg when I fell was a stroke of pure luck. With all my remaining strength I was able to stand up, now in waist-deep water, and pull myself back onto the sidewalk with some help from the guys. Shaken, I sat myself down on the closest porch steps and got myself together. After a few minutes I walked back over to Sand Flea to see if Duff and Marty needed a hand, but they were busy looking to the west where Big Jack, with its malfunctioning lights, was rumbling down the Promenade.

Across the Wedge on the north side of the blaze, disaster struck the Roxbury volunteers: their drafting pump burned out at approximately 2:00 A.M. Dozens of FDNY apparatus and over two-hundred city firefighters were now on the scene, rallying to Chief Pfeifer's calls for assistance, leaving the Roxbury volunteers no hydrants available from which to draw water. The rest of their fight, with Rockaway Point by their side, would be done with hand tools while assisting city units unfamiliar with Breezy Point to reach their assigned positions. It was back-breaking work for the already worn out volunteers, but they never faltered.

* * *

With the reunion of the Big Jack and Sand Flea crews, Point Breeze Volunteer Fire Department was at its best strength since we left the Clubhouse hours ago. Alongside Roxbury and Rockaway Point, Big Jack fought valiantly against the fires from the north. When FDNY showed up in force, the officers in command of Big Jack's crew came to the same conclusion we did and gave the professionals some room to operate. Mercifully, the Big Jack crew took over hose duty from the exhausted O'Briens allowing the Sand Flea crew to rest for a moment.

During our break, a plan was devised to check on several neighbors who we suspected stayed behind to weather the storm. Given the conditions of the smashed houses seen in the Wedge on the way to the fire, we thought it was worth the risk to search several blocks for survivors. All walkways were clogged with debris, especially parts of decks torn asunder from their homes. Bristling with nails and sharp edges, one mistake could end our search and rescue mission prematurely. We gathered the few remaining flash lights we could find and set out.

With a flashlight in hand, Pat and Tim Jr. led us down Lincoln Walk to check on Brian Quinn, a detective friend of ours, while I stayed alongside Tim Sr. in the rear. We had to climb over twisted and broken decks, move lawn furniture and other small debris, and navigate through tangles of wires ripped from the utility poles. On occasion we called out, "Point Breeze! Anyone need assistance? Is anyone home?" We found no one. The residents had either been rescued or evacuated, although we couldn't ignore grimmer thoughts when considering another explanation for the absent signs of life.

Soaked bunker gear limited our range of motion, while stiff muscles and aching joints combined to make climbing through the debris a miserable effort. Any thoughts I had of complaining were tempered by Tim O'Brien Sr. in front of me. Though nearly thirty years our senior, the elder O'Brien kept pace without a gripe. If it had been me at that age I would probably have given up a long time ago. Or better yet, I would be down in Florida with my old man, playing golf and drinking at the country club.

"I see a light on up ahead," said Pat. He pointed to a house fifty feet down the block. In the darkness you could make out a pale glow in one of the windows. Pat made it onto the wooden deck and knocked on the door. Inside a flashlight was turned on and standing upright on the living room table illuminating the room. We called out several times and looked inside, but no one was home. The owner probably fled in a hurry when the fire started and left a few things behind. There were no more signs of life on the block and the decision was made to head back to the rigs. If we went any further north the smoke from the fire a block over to our east would envelope us and that was the last thing we needed.

Tim Jr. helped the guys out with the hoses while his father sat inside Sand Flea for some rest. Ironically, despite the massive fire twenty yards in front of us, he was suffering from hypothermia and exhaustion. I was able to plug-in my phone to get a little charge and talked to Marty. After an hour, Tim Jr. pulled me aside while I was helping with the hoses, "Seabass, you mind taking a walk with me? My old man is done. I need to get him back to the other side of the fire where FDNY is set up so he can get checked out."

"No problem. Your dad is a real fucking trooper," I said, with one request, "Since we're going that way you mind if we pass by Essex so I can check out my house?"

"Sure, but let's get a move on. I don't know how much longer my dad's hip and leg are gonna last. He's in real pain but won't admit it."

Sitting in Sand Flea allowed him to catch his breath, but once he relaxed a little, the fatigue took over and he could barely move his legs. It took some effort, but Tim Jr. and I got his dad out of the rig and walking again though with a pronounced limp. Four blocks later we were at the end of Essex Walk. As expected, it was a disaster, but still untouched by the fire one block over. The O'Briens sat on the bench at the end of the block while I picked my way through the debris.

The house closest to the ocean, on whose deck I had taken pictures during the morning of the storm, was flattened. Across from it, the Dunn's house was swept off its foundation and was lying partially in the sand alley which runs between the blocks. It had crashed into the rear of another home on Atlantic Walk. As with other blocks throughout the community, debris choked the sidewalks and I found myself jumping from one broken deck to another. Finally, I reached my destination.

I fished my keys from my bunker gear and prayed, "Please God, don't let the inside be a total wreck."

We built high off the ground and were lucky since the first floor appeared to have no damage, although it was damp and reeked of smoke. I took a look at the finished basement and saw the water had flooded about four feet, but thankfully I had taken the time to move most of the valuables up to the second floor. The walls didn't show any signs of cracking, and although the deck was undermined, it appeared to be in decent enough shape. The fire was still a concern since it was less than a hundred yards from my front door and a shift in wind could easily sweep the blaze down my block. However, compared to what I had seen already, I knew I was lucky.

Getting to the house was hard, but leaving was even harder. The temptation to shed my water logged clothing and climb into bed upstairs was overwhelming. Just five minutes on the couch. "No," I said out loud. "You gotta keep going. Sleep later."

I snapped myself out of it, grabbed some bottles of water, and rejoined the O'Briens at the end of Essex Walk. Though there was still reason to worry, it felt so much better knowing what the damage was instead of playing guessing games all night. I lost my basement. So what? The next block over was beginning to catch fire, and at least six other homes on my block were total losses. Those people lost everything. I had nothing to complain about.

"You think it would be okay to grab a beer at the Sugar Bowl?" I asked Tim Jr. as we made our way east on the Promenade. The Sugar Bowl was a beach bar where Oceanside and the Promenade meet. They had only closed up for the season the weekend before Sandy after their annual Halloween Party. I was certain they would have a beer or two left behind.

"I don't see why not," replied Tim. "We'll bring some back for the guys after we drop my dad off. I think we earned them."

"Unless of course, the Sugar Bowl isn't there anymore," I joked. A minute or two later we were looking at a pile of debris where the bar used to be. The foundation was there, but the entire structure had been swept away. On the inside walls of the Sugar Bowl there used to be pictures of neighbors and friends going back two generations. As kids in the Wedge, we would go to the front part of the bar where ice cream and over-priced food was prepared by local kids trying to earn a buck. When I was a life guard it was our headquarters, and when I was old enough getting into "the Bowl" was a rite of passage.

I tried to make light of the situation, "So... no Sugar Bowl tonight?"

"Yeah, I guess not. That sucks," observed Tim, "You know this storm is really starting to piss me off. Wait here while I try and get something." He climbed onto the rubble and looked for a road sign for "Gorge Timmins Way" which had hung on a pole at the Sugar Bowl for years, in honor of the bar's original owner who had passed away a decade ago. Tim wanted to retrieve it and give it to his friend, John Timmins, who is George's son. Unfortunately the sign was never recovered, another of the countless sentimental items claimed by Hurricane Sandy.

Deprived of our chance to liberate a beer for the road, we turned north and navigated our way over the usual assortment of debris until we found a suitable house with a deck which we could use to cut through to the next block. Walking through other people's property via their side decks is a tolerated Breezy Point custom and a quick way to go from block to block without the hassle of walking to their ends. This is how we travelled from the alley behind 7th Avenue, over to Graham

Place, through the flooded Arcadia Walk parking lot, and finally onto 8th Avenue. We could see dozens of flashing lights from FDNY and NYPD vehicles at the intersection ahead.

"Only a few more steps Dad," encouraged Timmy. "We're almost there."

An Emergency Medical Service (EMS) worker saw us limping down the street practically carrying Tim Sr. between us. She approached the elder O'Brien and offered to help, but he just waved her off. We were headed to a house on 207th Street where friends were expecting him. With his last bit of strength Tim Sr. made it to that house and around to the back deck. Tim Jr. and I helped him take off his bunker gear then took him inside. We were greeted by a family who, despite flooding on the first floor, never evacuated. They offered us bottles of water while doting on their new injured guest.

"From a father's standpoint I was immensely proud of my two boys," Tim Sr. told me after the storm. "You could see the fear and the fatigue in all of our eyes, but we just continued doing what we had to do. I was worried about them, but they were among fellow police officers, and it made me feel like the proudest father in the world watching them work beside their fellow officers."

Tim O'Brien Sr. joined the firehouse when bell bottom jeans were still in style and was an active member for three decades. He went into retirement after suffering several serious permanent injuries, but was reinstated by the Chief the night of Hurricane Sandy. A man in his sixties, he kept up with firefighters half his age and never complained about the physical strain we endured that night, even after his past injuries became aggravated and caused him intense pain. After more than thirty years of volunteer service within our community, Tim O'Brien Sr. finished his final tour of duty the night of Hurricane Sandy, holding nothing back, sacrificing his health one last time for the people and the community he loves so much, fighting fires alongside his sons who proudly follow in their father's footsteps.

★ ★ ★

Reluctantly, Tim Jr. said goodbye to his father and we departed. The night wasn't over yet. At approximately 4:11 A.M. I made the following Facebook post for the residents desperate for information about the flood and fire:

> *"Breezy Point is in bad shape. Ocean Ave, Fulton, Hudson, and parts of Irving Walks are completely burned to the ground. Most houses on the waterfronts are destroyed. Essex walk is a disaster. All the homes near the water are either gone or unsalvageable. Fires are still burning. Update later."*

We made a brief stop at my house to get some bottles of water, and then rendezvoused with the rest of Point Breeze still fighting the fire from the Promenade. All of us were exhausted, our minds running on autopilot as we reconciled with all the horrible things we had witnessed so far. FDNY Chief Pfeifer raised a sixth alarm, summoning hundreds of firefighters from all over the city who were bringing the fire under control. After another backbreaking hour, we decided to take one of the trucks back to St. Thomas Moore Church where the evacuee center was set up so we could grab some food and water.

Marty was in bad shape and needed to rest. He could barely move his legs and his hypothermia had worsened. Tim Dufficy and Mike Scotko carried him into the last pew in the church and laid him down. In an interview after the storm, Marty told me about his time at the church from his own point of view: "The church was packed. I lay down on the oak pew and it was a great opportunity to stretch my legs but instead I started flopping around, shivering from the cold. I had been to Air Force Survival School and I'm assessing the situation and I know I have to get rid of these wet clothes. I knew if I stopped shivering I'd be in real trouble because it meant my core temperature had dropped. Ricky Savage came in and asked if anyone needed help so I told him to take me back to my house for a change of clothes and potassium tablets to help with the cramps and some water for dehydration. Then we went back to the church to continue rescue operations."

At 5:20 A.M., while at the church, I took a moment to update my Facebook page with more information:

"The Wedge is still burning but we've made amazing progress keeping it under control considering the circumstances. Ocean Ave, Fulton, Gotham, and Hudson Walks are all burned to the ground, as is Oceanside near those walks. Irving is on fire and we're having trouble with it.

Any house three houses from the ocean promenade are either destroyed, unsalvageable, or extremely damaged. All of BP was under 5 to 7 feet of water. We lost all the firehouses at one point or another and most of our trucks and equipment. Some amazing shit happened but I'll save the war stories for later.

The roads are still flooded and closed. Do not attempt to enter Breezy Point. I've been to almost every part of the point tonight. Ask me something specific and I'll try to answer."

At 6:05 A.M. I received a text from John 'Tiny' Fahy inviting me to join the rest of the volunteer firefighters at the Catholic Club across the street from the church. The plan was to regroup there for a few hours and then go back out. Pat and Brillo set up a series of chairs to lay on which were only big enough for one of them to sleep comfortably, so they crawled onto their makeshift bed together and spooned. The last thing Pat said before succumbing to fatigue was, "I don't even care how this looks. I'm fucking warm so let's just go to sleep."

I got a ride back to the Point Breeze Clubhouse where my car was parked. Inside awaited dry clothing and a charger for my phone. Water had destroyed most of the electrical system in my truck, but the engine started, the cigarette adapter had power, and the heater blew hot air. That was all I cared about. I had to get out of my wet clothes before hypothermia set in. My bunker gear went on the hood of the truck to dry while my jeans and shirt were draped over the roof. I was down to my boots, my socks, and my underwear. I sure as hell wasn't putting on clean, dry clothing over dirty, wet boxers. Despite the sun coming up and first responders all around me, I stripped off the last of my wet clothing and struggled, in all my naked glory, to get myself into new boxer shorts without accidently stepping in mud. Unbeknownst to me, several city firefighters gathered to watch the show. One of them whistled while several others shouted cat calls.

I honestly didn't care too much, but a good cop never passes on a chance to tease the FDNY if he can help it, "Glad you guys could make it. Hope you enjoyed the show!"

At 6:30 A.M., as I finished getting into dry clothes, FDNY Chief Pfeifer declared the fire contained, although it would smolder until dusk the following day, having lasted 45 hours. I climbed into my car and wrapped myself in an old Battlestar Galactica sleeping bag I had since I was a kid. The heat was blowing, my body was drying out, and my phone came back to life. I tuned the car's radio to the local AM news station, reclined the driver's seat, and settled in for a well-deserved nap.

CHAPTER 6

AFTERMATH

Tuesday, October 30, 2012

While we were sleeping, Ricky Savage and Marty Ingram had continued rescue operations throughout the morning with the help of Marty's son, Marty Jr., and his friend, Michael McEwen, both of whom are FDNY firefighters. Neighbors reported an elderly man stuck inside his house on Beach 221st Street. Upon entering the home they found him on top of a dresser where he spent the night to escape the flood in his bedroom. The man had lung cancer and could barely speak or breathe. They carried him out and drove him back to the church in Big Jack for medical attention.

"This older gentleman, who couldn't talk and couldn't communicate and we didn't even know his name, was smiling like a little kid because he was excited to get a ride in a fire truck." said Marty, "That was really incredible."

Soon after, another call came in for an elderly woman trapped in her home on Beach 215th Street as well as a buzzing transformer threatening to explode on Breezy Point Boulevard. The FDNY was still busy smothering embers in the Wedge and had already lost dozens of vehicles trying to navigate through the debris, tight turns, and undermined roads in the community. Units were called in from all across the city, and as a result were unfamiliar with the unique hazards of operating in the Breezy Point. We were needed.

Marty went into the Catholic Club where our guys were passed out from exhaustion and nudged Brillo, still wrapped up in Pat's arms, from his slumber. "Kevin you gotta wake up. We got two jobs going right now and I need Unit 7 and Unit 8 so get the guys going."

"Marty…" replied Brillo as he wiped the sleep from his eyes, "fuck you. I'm sleeping."

The Chief ignored the discourtesy. On a good day Brillo isn't a morning person and Marty understood how fatigued we all were, but people were counting on us and he persisted. "We have two jobs. They're our jobs. FDNY is busy and can't get to them. You want to ignore one and maybe someone dies?"

Despite only two hours rest, he woke the rest of the guys and got back into the action. I was roused by the sound of my phone chirping. It was 8:23 A.M. and Tiny informed me that the guys were getting up and returning to the Wedge. My body and mind strongly protested against anything which involved unwrapping myself from my blanket. I was sore from head to toe. Injuries I wasn't aware of last night appeared everywhere now as the adrenaline had worn off. No sooner had I convinced myself it was time to get moving than Pat showed up at my car looking for his gun. Last night in an attempt to safeguard our weapons, I locked them in my glove compartment. It was the best that could be done considering the circumstances. He had to go into work. My boss gave me the day off.

I hopped aboard Big Jack as it lumbered down the main road. The woman on Beach 215th Street was located and transported back to the makeshift medical center at St. Thomas Moore. We searched for the buzzing transformer but it was never found and most likely a product of someone's imagination running wild from shattered nerves. Power to the entire peninsula was out therefore we concluded a buzzing transformer was very unlikely.

Big Jack rendezvoused with Sand Flea on the Promenade. Last night we were too tired to properly pack up our hoses and equipment so we left them in place. Now it was time to collect our gear before someone else took it in the confusion. Despite our exhaustion we worked quickly and by 10:45 A.M. both trucks had recovered most of our lost hoses and were ready for action again. Sand Flea returned to the firehouse while Big Jack stayed behind to work over the still smoldering embers. I took dozens of pictures and videos of the fire zone, and then made my way back to Essex Walk. I wanted to get photos of every house to put online for my neighbors who were desperate for information.

On the morning after Hurricane Sandy, Brillo and another Point Breeze firefighter are awestruck by the ghastly results of the previous night's massive fire in the Wedge.

I climbed through the debris, following the same path as the night before, stopping at each house to assess the damage and take photos. My phone was full of messages from my neighbors looking for updates. In many cases I was the first to give them the bad news. I texted, "I'm sorry to say your house is completely destroyed. It's off the foundation and broken into several pieces in the back alley. Again, very sorry. Can't call. No service here." All they could send in reply was a quick thank you and wish me luck, and then it was onto the next message. It was a heartbreaking task but it was important and they wanted to know.

Inside my own house, I opened a bottle of water and sat down on my couch for a minute to collect my thoughts. The windows were fogged from the humidity caused by the flooded basement. At some point I would have to go down there and pump it out and remove the debris, but not today.

A decision had to be made.

I could pack up my things and head over to my brother's house in Staten Island where my sister was staying. No one would blame me for walking away now to take care of my own personal business. Hundreds of Breezy Point families would be doing the same thing. The homes which weren't burned down or washed away would have to be rebuilt. For some that meant tearing down and starting over, and for others it was just a matter of hanging new sheetrock. I was one of the lucky ones.

But I couldn't just walk away for all the same reasons I didn't evacuate the day before. I had been saving lots of vacation time at my job in the event I needed it someday. Well, today is that day. I love my job, and I'll do whatever they ask of me, but if I can get the time off I'm going to spend it here helping out at the firehouse and in the community. It was settled.

★ ★ ★

On the other side of Breezy Point, the O'Brien men went to check on their house along the main road. Tim Jr. got a ride into Rockaway to check on his apartment, then onto Bellmore to see his wife and kids. Kevin stayed for most of the day then left for Maspeth to get cleaned up before work the next morning. Brillo and the others went to check on their homes and assess the damage. Several members, who missed the storm the night before joined our ranks, and we were glad to have them.

Mike Schramm and his dog, Bailey, got a ride into Rockaway to check on his wife and daughter, who were staying with family in Dayton Towers at Beach 105th Street. He was covered with soot and reeked of smoke from hours of fighting the fire alongside the FDNY at Oceanside. Their route brought them through Howard Beach which had been hit just as hard as the Rockaways. A boat lay on its side in the middle of Cross Bay Boulevard next to a burned out FDNY fire truck.

The scene at his destination was no better. Dayton Towers consists of seven buildings, each with twelve stories, totaling 1,752 apartments. As Mike walked down the block towards the 105-00 building, he noticed every car window along the way was broken and looked as if looters had picked the vehicles clean. The people he passed who didn't wear blank expressions, returned predatory stares. Mike arrived at the darkened building onto a pitch black second floor hallway and knocked on the door. The distinct sound of a gun's slide being wracked was heard on the other side of the door. His sister-in-law is a court officer and wasn't taking chances.

Once inside, he was offered the opportunity to take a cold shower and something to eat. They didn't have clothing in his size, so he wrapped a bed sheet around himself like a Roman toga. He recounted his adventure in Breezy Point and listened as his family recalled their own tribulations of that night in Rockaway. With tears in his eyes, Mike broke the news to his wife and daughter about Maggie, their faithful dog, whose whereabouts were unknown, then fell asleep for the next fourteen hours from exhaustion.

I left my house just after 11:30 A.M. and headed towards the fire zone along Oceanside hoping I could get some information. Rumors were already circulating about mass casualties in hard hit areas of the Rockaways. My cellular service was out and I desperately wanted to check in with my girlfriend and my family, but at least I could still take pictures so I added another dozen along the way. The scene from the north was just as heartbreaking as that from the south, though suddenly I was stopped in my tracks as I passed Gotham Walk.

In front of me was a statue of the Virgin Mary, head bowed and arms extended at her sides. More than a hundred burned down houses smoldered around it, but this statue, although scorched by the fire, was otherwise perfectly preserved. I'm not an overly religious person, but I was moved spiritually and so were the people around me. In my opinion, it was a sign from God reminding us, despite all the carnage and suffering, we weren't forgotten. Over the coming weeks this statue became the symbol of the Breezy Point recovery effort seen all over the world.

The Chief and a few other guys were there as well. A reporter from The Daily News walked over to us and started asking questions about the events of last night. As a retired Colonel in the Air Force and former executive for the FAA, Marty had the right amount of savvy and professionalism to deal with the press. Before much could be said however, one of our members came over and drove the reporter off. He was also a city firefighter, and as a city employee, it's emphasized to never talk to the press unless specifically instructed to do so. In his defense, he thought he was doing Marty a favor. By the time the Chief explained the situation to him, the reporter was already gone.

"This isn't about attention whoring. The press is a reality we're going to have to deal with. They're going to tell the story no matter what, so we might as well help them get the details right. Besides it's a good story. It's an inspirational story." Marty continued, "We're going to need a lot of help rebuilding down here and to do that we're going to need help on the national level, so you better get used to the attention."

The iconic statue of The Virgin Mary, spared by the fire and flood which destroyed hundreds of homes around Her.

We made our way back to Big Jack which was sitting in the parking lot just north of the fire zone. In front of us were the charred remains of the Lapera house, burned down to its foundation. Marty's order to call off the rescue during the height of the storm weighed heavily in his heart and mind as the fate of Mary Lapera and her children was unknown. All of us, especially the Chief, were agonizing over the conflicting casualty reports of the people we were unable to rescue. These weren't strangers. Every loss would be a morale-crushing personal failure to the guys who risked so much to keep our community safe.

As we were contemplating this, two FDNY fire marshals approached us and stepped up onto the running boards to talk. They were already piecing together clues concerning the cause of the fire and wanted our account. When this was done we asked about the rest of the Rockaways since we had heard of a fire near The Harbor Light, a popular restaurant located on Newport Avenue and Beach 129th Street. We were told it had burned to the ground along with several other homes in the area. This was doubly sad for me since it had been the location of my first date with my girlfriend two weeks prior.

"How about injuries and fatalities?" I asked. "We're hearing a lot of rumors."

"We've heard anywhere from eight to twenty bodies have been recovered so far depending on who you talk to," replied one of the marshals, "but personally we haven't seen anything for ourselves."

The news was disheartening. I assumed we would have fatalities. There is no way the community could suffer a storm and fire of that magnitude without some. I remembered back to September 11th and how it felt to sift through the rubble hoping for survivors but only finding parts of the dead. I worked on Wall Street at the time and there was a chance of finding someone I knew, but this was different. In Breezy Point everyone knows everyone else. The fire zone in the Wedge is nearly a perfect match for the summertime paper route I did as a teenager. I knew these people. I grew up with them. We all did.

"If there's anyone recovering bodies it should be us," I suggested to Marty. "It's not something I want to do, but I think they'd appreciate us recovering our own neighbors."

Marty thought about it for a minute, "I understand what you're saying Seabass, but it's not our call. Besides, these guys have been through so much already. Would you really want to put them through that?"

"No, I guess not," I replied. "This whole thing is very frustrating and fucked up. We didn't see anyone else to rescue last night when we went looking. That means there's someone we missed or we got there too late."

"You're getting ahead of yourself," Marty advised. "You guys did an extraordinary job last night. So far we haven't seen any bodies in the Wedge, or anywhere else in Breezy Point for that matter. You're beating yourself up. Calm down."

He was right. We did the best anyone could have under those circumstances. The risks we took were outrageous, and we were lucky it was not us the FDNY was recovering. That sentiment was true for everyone who went out into the storm and fought the fire last night.

"Let's get back to the firehouse," Marty ordered. "We have a lot of work to do."

The firehouse was a wreck both inside and out. The flood had reached at least four feet inside and destroyed most of the interior. Utilities were shut off for safety reasons until they could be tested and repaired, therefore no gas, electric, or clean was water available. Most of our equipment was gone or broken. We had no access to food or fuel, and the mess inside meant the firehouse was unlivable. The radios were destroyed and the siren system, which we rely on to alert members about emergency calls, was down. The only way for us to get dispatched was by word of mouth, in which case assembling a crew was extremely difficult if we didn't stick together.

In the meantime, both Sand Flea and Big Jack were dispatched to the north side of the Reid Avenue parking lot in order to drain the flooded water main access tunnel. The plan was to use a drafting hose to suck the water out, and after some rigging we got it to work. Unfortunately, the water table was too high, and as quickly as we pumped the water out, more flooded back in.

At approximately 3:00 P.M. as we were packing up the rig, an older man in front of me started to have a seizure and hit the asphalt face-first.

"Everyone back up and give him some room," I shouted.

A woman approached, "Aren't you going to help him?"

"I am helping him. He's having a seizure. You don't try to restrain someone unless they're a danger to themselves and he's not," I explained. "All I can do is put my glove in his mouth for him to bite down on so he doesn't cut off his tongue. We just gotta wait it out."

When the seizure finally ended, firefighters Mike Scannell, Gerry Carney, and Dylan Dombrowski helped me get him onto a backboard and we loaded him on the bed of a commandeered pickup truck from Breezy Point Security. We drove him down to Rockaway Point Volunteer Fire Department where a triage center was organized. Since Rockaway Point lost their fire trucks and ambulances they took over medical services and logistics. Soon, between the Catholic Club and activity center next door, their location would serve as the major hub in Breezy Point for the recovery effort.

As this was happening, the NYPD utilized its large five ton barrier trucks to shuttle residents from their cars parked alongside the road in front of the main gate and into the property. Rockaway Point Boulevard was still flooded near Beach 203rd Street in front of the Co-op offices and the stores. The water was deep enough to restrict access to all but the largest of civilian vehicles. Sedans couldn't make it and were waved away by security along the road. A significant traffic jam ensued as vehicles were barred from entering the property and were forced to turn around on the two lane road. Many simply pulled to the side of the road and walked.

The traffic jam was more than an inconvenience. By clogging the road with civilian vehicles, it restricted passage to trucks carrying desperately needed supplies. Furthermore, since the road was our connection to Roxbury, our response time during an emergency became dangerously prolonged. Like us, the Roxbury Volunteer Fire

Department suffered manpower and material losses after the storm. A serious incident there could escalate quickly while we were stuck on the road.

We discussed these issues amongst ourselves, and as the day drew to a close it became apparent the firehouse would have to make the same decision I faced earlier in the day. Leaving meant shutting down the firehouse and stranding the community without the coverage we provide. FDNY was on the scene, but they were already stretched thin and also suffered significant material losses during the storm. From the information we had available, this was especially true of their light four-wheel-drive vehicles. If another fire broke out, our presence could be the deciding factor.

To most of us, the idea of shuttering our trucks in the firehouse was simply unacceptable in light of the miracle it took to get them started. Rockaway Point, unfortunately, had no working trucks or ambulances and Roxbury had one damaged fire truck and no ambulance. We had the manpower and two working fire trucks, but living in the firehouse wasn't an option until it could be cleaned out. The only way for our plan to work was to pool our limited resources under one roof.

Tim Dufficy volunteered his house to serve as a barracks for any Point Breeze firefighter looking to stay. His house is on the bayside only a few homes away from the fire at 5 Bayway. The basement, like mine, was flooded and destroyed but the first floor was intact. We collected as much food, fuel, and water we could find and loaded it into Sand Flea. We left Big Jack at the firehouse for anyone who responded there during an emergency. The electrical issues were getting worse and the older Sand Flea was more reliable.

We combat parked at the end of Duffman's block along the main road and moved the supplies inside. In the failing light of day, we got the generator working and organized our resources. The limited electricity provided by the generator was fed to a power strip to charge cell phones, the refrigerator and the TV to watch the news. With the remaining available power we strung up Christmas lights for illumination. Unfortunately, electric heaters were too much of a drain and we would have to do without the comfort of artificial heat.

Wet clothing was replaced by Tim's own personal wardrobe bolstered by a few donations we collected here and there. Many of us required first aid for cuts and scrapes. In the case of Kieran Carley, his legs were covered in friction burns from wearing firemen's boots with inadequate protection for his legs. A bottle of Motrin was polished off very quickly, chased down by whatever beer Duffman had sitting in his fridge. Phones were tested but didn't work.

Inside "Camp Duff" a dozen of us crowded onto two living room couches. None of us had showered or brushed our teeth. All of us reeked of fire and dirty floodwater tainted by open cesspools, but that didn't matter. We cracked jokes, talked about the things we had seen, and busted each other's balls. It was therapeutic. Our first day after Sandy ended with the firefighters of the Point Breeze Volunteer Fire Department huddled together under blankets just trying to stay warm.

CHAPTER 7

CAMP DUFF

Wednesday, October 31, 2012

Being the oldest had its advantages, so when I took the second floor guest bedroom the guys granted me that luxury without complaints. I woke up to light streaming into the room which meant the dismal weather must have cleared up overnight. It was freezing! I could see my own breath as I lay in bed wondering what this new day would bring. The hum of the generator was gone, so I figured it had stopped operating sometime in the night from a lack of fuel. We would have to work on that.

I looked over at my phone for the time and was surprised to see several missed calls and voicemails. During the night service must have reached us and then shut down again in the morning. Work was calling me back in tomorrow. My girlfriend left a voicemail and text messages wondering if I was alive or dead. I couldn't reach her, or anyone else for that matter, to let them know what was going on. If I kept the phone on, the battery would run down very quickly while searching for a signal, but if I shut it off or put it on Airplane mode; I would never know if a signal was available.

Our dependence on electronics, and the consequences of losing the services of those devices, was becoming very apparent. As a child of the Reagan era I could remember a time before cell phones and the internet were in every home. Everyone else in Camp Duff, except Tim Dufficy, was in their early twenties. As a result of our un-plugging from the online world we all went through electronics withdrawal. There were no Facebook statuses to update, no information at your fingertips whenever you needed it, and most of us had become too lazy to remember important phone numbers even if we could find a working line.

After several minutes of contemplating these issues, biology forced me out of bed and into the bathroom. It was a mess, but at least people were sticking to the "no shitting in the house" rule we agreed on last night. Toilets didn't flush due to the lack of running water and no one wanted to stink up the house any more than we already were. A bottle of water and a toothbrush from my bag provided me a little bit of personal hygiene.

Walking down the spiral stairs I looked down and saw the rest of the guys still huddled under the blankets together trying to stay warm. One of the couches pulled out to become a sofa-bed straining under the weight of five men, some of them spooning each other.

"I hope I'm not interrupting anything," I said to Brillo as I made my way into the living room.

He gave me an exhausted look, "It's fucking cold."

"You guys look like you all had a nice, cozy night."

"Yeah, well…prison rules," he quipped. "Don't ask; don't tell."

Kieran had an interesting question. "Is it a bad thing I haven't taken a shit in three days? I've got one in the chamber but there's no place to go."

"We're in an apocalyptic disaster area and you can't find a single place where you can take a dump?"

"You want me to just drop my pants and take a shit on the beach?" he asked.

"Well…maybe not right now in the daylight. Can you wait until tonight?" I asked. He groaned in reply.

All we could do was laugh. It was a good sign the guys were finding humor in the situation. When I went to bed last night, I thought by morning we would know for sure if staying at Camp Duff was something which could be realistically sustained. For me, that first night was a test of who was committed and who was having second thoughts. We wouldn't have blamed anyone for leaving. Some of these guys lost their homes and all their belongings. Others had jobs and real life responsibilities. To my eternal admiration everyone was in good spirits and ready to start the day.

Tim gave me a Point Breeze FDNY pullover sweat shirt, not knowing at the time he would never get it back. I wore it for almost two months straight, and you can see it in many pictures taken of me during the recovery. It smelled like fire and gasoline, but it was sturdy, warm, and very comfortable. My girlfriend teased me about it mercilessly, and I still have it in my closet today.

Our new home at Camp Duff.

First on the agenda was fixing up our new residence. The basement was flooded and needed to be pumped and debris removed from the exterior of the house. A new set of steps was constructed, to replace those swept away by the storm, by piling cinderblocks on top of each other. Much of the material we used to make repairs was from the house next door which had been pushed off its foundation and was crumbling into the flooded basement below. The house was a summer bungalow and not emptied of personal items before the storm. When the residents showed up to survey the damage, we crawled inside the ruins to retrieve valued family heirlooms. It was the least we could do.

Inside Camp Duff, Nicholas Ecock organized and cleaned the mess we had created. Nick and his brother, T.J., both attend SUNY Maritime and joined us after the storm since their school had closed. On the night of Hurricane Sandy, they weathered the storm in a hotel room in Times Square, ordering room service and watching television. They never even lost power, although T.J. tearfully recounted his harrowing episode with the snack machine in the hotel lobby that wouldn't accept his crumpled currency. Their good fortune and cozy accommodations, while we nearly drowned, lead to a lot of friendly ribbing. However, both Nick and T.J. made a tremendous effort during the recovery and more than made up for missing the action that night.

A proper sign for Camp Duff was made on a long piece of white plywood and hung from the front porch. Some went into the basement to set up the pumps while the rest of us rigged a pole and raised the American flag in front of the house. Satisfied we had done all we could, the guys loaded up our gear onto the truck and made the short trip over to the firehouse. We found Robert Johnston working on Big Jack. A retired firefighter and mechanical wizard, Rob has forgotten more about fire trucks than we'll ever learn. Whatever his diagnosis of the situation with Big Jack, it was probably correct.

"This rig really had a number done on it," he said. "You guys drive it into the ocean?"

"It runs though, right?" I asked.

He just looked at me, knowing full well I don't know a thing about fire trucks, "It only goes into four wheel drive some of the time. All the wiring and electronics need to be replaced. And the pumps might not work. I'm trying to fix that but we don't have the parts."

"Well, Marty and I are meeting with FEMA people at the Co-op office tonight," I told him. "If you make a list of stuff you need maybe we can get some of it."

Rob just stared at me, trying to judge if I was serious or pulling his leg. In retrospect, our expectations from FEMA were comically optimistic and he was cynical enough to know better.

We split up into groups to attend to their homes. Those whose houses had burned down or washed away came first. We crawled through the wreckage to recover personal items the fire and water had spared. In most cases, singed clothing, flags, picture albums and other small trinkets were all that survived. The more fortunate ones, myself included, had homes which could be repaired. Pumps were set up to drain the basements filled with brackish seawater, and some was debris removed. We didn't have the tools to do much else, but it was a start.

On Fulton Walk, Karen Donnelly and her two sisters wept over the scorched foundation of their burned down home. They did not grieve alone. None of the thirty houses on their block survived the fire. Karen spent the night of Hurricane Sandy in her apartment in the Bronx. A neighbor knocked on her door that evening with bad news, the high winds had knocked down a tree branch which had pulverized her car. She was upset, having just made the final payment in August. As she went to bed early on the evening of the storm, Karen thought, "How can this night get any worse?"

Early the next morning her sister called, sobbing over the phone. Karen later told me, "I have one brother who is a firefighter and another who slept down in Breezy Point the previous night to keep an eye on the house. I think I timed it. For the next fourteen seconds as my sister cried over the phone, I was overcome with horror, worried about what she was going to tell me. So when she told me the house was gone, I was initially relieved because in my mind I was already thinking one of my brothers might have died. That's the fear you live with when you have a fireman or cop in the family. It's always there in the back of your mind that one day a phone call might come saying they're gone."

The reprieve was short lived as the words finally sunk in. "What do you mean the house is gone?" asked Karen. She hadn't turned on the television yet and heard nothing of the drama which had occurred in the Rockaways throughout the night.

"There was a fire in Breezy Point," her sister replied, "I think the whole Wedge is gone."

"We drove down from the Bronx and had to park out on the road. To get to Fulton Walk we had to travel behind the stores because the main road was too deeply flooded to walk through. We made our way up Ocean Avenue but you couldn't see the fire zone until you were right on top of it. It was like a slap in the face. We thought we knew what to expect from seeing it on television, but seeing it in person—with the smell of fire heavy in the air—was a total shock. We had to find Fulton Walk, and then find our house, with nothing to guide us but memories of where things should have been. Finally we found our house, but there was nothing which could be saved. However my niece points out a bright red object in the flooded foundation. It was an American flag, charred but not burned."

The flag was recovered and unfolded. Karen noticed that the metal frame of her neighbor's awning was still standing, so with the help of several others, they hung the flag across the frame for all to see. A crowd had gathered and photographs were taken. The Donnelly women didn't know it at the time, but they had taken the first step towards rebuilding the Wedge. The image of them raising the flag over their collection of flooded and fire ravaged foundations would appear on the front page of the New York Post and other publications throughout the country the following day.

✶ ✶ ✶

As the day turned into night, the rest of the guys went back to Camp Duff, while myself and Chief Marty Ingram went to the Co-op offices for a meeting.

The streets in front of the office were still flooded so we needed to take Sand Flea to get through. Aside from a few portable light towers set up by the NYPD, the entire neighborhood was blacked out. One such light tower was positioned outside the office and a power cord was run up to the second floor to run a handful of laptop computers and phones. We entered a large office with a table running nearly the entire length of the room with enough chairs to seat twenty to thirty people. There we met with Denise, from the Co-op, to discuss our situation. The expected FEMA representatives were unable to attend but asked Denise to make a list of our needs and pass it onto them in the morning.

We told her about the damage to the firehouse and made up a list of items which needed to be replaced as soon as possible. She discussed the situation within the Co-op's borders. It wasn't good. Power and gas were out across the peninsula and the water mains in Breezy Point were destroyed. The FDNY, NYPD, and DSNY were doing all they could with the limited resources available. FEMA and OEM were getting organized and the first meeting would be held in the morning.

I asked, "Do you have information about fatalities or injuries? We're hearing different things."

"I'm sorry," she said, "I have no information about that. We've heard a lot of rumors ourselves."

"In this case maybe no news is good news," added Marty. He was right, as usual.

Just as we were finishing, a Homeland Security agent came into the room wearing full tactical gear. Green fatigues, body armor, assault rifle, side arm, helmet…the works. Outside was a dark blue, 16-ton, four-wheeled armored personnel carrier with agents around it, all dressed up for war. It took a lot of effort to suppress a laugh. Since I was carrying my own off duty Glock, I figured it would be wise to let G.I. Joe know I was a police officer before he got the wrong idea.

"Good evening," he said. "We're here to check in on some of our assets. Do you have a map we can borrow?"

"Yeah, we can lend you one we carry in the truck. Where are you looking to go? Maybe we can show you," I replied.

He said to me in his best professional tone, "The names of our assets are classified for their protection." You can tell he was really enjoying his chance to buff out.

"Oh you mean the…." as I rattled off a half dozen names of people I knew to be his assets. It's a small community. We all know each other. He looked annoyed.

"Look, we're all on the same side here," I told him. "We've been through hell. You want to drive around in your tank, caving in undermined roads and sidewalks along the way? But what do you care? Well, we do. When you get stuck I'm calling dibs on your APC, and down here dibs is passing for law right now."

"We can go through the sand," he said, even more annoyed now.

"No, you can't. First of all your vehicle isn't sand rated. Do you know what ground pressure is? No? Well I do. Even if you didn't get caught in a sink hole or stuck in a sand trap, which are much worse in the off-road areas, your vehicle's gross weight is too heavy to get through soft sand. If it were dirt or grass you'd be okay, but sand is a no go. Ask your driver, he'll tell you."

With that he bid us farewell and went outside to confer with his men. Marty just looked at me and laughed. We finished up with Denise and headed over to Sand Flea. The armored personnel carrier was still there, with the guys standing around the light tower warming their hands with the exhaust. They were debating what to do next. I told Marty to wait for a few minutes while I went over there to make amends. After all, I'm a police officer and despite all the fun and games, he was trying to check up on his fellow agents and I respect that.

"I think we got off on the wrong foot," I apologized. "Sorry if I was a dick back there but it's been a long couple of days. It's frustrating to see you guys come in here with your tank and machineguns ready to fight World War III, meanwhile we haven't gotten any food and water yet."

We made small talk. He told me how things were going in the rest of the city. It sounded bad. After getting him a map and showing him the best route to take, we said our goodbyes, but I still had one more favor to ask him.

"One of your assets is my girlfriend," I told him. "She lives in the area and I haven't heard from her in a while. My phone doesn't work and I have no way to leave to check up on her. If you find her can you tell her I'm alright?" I gave him my name and her information too in case she was still at her parent's house. We shook hands and went about our separate duties.

"Remember man," I said to him as I walked away. "Dibs!"

He just laughed. Apparently G.I. Joe was issued a sense of humor to go with that kung fu grip. I climbed aboard Sand Flea and headed back to the firehouse and then Camp Duff. Marty came with me to check out our new quarters, and along the way we discussed a few ideas about the long term plans for the Point Breeze Volunteer Fire Department following Hurricane Sandy. Even though at the time I was only a firefighter in rank, my age and experience gave me perspective some of the other guys hadn't gotten yet and it wasn't uncommon for Marty to talk about his concerns with me.

"We need to reconstitute the firehouse," he said. "It's important for the morale of our guys and for the community."

"I agree. We have about a dozen guys who decided to stay for the time being. I don't know how long that's going to last without a steady supply of food and a way to keep ourselves warm. Some of the guys have minor injuries we can barely treat," I warned.

"Keep an eye on them. Duffman is in charge but you've been a big help getting things done. Its good you're staying together, but don't let this turn into a frat house," Marty warned. "People are watching."

"I got it. I'm not saying we're not going to fool around and unwind, but we'll keep the place clean and organized. I think that's important. If we start letting the place become a mess it's not only unfair to Duff but it'll breed apathy," I said. "We'll do our best to get things organized and clean. If we can keep the house looking professional, we'll stay professional. If it becomes a mess, they'll act like a mess. That's my personal experience."

"Exactly," Marty agreed. "Also, you know how the press is. There's always going to be a few of them looking for a scandal. Don't give them an easy one."

I thought about that for a minute, "How do you want to handle them?"

"I'm not sure what the other firehouses are doing, but I think we should play nice with them," Marty suggested. "If we don't talk to them, someone else will."

"You're right," I said, "but I think it's important to send the right message and present the right image. We don't want to be seen as glory hogs looking to get our names in the papers. This is about survival. I think it's good we get the story out there and ask for help because we really need it. The last thing we need is someone with a PBFD shirt on letting the stress get the better of him and saying something stupid in front of a camera."

That got a laugh out of Marty and our driver, Ricky Savage. He knew I was right. All it would take is one bad interview to turn this whole thing sour. Talking to the press is a risk. They have jobs to do too, and scandals sell more papers than feel-good stories, though scandals about feel-good stories sell even more. We had no public relations officer before Sandy, but we needed one now.

As I mentioned earlier, Marty is a retired military officer and FAA administrator with professional experience dealing with the press. He's clean cut, a natural leader, and as wholesome as they come. That's why he's our Chief, and lucky for us we couldn't have asked for a better spokesman for the department. It was agreed if Marty wasn't available, Tim Dufficy and I could handle things in his absence.

As with many things during Hurricane Sandy and the recovery, impromptu conversations would lead to important decisions with far-reaching consequences down the line. The choice to actively engage the media, in an effort to raise awareness of the situation in Breezy Point and reconstitute the fire department, was game changing. The Point Breeze Volunteer Fire Department is funded solely by grants and donations from within the community. The amount of material and equipment we lost was staggering while at the same time nearly all of our benefactors would need to be more frugal as they rebuilt their homes. It would be unreasonable to expect them to continue the same level of financial support in the near future. We needed help from outside the community, probably outside the city and other storm-ravaged areas.

Sand Flea pulled up to Camp Duff and Marty went inside to take a peek at our new living space. The place looked pretty good, all things considered, although the smell of a dozen men sharing the same space with no chance to bathe didn't improve the ambiance. The Chief made a short pep talk then left to handle some personal business. The rest of us sat on the couch and went over the day's events. We turned on the television and spent the rest of the night enjoying one of the few creature comforts still available to us, even if it was whatever shitty programming the antenna could tune into.

It was Halloween night but no one cared. There was no candy or costumes anyway. This year we were all going as dirty, hungry, freezing, refugee firefighters.

CHAPTER 8

ALL SAINTS

Thursday, November 1, 2012

The sound of the generator humming away on the deck outside made me smile as I rubbed the sleep from my eyes. Unlike the night before, we were smart enough to top off the fuel tank before going to bed. It also meant my phone was able to charge through the night and I was greeted by the same flurry of messages and voicemails as the morning prior. The most important one was from my girlfriend.

She wrote, "I'm so happy u r alive!"

Looks like G.I. Joe kept his promise and gave her the good news. Earlier yesterday she left me a voicemail about a rumor of a missing volunteer firefighter and she was afraid it was me. She left another voicemail, right around the time we had our meeting last night at the Co-op offices, begging me to call her and let her know I was okay. The situation was frustrating and taking an emotional toll, so it was a tremendous relief when I read her text message that morning.

I crawled out of bed an hour before my boss was expected to pick me up at the firehouse. Today was my first day back to work since the storm. Normally this allowed me enough time to shower and get dressed for the day ahead. But in a post-Sandy world with no running water my routine had changed into putting on the same dirty clothing as yesterday and brushing my teeth with a bottle of water. The police department expects a certain standard of hygiene and personal appearance, and to be honest, I wasn't sure how my supervisors would react to my present condition.

As the expected rendezvous time approached, I made my way to the firehouse and waited. The garage door was still stuck in the up position from the night of the storm so I went inside and grabbed a broom. I might as well clean the place up a little while I waited, but no sooner had I started sweeping when my boss showed up in the precinct's SUV to take me into work. In the passenger seat was Mike, my union representative, who decided to come along for the ride.

Mike evaluated my appearance and asked, "How are you holding up, Seabass?"

"Okay, I guess," I said quietly, not sure if I was in trouble or not. "It's been a rough time. We had a big fire and the water doesn't run so I can't shower or shave."

"Hey man, don't worry about it," he cut me off. "We understand. You're not in any trouble."

For the second time today, I felt as if a huge weight had been lifted off my shoulders. "I was kinda worried for a minute there."

My boss chimed in, "So, where was this fire?"

I directed him from the firehouse to the Beach 208th Street parking lot just north of the fire zone. Burned out cars littered the parking lot and a grey haze still lingered above the charred remnants of over one hundred houses. It was early but there were already residents sifting through the ashes. The scene was heartbreaking and all at once it started to hit me. My eyes started to tear up and my hands began to shake. It took every ounce of self control to avoid a total breakdown.

"Jesus," Mike whispered. "We heard there was a fire, but nothing like this. Is everyone okay? Are you okay?"

"We don't know yet," I explained. "No one has given us an official number but we've heard it's somewhere between eight and twenty. But last night in the meeting, we were told no notifications have been made yet so nothing is confirmed."

As my boss circled around the lot to get back to the main road he said to me, "Let's get you back to the command so you can take a shower and get cleaned up. I brought you a change of clothes from my house. Are you hungry?"

"Starving," I replied. Since the storm I had barely eaten much at all and had noticeably shed a few pounds. We made our way across the

Marine Parkway Bridge and up Flatbush Avenue to George's Luncheonette. Along the way I surveyed the destruction Hurricane Sandy had dealt in Brooklyn, and while it wasn't as bad as Breezy Point and the Rockaways, it was still odd to see boats washed up onto the street and cars bobbing in the water.

"Looks like you guys had a rough time too," I said to Mike.

He told me about the precinct's own trials and tribulations the night of Hurricane Sandy in Brooklyn. Much like Hurricane Irene the previous year, there was flooding in Mill Basin accompanied by the expected downed power lines and fallen trees, although more severe. A looming fuel shortage was causing some gas stations to run out of gasoline, and the accompanying disputes were stretching thin an already over-worked police department.

Fuel was quickly becoming my greatest concern. Donations of food and clothing had already started to trickle into the firehouse, but without a steady supply of gasoline we wouldn't be able to stay in Camp Duff or operate our vehicles. The pumps operated by the Co-op were damaged during the storm and contaminated with seawater. At the time, my hopes rested on FEMA showing up with the necessary supplies to keep us going.

We reached the precinct and sat in the Special Operations office where I devoured my bacon cheeseburger in record time. Next I went upstairs with my towel, soap, and a change of clothing my boss donated to me. I accepted it graciously even though it was a Yankees sleeveless shirt and any devoted Mets fan will support my assertion, despite all the records and statistics, our rivals in the Bronx are the inferior team. Beggars can't be choosers though, and that point couldn't have been driven home more as I stepped into the moldy shower on the second floor of the precinct. In five years I hadn't showered at work, and for good hygienic reasons, but considering my current situation it might as well have been a luxury spa.

Clean and refreshed, I went back downstairs to another surprise my boss was giving me the rest of the week off and Mike was waiting to take me back to Breezy Point. Apparently the picture I presented was one of such severe desperation and stress, he took pity on me. His parting words to me before I climbed into Truck 5153 for the trip back to the firehouse were, "What you're doing over there outweighs anything I can find for you to do here. Check in with me and let me know you're okay. Stay safe!"

I bid Mike farewell at the firehouse. One of our members told me Steve, a good friend of mine and a detective at my precinct, came by to drop off a few pizza pies from L&B Spumoni Gardens. Apparently I had just missed him because the pizza was still warm. Just then Marty showed up and told me we were helping run large bore fire hoses from the flooded parking lot in front of the Co-op offices to the bayside. The Chief of the FDNY Marine Unit, James Dalton, had secured several pumps but was short on manpower.

I packed up the pizza and drove Marty in my battered, but functional, Honda Pilot to the lot. We followed the trail of thick red hose northward, as it wound its way through sand alleys and sidewalks, until we reached the bay. There we found Rockaway Point and Point Breeze firefighters working together to drag the heavy hoses through the sand to the water's edge. The pizza was gone in minutes.

* * *

As we drove back to the firehouse, Marty saw the Fire Marshalls from the day before sitting in their truck alongside the main road. I made a U-turn and pulled up alongside to see if they had any more information about casualties in Breezy Point. We feared the worst and braced ourselves for bad news.

"No one told you?" they asked.

We looked at each other, sharing an apprehensive look, "No one has told us anything. How bad is it?"

"Well then, let me be the first to congratulate you. We haven't found a single fatality. There are some in Rockaway, but in Breezy Point you got the ones who couldn't save themselves. All of them! You guys did an incredible job."

We were speechless. It was the result we were hoping and praying for, but looking at the aftermath of the storm, especially all the burned down houses in the Wedge, we expected to find dozens of dead friends and neighbors. Marty and I were so happy we were on the verge of tears. For the rest of the ride home neither one of us said a word. Finally, when we pulled into the parking lot in front of the firehouse, Marty breathed a long sigh of relief.

"Jesus," he whispered.

"Yeah," I replied. "He definitely had something to do with it."

* * *

In Rockaway, at Dayton Towers, a happy reunion was underway. The day after Sandy hit, a woman named Ann Lewis came to Breezy Point to take photographs and see the damage for herself firsthand. She and her partner couldn't drive onto the property so they parked their car just outside the main gate and walked in. At Reid Avenue North, while taking pictures, she noticed a rope tied to a pole which looked like it was moving. Ann followed the line under a Ford pickup truck and at the end of it was a filthy, shaking, frightened dog without a collar.

She untied the rope, coaxed the dog into her car, and drove back to Brooklyn. In Ann's apartment in Bushwick, which was untouched by Sandy, a warm bath was prepared along with some dog food. A photographer by trade, she took several photos of the as yet unidentified canine and posted them online. She created a Facebook page titled, "Found Female Dog in Breezy Point," and registered the pooch on Fidofinder.com, both which can still be seen today.

The following morning, after a desperate search of their own, the Schramm's recognized a dog they thought could be their beloved Maggie in Ann's photographs. Just after noon a call was made to Ann, who immediately drove to Rockaway, hopeful she had found the owners of the dog she had rescued. Maggie burst from the car and ran into the arms of Gracie, Mike and Sheila's daughter. Long after the storm, during an interview with Mike Schramm in his newly rebuilt kitchen, he recalled the story while choking back tears.

Sheila and Gracie Schramm are reunited with their dog, Maggie, who had gone missing the night of the storm.

"She found the dog, gave her a bath, and really took care of her. It was really nice. I'm crying just thinking about it. We weren't sure though and all we kept thinking was, 'Please God, be Maggie!' You can kinda tell from the pictures but we really didn't know. My wife was like, 'I really hope this is the dog because Gracie is gonna be crushed if it's not.' I wasn't there for the reunion—I was down in Breezy Point gutting the house—but when my wife pulled into the lot with the dog, Maggie popped out of the car, her tail was wagging, and ran right up to me."

The Schramm family was complete once more.

* * *

Sometime around 4 o'clock that evening it was decided a fuel and supply run was needed, so Kevin O'Brien drove Sand Flea with Pat Dempsey and me into Brooklyn. We pulled into the NYPD's Highway 2 base on Flatbush Avenue and filled up the nearly empty tank with diesel, then headed towards the Marine Park area to see what businesses were open. The Floridian Diner was running on limited power but still serving food, so we decided to get some cheeseburgers. While our meal was cooking, I went into the pharmacy next door and bought soda, 5-Hour energy drinks, and cigarettes—enough to satisfy a wide range of vices.

By the time I was done my wallet was $300 lighter, but I thought the boost to morale my purchases would bring was worth it. I climbed back into Sand Flea and we drove back down Flatbush Avenue towards the storm-battered Breezy Point. We impatiently tore into the bags of food, removed the aluminum trays, and grabbed handfuls of fries and onion rings. I opened my tray and bit into my cheeseburger only to find an essential ingredient missing.

"Hey, any of you guys missing the burger from your cheeseburger? How the fuck do you screw that up?"

Pat lamented, "Mine has no meat in it too! All I got is cheese, lettuce and tomato. They didn't even add the fucking bacon!"

"Mine too!" added Kevin.

"Serves us right for not buying for the other guys."

Burger or not, we ate every last bite as Sand Flea rumbled back into Breezy Point. We dropped Pat off at his rental truck and headed over to Camp Duff where the guys were waiting. Kevin said goodbye and left to rejoin his family out in Long Island. Spirits were high despite the worsening conditions. There were plenty of cigarettes and soda to go around, and even a cigar or two for the non-smokers like myself. We were ready to settle in for another night in our makeshift barracks on the bay when there was a knock at the door.

Disasters like Hurricane Sandy bring out all sorts of people. Most are good folks trying to help, while some are looking to take advantage of the situation and either make a quick buck or steal whatever they can. There are also crazy people who are attracted to chaos like flies to honey. As a police officer I have to deal with emotionally disturbed people all the time. Some are just eccentric, socially awkward people who are harmless with good intentions. That's the kind of person who showed up on the doorstep of Camp Duff that night.

Dan was the former roommate of Captain Kevin O'Brien, when they attended school at SUNY Maritime together. He saw us on the news and decided to lend a hand, which is very admirable and clearly his heart was in the right place. Dan had an intensity about him. Maybe it was the fact that he was wearing his bunker gear, helmet and all, during the car ride in; or that he had three different radios on him—one of which could be used to summon the Coast Guard, or perhaps it was him drinking three 5-Hour energy drinks in front of us over the course of ten minutes. Whatever the case, Dan had lots and lots of extra energy and wanted to put it to good use, right now!

The department teaches us "verbal judo" to use to talk to people in order to avoid conflict, and that was exactly what I planned on doing. I convinced Brillo and a few others to join me checking out Dan's new pickup truck, partly because I would need a hand unloading supplies, and also because I wasn't entirely convinced Dan wasn't planning on putting my head in a jar of formaldehyde. When we reached his truck everything happened more or less the way I expected. Dan started the engine, turned on the radio, cranked the volume to its maximum setting, then played "Welcome to the Jungle" by Guns 'n Roses while throwing things at us from the bed of the pickup.

A kayak was politely declined, as were several lengths of thick tugboat rope. Bottles of propane were tossed to us with reckless abandon, and it was a small miracle nothing exploded. I watched Dan consume another energy drink as he plucked item after item from the pile at his feet and carelessly throw them in our direction like a lunatic Santa Claus. It was magnificent.

When the pile was depleted, he hopped down and asked me where he could pump and gut a home. I politely explained it was dark and very unsafe to go walking in Breezy Point at night with the looters running around. Rummaging through people's houses to rip out sheetrock and insulation at this hour was ill advised. He looked dejected, but I appreciated the offer and immediately decided I should send this guy down the road to our friends at the Rockaway Point Fire Department. Perhaps they could find work for him. I shook his hand and sent him on his way, confident they would appreciate our gesture of good will.

It's my understanding Dan knocked on their door but no one answered. Undeterred, he decided to set up road flares along Rockaway Beach Boulevard for a purpose known only to Dan and whatever God he talks to. An argument with an unknown local authority ensued over his impromptu checkpoint and the police were summoned to escort him off the property. I never found out what happened to Dan after that, but days later I ran into several firefighters with bunker gear from the same fire department where he was allegedly a member. Despite my assurances that everything was fine, one of their Captains turned pale when I mentioned Dan and described his adventure with us.

CHAPTER 9

THE RECOVERY BEGINS

Friday November 2, 2012

I leaned over and whispered to Marty, "Are these guys serious? Do they have any idea what's going on here?"

"They're planning for the long term, we need help now. Let's see how the rest of the meeting goes, Seabass."

We were approaching the second hour of our first Office of Emergency Management (OEM) meeting in the Co-op offices in Breezy Point. Representatives from every city agency and utility company in the area were in attendance, perhaps fifty people, crammed into a meeting room designed to hold thirty. For us it was standing room only, so me, Marty, Chief Valentine from Rockaway Point, and Chief Coloran from Roxbury volunteer fire departments huddled in a corner to stay out of the way. The table was littered with laptops and iPads, all tethered to power cords sucking energy from a few power strips fed by an NYPD light tower outside.

Nobody had any real answers yet, just estimates, but even those didn't sound very encouraging. It would take weeks before we had any running water, months before the power could be restored, and perhaps the gas would be back as early as next spring. Almost every main, pole, wire, cable and pipe line had to be ripped up and replaced in the Wedge. Work crews were being brought in from all of the country, but it would be days until they arrived.

The Commanding Officer of the NYPD's 100th Precinct gave us an update, as did the FDNY and DSNY. The information they provided was more relevant for those of us involved in the day-to-day operations although we knew most of it already from being in the field alongside those personnel. The update was more for the benefit of the attendees who were managing the Hurricane Sandy recovery from elsewhere.

To our frustration, the focus was on long term recovery efforts and not much was said about the here and now. There was no mention of the supplies we requested or the equipment we needed replaced. The only FEMA presence we had seen thus far was G.I. Joe and the real American heroes in their big blue tank a few days prior. One of us finally was able to ask a relevant question, "What about food and water for those of us still down here?"

Looks were exchanged around the room but no one had an answer. Some people shifted in their chairs uncomfortably. Finally after a few awkward moments someone finally spoke up, "How about the Red Cross? They should be in the Rockaways by now."

Heads nodded and everyone seemed satisfied with that answer. Everyone, that was, except us. The roads were clogged with residents driving into Breezy Point to check on their homes, and because fuel was in short supply, the Rockaways might as well have been on the other side of the country. Using the rigs for supply runs was already risky and done only at night when the traffic on the main road had diminished. All our personal vehicles were destroyed except my truck, and the gas tank was just about empty from ferrying people back and forth in an effort to save fuel for our fire trucks.

In the end it didn't matter. After asking the OEM for details, they informed us that the Red Cross had extremely limited supplies at the moment and usually had no extra food available for us. Even when they did, only lunch was served and their food trucks left the Rockaways at night, which was the only time we could spare a truck and crew to meet them. We were on our own.

Marty had a conference with the other Chiefs while I waited downstairs and talked to the Commanding Officer of the 100th Precinct. When Marty's meeting concluded we drove to Camp Duff to pick up the guys. No sooner had we arrived when a call for an odor of gas was reported on Tioga Walk. We stepped into our cold wet bunker gear and boarded Sand Flea for the short trip to the western border of the Wedge where the job was reported. Rob brought Big Jack from the firehouse for support.

Tioga Walk is unusual because the southernmost half of the block is a paved road while the rest of the walk is a double-wide sidewalk only wide enough to accommodate passenger cars. However, our small truck could fit and we were soon flagged down by an elderly woman.

"That man back there was pouring gas into his generator and got it everywhere! There could be a fire."

"Okay, thanks, we'll check it out. You stay here."

We made our way onto the back deck of the house she had pointed to and found the culprit. The man in question had purchased a new generator so he could run his pump to drain the water from his basement. The problem was he had never used a generator before and spilled gasoline all over the wooden deck, the generator and himself. With no running water he couldn't wash any of it off with a garden hose. Luckily, his inability to start the generator was the only reason he didn't blow himself up and light his house on fire.

"Whoa there buddy, what are you trying to do?"

He replied, "I gotta get my pumps working."

"I can understand that, but you're covered in gasoline and so is your house. That's a combustion engine, not electric. If you start that thing up all covered in gas, it's going to catch fire," we told him.

"Are you sure?" he asked, skeptical of us.

"It's a miniature version of the engine you have in your car. Would you pour gasoline on your car engine? No, because it would start a fire, right? Same thing applies here," I said.

Another firefighter added, "Besides, you gotta prime it first. It's never going to start like that."

He was right. Apparently the directions which came with the generator were written only in Spanish and Chinese, and the trial and error method clearly was not working. This was a problem we would run into many times during the recovery. People were suddenly thrust into situations for which they were not prepared. With thousands of flooded homes needing to be pumped out, someone was bound to get seriously hurt.

We gave the guy a crash course in gas generator operation and helped him clean up a little so he wouldn't start a fire. On the way back to the firehouse, I couldn't shake the feeling that we could be doing something more to help these people. The firehouse had one or two operable portable generators. If we could get some pumps, we could start on our own homes first and carry on from there. It was something to consider for the near future, but not today. We had bigger problems to deal with first.

On Rockaway Point Boulevard, we encountered a NYPD Emergency Services Unit (ESU) pickup truck with a light tower and generator combo in tow. They were lost. I explained our situation and got permission to deploy the light tower and generator at the firehouse. Within the hour, the diesel motor was humming outside the engine deck. It didn't solve our fuel or power problems at Camp Duff, but at least the firehouse had electricity and the tower's four powerful spotlights could light up the immediate area. The generator had a full tank of gas—enough for 48 hours of operation. They left me the number for ESU Truck 9 and went on their way with our thanks.

The fuel crisis was getting worse and our supply of gasoline was running out with no hope of replenishment. Our requests to OEM and FEMA had gone unanswered, and it was only through guile and a little bluffing that we were able to fill the trucks with diesel. Regular gasoline was another story. The hurricane had blocked portions of the harbor and damaged the infrastructure. The supply of gasoline to New York City had to be brought in by truck while the tankers offshore were re-routed to other ports. Even tanker trains weren't an option. Despite the hundreds of miles of tracks running through the five boroughs, they are not of the national gauge.

Nick Ecock, the Camp Duff custodian, gave me the bad news, "There's maybe 30 hours of fuel left."

"We can stretch that if we shut off the generators during the day time, right?" I offered in reply.

"That still doesn't solve the problem. It might buy us a few more hours, but after two days we'll be right back in the same situation."

"We'll take one of the rigs, make a run into Brooklyn tonight and see if we can buy some fuel," I told him. "We topped off Sand Flea the other night, so we'll take Big Jack this time."

"You're going to pay for it yourself?"

"Yeah, well, we don't have any other choice."

I left soon after our conversation ended and walked the short trip from Camp Duff to the firehouse, pondering the fuel issue along the way. If I couldn't get some gasoline tonight or tomorrow we would have to pack things up and shut down the firehouse. After all we had been through so far, it was the last thing any of us wanted. The guys were standing around a new-looking black Dodge pickup truck when I arrived.

"What do you think, Seabass?"

"Is it ours?"

"Yep, the guy from 5 Bayway donated it to us as a thank you for putting out that fire. I heard he owns Western Beef or something."

"No fucking way! That's awesome. Does it have gas?"

"A full tank I think. The keys are in the ignition."

"Nice! Let's take it for a ride to Rockaway Point and pick up some supplies." Due to their location on the main road and plenty of room for parking and storage, they became a medical, logistics, and information center. Most of the supplies trickling into Breezy Point were there, and it was from that stockpile which we helped ourselves occasionally.

As we pulled up, I noticed several NYPD officers in blue Community Affairs windbreakers unloading cases of bottled water from a party bus. I introduced myself and helped them off-load their cargo. After we were done, one of them pulled me aside and asked if there was anything we needed besides water.

I told him about our gasoline situation: "Frankly, if we don't get some fuel tonight I think we're gonna have to pack it in, and that sucks because we're still responding to jobs and helping people out. We've been here since the night of the hurricane. We fought that big fire too. There's a dozen guys living at one of our member's houses and nobody is ready to leave yet. It's fucking freezing at night and we need gas for our generator."

He gave me his card and said, "Go to Highway 2 and tell them Commissioner O'Connell says to give you anything you want. Here's my number. If you have problems call me."

I was floored. Regular street cops like me don't walk up to Deputy Commissioners and start bitching about how bad their day is. If I had known who he was I also would have toned down the language a little. All I could muster was, "Yes sir! Thank you. You don't know how much this means to me and the rest of the guys. I'll call you if there's any problem."

"Who was that?" asked one of our firefighters as we drove back to the firehouse.

"That," I said, "was our fucking savior."

* * *

In Hernando County, Florida, Erin Concoran-Daly was having fuel problems of her own. She had watched the storm on television and followed the drama unfolding in Breezy Point through social media. Friends of hers, able to post online but unable to get a call through to 911, reported a growing fire in the Wedge. Shortly after midnight she received a frantic call from her teenage cousins who couldn't contact their mother, Debbie, who stayed in Breezy Point. Ten anxious hours passed before news reached Erin that Debbie and her boyfriend had been rescued. They had stayed overnight pouring seawater, which was lapping against their front deck, onto flaming embers which were raining down on the house.

Erin contacted her childhood friends, John Norton and Kevin Adams, and informed them she and her husband, Bill were driving from Florida to Breezy Point over the weekend. John and Kevin were in desperate need of supplies, especially fuel. In the bed of her pickup truck, Erin had 27 full, five-gallon gasoline cans, and in her lap was a fire extinguisher. Behind them was a motorcycle trailer full of clothing and supplies donated by the sympathetic Floridians who were all too familiar with the devastating effects of hurricanes.

Two miles into their journey disaster struck when the trailer buckled and forced them off the road. Only by sheer luck did the gasoline-packed pickup truck not catch fire. A few hours later the motorcycle trailer was towed back to its owner and replaced by a box truck driven by her husband. Hours behind schedule, but back on the road, Erin and Bill were on their way to Breezy Point for what they both thought would be a couple of days of backbreaking work pumping and gutting their home on Reid Avenue by the bay.

"I need everything you guys can find that can hold some gasoline," I told them. "Beg, borrow, and steal whatever you have to. We might only have one shot to fill up and I want to walk away with as much fuel as we can. The more fuel we bring home the longer we can keep going."

It was freezing cold and dark in front of the firehouse as we loaded every can we could find into the bed of the Dodge pickup, christened Unit 9. In a few minutes I was taking the pickup across the bridge and onto Highway 2 to see just how good a Deputy Commissioner's business card really was. A quick survey of the cargo bed told me we could carry about 80 gallons of gasoline. If we were able to get that much fuel, we would be good for another two to three days. In the event Highway 2 was out of fuel or we were refused, we would be packing our things tomorrow and going our separate ways. No one wanted to think about that.

The truck was used but drove like it was new, which was great because my Pilot finally gave out a few hours earlier. The corrosion caused by the saltwater had already severely damaged the electronics, and that afternoon it wouldn't start. I can't complain. To the best of my knowledge, my truck was the only civilian vehicle to spend the night in Breezy Point the night of Sandy and still work the next day. It had served us well.

Our first stop was Walgreens, at the intersection of Utica and Flatbush Avenues, to buy more smokes, food and medicine. I was paying the bill again but I figured it was worth it, though as a non-smoker the price of cigarettes is appalling. Our next stop was the NYPD's Highway 2 base on Flatbush Avenue where I approached the desk officer, informed him of the situation, and requested the fuel card to work the pumps. I half expected an argument, or at the very least a few questions, but he understood who we were and where we were coming from. An officer was sent outside to assist us.

One by one we filled up the cans, even those with no caps. Every regulation gas can has a fill line on it which you're not supposed to cross, but we passed it until each can was filled to the brim. The rubber lined bed of the pickup truck was filled with spilled gasoline as fuel sloshed around in the over-flowing containers. To say we were tempting fate is an understatement as I drove the pickup down Flatbush Avenue and over the Marine Parkway Bridge, knowing at any moment an errant spark would turn Unit 9 and everyone inside into a funeral pyre.

"Duffman," I said over the phone, since the best thing to do when driving a two-ton bomb is to distract yourself by talking on a cell phone, "get everyone ready. We're coming in hot. There's gas all over the truck. Bring out a case of water so we can wash this thing down before we all go up in flames."

"We'll be waiting," he replied, laughing at our predicament.

Unit 9 came to a stop at the end of Duffman's block, next to Sand Flea, where the guys were waiting, water bottles in hand. The truck bed was given a healthy rinse as the gas cans were carried onto the deck of

Camp Duff. I did a proper inventory and counted 78 gallons of gasoline, which should be just enough to keep us going for the next three days.

We relaxed in the living room on the couches where the guys slept, watching whatever signal the digital antenna atop Duffman's television could pick up. The younger Ecock brother, T.J., expressed his growing concern over the reported destruction of the "Smush Room" from reality show *The Jersey Shore*. We cheered the cancellation of the New York City Marathon which had been tying down an enormous amount of resources we felt could be put to better use in the storm-battered parts of the city instead.

Bouncing along the sand tracks in front of Camp Duff was a red, white, and blue converted ambulance belonging to Norton Mechanical. The company owner, John Norton, brought his friend, Kevin Adams, along for a ride on the bayside. Since we were one of the few occupied houses in the community, they stopped by to say hello and have a beer or two. Kevin is a FDNY firefighter from Engine 48 in the Bronx and Norton's longtime friend. Kevin was vacationing in Vermont when Sandy hit and offered to come down and help pump out the houses of his many Breezy Point friends.

Their efforts to pump out Norton's basement were frustrated by the saturated ground all along the peninsula. The pumps would push the seawater out, but the basement would fill with water again overnight. They had been at it for two days already. As Kevin put it, "The saving grace was you only had to pump the dirty water out once. The water that came up through the cracks in the foundation afterwards was filtered through sand and soil, so it was pretty clean." We took his word for it.

After they left we watched the one-hour, commercial-free benefit concert *Hurricane Sandy: Coming Together*. The $23 million in proceeds went to the American Red Cross. We saw a lot of pictures of Breezy Point on the television that night, including one I believe was taken from the Point Breeze Fire Department's own Facebook page. In my experience, what we didn't see then, or even a month later, was the Red Cross in Breezy Point in any meaningful way. Whatever they were doing, they weren't doing it here when we needed them the most, but they sure as hell didn't mind capitalizing on our suffering.

✱ ✱ ✱

At another part of Breezy Point, in a house ravaged by the ocean he loved so much, our Chief lay awake on a wet mattress set on the floor. He needed some time alone to process the events of the previous four days. The stress caused by countless decisions he was forced to make, many of which could have easily ended in tragedy, was starting to take a toll. He had gambled and won, but so many of his decisions were close calls. It was too much. Marty Ingram, the indomitable personality who flawlessly led us through the toughest challenge our firehouse has ever had to face, rolled over and cried himself to sleep.

CHAPTER 10

REUNION

Saturday, November 3, 2012

My alarm was set for early this morning but I was up before the claxon ever had a chance to blare. Concerns of keeping the firehouse supplied and about the well-being of the men one floor below me, still huddled together trying to stay warm, caused a restful night's sleep to elude me. Chronic fatigue was starting to set in. Each night I was sleeping less than the one before. The tempo of our operations combined with the dietary and sanitary situation was wearing us down. We looked and smelled like shit, and it was only getting worse. Most of us had limited contact with our loved ones since before the storm and it added an emotional element to my concerns. Although the guys were in good spirits, I would catch them alone from time to time looking off into the distance with a thousand yard stare. We needed a break, even if it were just for a few hours to get cleaned up and enjoy a hot meal.

At 5:25 A.M., I turned to Facebook looking for help: "There are approximately ten volunteer firefighters with me here at Camp Duff that have been going non-stop since hours before the storm. Almost all of them haven't had a shower or any time to unwind. Right now we all have chronic fatigue and the weekend is expected to be very busy. We're largely cut off from the world and information about life past the security booth. Anyone know of a place close by where I can get these guys a shower, a hot meal, and some time to put themselves together again—even just for a little bit? I'll pay whatever the cost is."

Many offers were made but all of them were too far away to be practical. I considered taking them to my precinct, but with the fuel crisis in full effect and a manpower shortage, I ran the risk of being immediately recalled to duty and that wouldn't help us at all. It would have to wait.

Today marked the first weekend since the storm and we expected a large turnout of residents and volunteers. For us that meant a few extra hands to clean up the firehouse, though it brought an increased chance of being called into action as well. The expected traffic jam would cut us off from Roxbury and that concerned us. If a fire erupted it would take a long time to travel the one and a half miles from our community to theirs.

No sooner had we arrived at the firehouse when a call came in for a missing hypothermic person who was last seen on the bay side. I parked Unit 9 near Beach 219th Street and made my way onto the dunes overlooking Jamaica Bay. Several other firefighters, volunteers and city alike, were combing the shoreline for the missing person. After an hour of fruitless efforts, the search was called off. We conferred with FDNY leaders on the scene and determined the call was a mistake. It was not an uncommon occurrence; emergency calls often end up as unnecessary or unfounded.

I drove Unit 9 back to the firehouse through a swarm of vehicles and volunteers along the main road. It was a mad house. Hundreds of residents showed up looking for equipment and tools to pump out their homes. Some of our members, who were not with us during the storm, came looking for help, especially manpower, and we did our best to accommodate them. What little supplies we had quickly disappeared. One member took our last functional spotlight to work in his basement.

This had to stop.

I found Marty and made him aware of the situation. "They're taking everything! The hand tools, the big crowbar thing, even the axes and sledgehammers. The generator is missing along with two red plastic five-gallon cans of gasoline. One guy took our last fucking flashlight!"

"That stops immediately," he ordered. "No more borrowing our equipment no matter who they are. I'll talk to the members who took things and try to get them back."

"Thanks. I'm sorry for yelling," I said, calmer now that I had an opportunity to vent. "I'm pissed off. We're barely holding on here and these guys show up out of nowhere and loot the place."

"You're doing a great job, Seabass. Hang in there. Go for a walk and cool down a little. I'll straighten things out."

I took his advice and strolled toward the Wedge to check on my house. It had been a few days since I was there and I was dreading going back. The reality was, despite all my storm preparations and moving the most valuable items to the second floor, the majority of my personal items were in the flooded basement. Most were probably destroyed and I tried not to think about it. The stress and fatigue of my firehouse responsibilities were slowly overwhelming me. I wasn't ready to face this other deeply personal challenge yet.

Halfway to my house, I turned around and went to the fire zone instead. People were crawling through the ruins of their homes looking for anything which might have survived. It was heartbreaking and helped put my feelings of personal loss into perspective. I felt ashamed for being upset over a few personal items when so many people had lost their entire house. They lost everything. A family only a few yards away from me was huddled together, staring into the charred remains and crying.

I made my way down Gotham Walk to where we made our stand that night and climbed onto the deck of one of the houses. Four days ago, Pat and I stood on this very same spot working our fire hose, spraying water onto the blaze, hoping the elevation might make up for the lacking water pressure. The side of the house facing the fire was blackened by the heat as were parts of the deck.

"Excuse me?"

"Sorry," I said to the man behind me. Apparently this was his house. "I was here during the fire, on your deck. It looks so much different between then and now. I'm sorry we couldn't do more. I'll get out of your way."

"It's not a problem," he replied. "Come back any time."

* * *

I took a walk over to the Rockaway Point firehouse to see about getting some food. The military had set up a long beige tent in front of the Catholic Club from which a hot meal was served by the FDNY firefighters from the Bronx. It began when firefighter Bobby Eustace of Ladder 27 started cooking trays of food in his firehouse and driving them down for the volunteers in Breezy Point when he was off from work. Today he brought down the firehouse's six-foot grill and cooked hot dogs and hamburgers. For the next 25 days, on their own time and at their own expense, the Bronx firefighters cooked for an ever increasing number of hungry residents and volunteers looking for a warm meal.

* * *

At three o'clock I went back to the firehouse after checking in with Nick Ecock at Camp Duff, feeling a little less frustrated but still plenty stressed out. Something needed to change. We had been lucky, but with the limited support we received from FEMA, the City's over-stretched OEM system, and with me paying for every purchase thus far, we wouldn't be able to keep operating much longer. I walked around the rear of the firehouse, through our parking lot, looking for Marty so we could have another chat. What I found was so much better.

My girlfriend was there looking for me. It was the first time I had seen her since the morning of the storm. Suddenly all the stress and frustration seemed to fade away. She turned around as I approached. We both looked at each other for a moment before embracing, not wanting to let go. She told me about her ordeal that night and the days after. A fire broke out in the Rockaways only a few blocks from her parent's house, razing dozens of homes and businesses. The description she gave me, of life in the Rockaways, sounded like a lawless nightmare where looters broke into evacuated homes at will. I held her as she cried when she told me her new house in Roxbury was flooded and needed to be pumped and gutted. She had no insurance.

A call for an odor of gas, relayed to us from the security office, cut our reunion short as the troops were rallied. I had to leave, but not before promising we wouldn't wait another week before seeing each other again. I climbed onto the back step of Big Jack as we made our way out of the parking lot, looking back and waving, wondering what kind of idiot would leave a girl like her behind a second time to go fight fires.

* * *

Later that night while refilling the generator on Duffman's balcony, we saw boats coming across Jamaica Bay from Brooklyn toward us. They stopped along the beach at the washed out dock near Kennedy's restaurant 250 yards away and the passengers disembarked. The wind carried their voices to our perch. Whatever they were yelling to each other wasn't in English. They were looters circumventing the NYPD checkpoint along the main road by using small boats. I had heard a rumor about this sort of thing earlier, but dismissed it as paranoia, although seeing it firsthand cast aside any doubts.

I watched them, magnified through a Leupold scope, when the eastern horizon flashed and backlit the houses along the bay, followed by the crack of gunfire. We weren't the only ones to take notice of our seaborne guests. Someone had fired a warning shot, apparently to scare our unwelcome guests away. Surprised, our visitors froze for a moment then fired a reply of their own. The situation was quickly getting out of control. If these men were able to cross the beach and make it into the houses, who knew what tragedy would possibly befall anyone they encountered. My phone didn't have a signal and our radios were dead so we couldn't call for help. The cold November night was thick with tension as the intruders looked around, unsure of what to do. Clearly they had not expected resistance but were armed anyway.

Suddenly, the reverberating sound of rotor blades broke the spell, as did a spotlight swinging its beam in wide arcs along the waterfront.

Someone had heard the gunfire and called the police. An NYPD helicopter from Floyd Bennett Field was searching for signs of mischief. The men scrambled back into the boats and hastily motored away back towards Brooklyn with the Aviation unit apparently in pursuit. I sat outside for a while, considering what might have happened if things had gone differently. The looting was getting worse every day. I decided to give the guys a crash course on gun safety. Tomorrow I would begin carrying my off-duty weapon with me, especially at night.

CHAPTER 11

OPERATION PORT-A-POTTY

Sunday, November 4, 2012

I didn't bother setting my alarm. We had a call just before midnight and everyone downstairs was wiped out. I fell asleep for a few hours out of sheer exhaustion, but had been awake since before dawn thinking about fuel, food, and morale as well as my own personal problems. Last night before bed we joked about the cacophony of smells wafting through Duffman's house. It was a mix of body odor, sewage, fire and moldy dampness from our clothing and his basement. We needed to get cleaned up.

The best offer came from a friend, Aileen Mullins, whose father also happened to be Duffman's boss. They lived in Marine Park only fifteen minutes away. She came to Breezy Point the day before and dropped off cigarettes, chewing tobacco, soda and some food. I grabbed a gas can and filled up the generator on the balcony, then gave her a call.

"Are you sure you don't mind?" I asked her.

"Don't be stupid! Come on over! We'll make you breakfast."

It was too good an offer to pass up. I went downstairs and told Brillo about the offer. We agreed to leave both Sand Flea and Big Jack behind, and take Unit 9 instead. The limited seating capacity of our new pickup dovetailed nicely into the next issue, who would go and who would stay behind to man the firehouse. We could only take five guys. The others would have to wait for the next opportunity.

Brillo volunteered to stay as did a few others. I climbed into Unit 9 with Mike Scannell, the Ecock brothers, and Kieran Carley and drove toward Brooklyn. The Mullins family cooked us a veritable feast of bacon, eggs, bagels and orange juice while we took turns in the upstairs and downstairs showers. After breakfast an offer for haircuts on the back deck was accepted by Mike and myself while the other guys watched. I've been keeping my hair cut short for a few years now, but Mike had long wavy locks which must have taken him a year to grow out.

We thanked the Mullins family who were so generous to us and said our goodbyes. They gave us some food, clean clothing, and hygiene products to bring back to the guys who couldn't make this trip, and offered an open invitation for anyone who needed to get cleaned up and something hot to eat. The five of us climbed back into Unit 9 smelling clean, in new clothing, bellies full of bacon and eggs, and in the case of Mike and I, hair cut down to our scalp. We felt refreshed, like new men, as I drove the pickup southbound on Flatbush Avenue back to our disaster area which we called home.

As we were getting cleaned up in Marine Park, Erin Concoran-Daly and her husband, Billy, were pulling into Breezy Point to meet with Kevin Adams and John Norton. Their U-Haul box-truck full of desperately needed supplies, which were nearly lost during an accident at the start of their journey from Florida, arrived safely as well. She and her husband brought food, drinking water, generators, gasoline and other tools and equipment to work on their home on Reid Avenue. What they were not prepared for, however, were the sights, sounds and smells of the devastation throughout the community. Seeing it on television a thousand miles away was very different than in person.

Their first stop, after checking the damage to their own home, was the Rockaway Point Volunteer Fire Department to drop off a generator. Erin and her husband rendezvoused with Kevin and John to plan for the next few days. "Kevin showed up at my house early on Monday with ten firefighters," recalled Erin during an interview after the storm. "They gutted my basement since the water didn't reach the first floor. For years I had been storing stuff down there, so the pile of stuff nearly went from the floor to the ceiling. Next we went to Kevin Whalen's house on Newport. All this time I'm running back and forth getting food and supplies for the guys. More and more firefighters kept showing up out of nowhere on their day off looking to help. Kevin and I spoke and decided we needed to get better organized."

"We needed to do in Breezy Point what we did in Hurricane Katrina," said Kevin Adams, who went with the FDNY to New Orleans in 2005 to assist that beleaguered city. "We gotta gut these houses. We gotta pump out all the water. We gotta gut and pump! Gut and pump!" An idea was taking shape. There was no shortage of firefighters who wanted to volunteer, but he would need equipment and material to keep them supplied. To run an operation like that he also needed to stake out an area to store everything and a place where volunteers could meet and be organized. Most importantly, he needed someone with the people skills and organizational ability to keep track of it all.

He needed Erin to stay in Breezy Point just a little bit longer.

* * *

Waiting for us at the firehouse were Matt Robert, Corey Gelato, John Crean, Tim Finnegan and James Barlow from South Blooming Grove Fire Department located in Monroe, New York. The five of them drove all the way down to Breezy Point with their bunker gear and hand tools to help us. They didn't have to wait long. After a brief introduction the first call came in.

"We have smoke coming from a roof, maybe a fire, on Breezy Point Boulevard near Queens Walk."

"Two of you go with Duffman on Sand Flea," I said while pointing at Unit 8 as Tim turned the engine over. "The rest of you come with me in Unit 9. The ride can get a little bumpy and don't mind the smell of gasoline. That's perfectly normal."

One of them chuckled, "Whatever you say dude."

Sand Flea arrived first. Duff quickly identified the problem and climbed onto the roof of the house. It was the solar panels. The panels were still functioning, absorbing the sun's rays and converting it into usable energy, but the current was running through damaged wires and starting to overheat them, resulting in the reported smoke. Duffman is an experienced engineer, and solved the issue with a set of insulated wire cutters.

"Well, that was anti-climactic," I said to the guys in the pickup, "but in a good way."

"Where's the FDNY?" one of them asked.

"They'll be here soon. The city is stretched very thin at the moment. The gas shortage isn't helping. I'm a cop and very lucky to have gotten the week off. I gotta go back on Tuesday though. I think this is them now," I replied, as several city trucks turned onto the block. "Let's get out of here before we get boxed in."

Corey Gelato asked, "Where did the big fire happen?"

"Just down the road," I said, "I'll show you."

I drove eastward down Breezy Point Boulevard and onto the Promenade, retracing the steps Sand Flea took the night of the fire. They were speechless as we passed block after block of shattered houses, smashed apart by the Atlantic Ocean only a few nights ago. We arrived at the end of Gotham Walk and I gave them a tour, describing the events of Hurricane Sandy as we went.

"It's so much different in person," one said. "It's nothing like on TV."

"I've heard we've been in the press, but haven't seen anything yet. Is that how you guys decided to come down here?" I asked.

"Are you kidding? You guys are all over the news. That's why we decided to come and help you out."

"Well, I'm glad you're here. We could really use a hand."

I lead them down to the end of the walk and to the statue of the Virgin Mary which had become a symbol of the Breezy Point community and Hurricane Sandy. Several people approached us to ask questions and take pictures. All the attention took some getting used to, but if it brought hope to these people sifting through the ashes of their homes I thought it was the least we could do.

An older woman pulled me aside, "Would you boys mind going into my basement and getting some photo albums? They're in a dresser. I can see the top and it isn't burned so I think they're still in there."

"We'd be happy to ma'am. Just show us which house is yours."

She brought us to a foundation filled with charred timbers and rusted appliances. "It's right over there. Please be careful."

I cautiously climbed in with Corey and another firefighter. The footing was unstable and the foundation was half full of water. After carefully climbing over to the dresser I reached my hands into it and pulled out several albums, wet but untouched by fire. The other firefighters recovered various personal items as well, previously presumed lost, much to the delight of the homeowner.

"Oh my! I can't believe you found this!" she cried as we handed her one thing after another. When we were finished she gave each one of us a hug and a kiss before going back to her car with an armful of memories. "Thank you so much!"

"Do you think you can help me out too?" asked a man who looked to be in his fifties. "I have a few things I'd like to get out of my house while there's still time."

The conditions of his foundation were similar, but after a few minutes we recovered several albums, flags, pins and coffee mugs. We also found a case of cold Bud Light and several bottles of liquor.

"Thanks a lot guys. Keep the booze, you earned it!"

I popped the cap off a beer and had a taste. "It's still pretty good," I said as I handed another to one of the South Blooming Grove firefighters.

"This tastes like saltwater!" he observed while the other guys laughed. I took a look at the beer in my hand and noticed the inside of the bottle cap had sand in it.

"Suit yourself," I told him. "After a few days in this shit you'd be happy to have a cold one!"

"I'll drink to that!" he said, taking a courtesy swig then tossing the bottle aside. The hard liquor was left on the foundation for anyone interested.

We spent the next hour going into wrecked homes and pulling out whatever personal items we could find. Despite a blazing inferno above, the seawater did a fairly good job protecting any submerged items. Hundreds of cherished belongings were recovered. A 10-speed bike, a box of toys, lots of photo albums…you name it. After a few close calls I decided we had pushed our luck long enough. It was only a matter of time before one of us slipped and had a serious injury. Reluctantly, we left the fire area and made our way back to the pickup and drove back to the firehouse.

As we bounced along the sand track running parallel to the Promenade, I checked my voicemail and messages. One in particular was of great concern. My sister had arrived in Breezy Point and went to the firehouse looking for me. She found several volunteers looking to help so they went to my house and gutted the basement. The pumping and gutting needed to be done, and I wasn't ready to confront the painful task of sifting through my personal belongings.

What worried me most was her discretion concerning items that could be saved and those which were a total loss. In her mind everything fell into the latter category. I love my sister, but she once threw out my grandmother's cook books because they looked old. She's not the type of person you want determining the fate of your sentimental objects and in a pile of rubble was exactly where most of my beloved things ended up. I waited too long.

I put these concerns out of my mind as we pulled off the main road and into the firehouse parking lot. Marty was waiting for us with a special request, "If you don't mind there's an older gentleman, Mr. Gormley, in the house right over there who could use a hand cleaning up his house. He could really use an extra set of hands."

We grabbed some tools, including several chainsaws, and walked the short distance to the Gormley residence. The family, already removing debris and tearing up their mangled deck, was happy to see us. I started hauling flotsam, which had washed onto the property, while Corey and the South Blooming Grove firefighters started up the chainsaws and cut the deck into manageable sections. Mike Schramm and several of our guys joined us and soon we had the house stripped bare. The eldest Gormley was visibly upset. Someone told me he built that house with his bare hands thirty years ago.

The fading light of another November day heralded the departure of our volunteers from Monroe. We said our goodbyes and thanked them for all their hard work. Those of us staying at Camp Duff made our way home, going over the day's events.

"I have to take a shit," griped one firefighter. "Where the fuck is the port-a-potties?"

"Dude, there are none. Go on the beach."

"That's bullshit. I was down at the FEMA headquarters today in Fort Tilden and they had a dozen of them lined up against the fences."

"Is that true?" I chimed in.

"Yeah, they got a whole bunch of shit just sitting around and no one is able to use it."

"Interesting," I thought. Here we are on the sixth day since the storm and still no food, no water, and no toilets from FEMA. I wouldn't blame them if they didn't have any, but our trips into Brooklyn revealed a veritable cache of badly needed supplies just sitting across the bridge at Floyd Bennett Field. FEMA had set up a massive depot of food, water, fuel, medicine, tents, survival gear and personal hygiene materials which we desperately needed. By our estimate there wasn't a single port-a-potty in all of Breezy Point. I took a ride in Unit 9 down to Fort Tilden to see for myself and make FEMA aware of our situation.

Sure enough there was a luxury camper and giant heated tent set up in the parking lot, and behind the tent were a cluster of port-a-potties. The lights in the camper were on so I walked up to the front door and knocked. I think I caught them at a bad time. Among the laptops and papers strewn across their kitchen table were various sandwiches and sides. They even had a coffee machine percolating in the corner. Clearly my presence made them uneasy, like kids caught with their hands in the cookie jar.

I introduced myself and described the situation, "My guys have been living down here for a week now. We're on call 24 hours a day and answering fire jobs between clearing debris and helping the residents fix their homes. So far we haven't got much in terms of food, water, or other supplies and we need a bathroom. I see you have eight port-a-potties outside. We only need one. Can you help us?"

For a moment they looked at each other, then down at the table perhaps hoping I would just go away. One of them told me to leave my name and phone number, and they would send my request up the chain then get back to me. I spent enough time in government service to know when I'm being given the run-around. After that I was ushered out of the camper with a pat on the back and a, "We'll get back to you."

A short while later I received a voicemail, "This is Gigi Perez the FEMA manager for Breezy Point. I talked to my boss and because we're under Federal contract through the GSA we can't lend you any port-a-potties without the proper paperwork because without it we will get in trouble. I'm sorry I can't help you on this occasion. Take care and be safe."

I looked down at my phone, "Fuck you."

I'm not an unreasonable guy, but this was starting to really get to me. We had been asking for help for nearly a week now with nothing to show for it except my growing credit card bill. All the supplies we needed were sitting a few miles away but we couldn't get to them because we didn't have the proper paperwork. I laid out my plan to the guys in Duffman's living room, "I need a couple of volunteers. We're taking Unit 9 and coming back with a port-a-potty and whatever else we can carry. Anyone interested come with me."

Eight of us climbed into the pickup, three of them onto the rear bed since there wasn't enough room in the cab. We drove along Rockaway Point Boulevard towards Fort Tilden and stopped just outside of the parking lot. As expected the FEMA people cleared out right after I left, but a patrol car was making lazy circles inside the lot where the port-a-potties were standing. I walked up to the U.S. Parks Police officers and gave them my spiel, but they weren't going for it.

"Time for Plan B," I said as I got back into the truck.

We crossed the bridge and drove into Floyd Bennett Field where FEMA had set up its headquarters for the Rockaway and Breezy Point relief effort. We had seen some of their operation from Flatbush Avenue, but what we saw from the inside gave us a sense of hope and depression at the same time. Dozens of fuel trucks were lined up near the old control tower, along with ambulances and fire trucks idling with their turret lights on, burning fuel we desperately needed. Massive tents, like the one at Fort Tilden, were everywhere with hot food and cots inside. In the back field were trailers full of supplies as far as the eye could see, and lined up along the road were hundreds of port-a-potties.

I stopped the pickup again and again. We were directed to one office after another where each person directed us to yet another office, until someone finally had the common courtesy to tell us the truth and put our dream of shitting somewhere other than a hole in the sand out of its misery. "I'm sorry fellas, but unless you have the proper authorization these toilets aren't going nowhere. We're accountable."

Well, at least we could say we tried to do things the right way. It was not our fault we didn't have the proper forms to cut through the red tape. I had to consider the hygiene needs of my men over the paperwork requirements of the bureaucrat in the FEMA trailer, so I maneuvered Unit 9 around several barriers and onto an unlit road. From there I figured we could explore other options and, at the very least, make use of the port-a-potties while we were here. If one of them accidently ended up on the back of our truck, so be it. They could bill me for it later.

At the end of the old tarmac we found a trailer with a few NYPD cops standing around outside while another worked a forklift. One of them escorted me inside to talk with an Emergency Services Unit (ESU) Deputy Inspector. By this point I had gone over our tale of woe too many times to put real feeling into it, but I told him about our ordeal anyway. He thought about it for a moment then called for another cop standing outside the trailer door.

"Ricky," he said, "grab one of the shitters and load it into their truck for them will ya?" He looked back at me, "Is that all you needed?" It was that simple. Once again the NYPD came through for us when we needed it most. I was shocked, and embarrassed him a little as I repeatedly gave thanks for his help. He probably never saw anyone so happy to get a plastic booth half full of human waste. The forklift driver found the least used of the bunch and loaded it on the bed of the truck for us.

As we raced along the road traversing Floyd Bennett Field past the FEMA offices which rejected us earlier, a few confused looks were aimed our way. We had the radio at full volume, blasting Toby Keith's *Courtesy of the Red, White, and Blue* and singing along while the guys in the back clung to the port-a-potty for dear life. You would think we just won an epic victory against an insurmountable giant, and in some ways I guess we had.

CHAPTER 12

ESCAPE

Monday, November 5, 2012

At dawn I walked over to the firehouse early after another sleepless night. There was too much on my mind at night to rest peacefully. Tomorrow I was scheduled to return to work at 4:00 A.M. and much needed to be done between then and this evening when my girlfriend and I planned to escape. Last night we set up the port-a-potty in front of Duffman's house, and Brillo scrubbed it down with Clorox wipes. Food and other supplies, especially fuel, were running low. I would have to take care of that before I left. I was deep in thought, walking around the firehouse on autopilot, picking up little bits of debris and putting them in a trash bag.

Suddenly my introspection was interrupted by a man in green fatigues. "Sir, is this the Point Breeze Fire Department?"

"Yeah, what's left of it. Can I help you?"

"Actually sir, we were looking for a place to sit down and eat but I believe we can help you. We're from the 8th Engineer Support Battalion, United States Marine Corps. We've been sent to Breezy Point to see if we can be of any assistance."

"Here's our Chief now," I said, as Marty walked through the front door of the firehouse. "There's tons of stuff that needs to get done, but he'll tell you what we need most right now."

Marty and the Marine officers made introductions while I talked to the enlisted men. It wasn't long before they were carrying out the heavy debris and appliances which littered the firehouse since the night of Sandy. Crowbars were passed around and the water soaked sheetrock was torn from the wall studs all around the room. After an hour or so, I made my way over to Camp Duff to get the guys into gear. They were munching on chips and soda for breakfast when I arrived.

"The Marines are here. They're gutting the firehouse for us. Let's get over there and help, okay?" I stepped outside to take an inventory of our fuel and top off the generator while Brillo got the guys up and moving. We were down to less than a day's worth of fuel, and with the departure of the Ecock brothers, the house was starting to look like a mess again. Duffman's basement was still a wreck and we promised him we would take care of it while he was at work.

Two Marines, Cpl Zachary Wiener and Petty Officer Jeremy Whitaker, from the 8th Engineer Support Battalion, 2nd Marine Logistics Group help gut the Point Breeze firehouse.

By the time I returned to the firehouse it was almost ten o'clock. A friend of mine from the 63rd Precinct Conditions Team, John Fatorrusso, had arrived with his girlfriend, Megan, and were gutting Schramm's house. He joined me a short while later and we began ripping down lime green painted sheetrock in the firehouse office. John had construction experience and gave me a crash course on how to rebuild everything we were tearing down with such gusto.

The arrival of Bill Flynn, from FEMA, cut my time with John and Megan short. Bill and I made our way over to Essex Walk to have a look at my house and fill out some paperwork. There was a giant pile of garbage and debris at the front of my block, and although I tried not to look, it was painfully obvious many of my things were scattered among the trash heap. Plastic toys from my childhood which I had hoped to one day give to my children were mixed with my clothing and other items that could have been easily saved with a bucket of water and some Lysol.

"She threw out the fish tank," I whispered.

"I'm sorry Sebastian, what did you say?" asked Bill.

"Nothing. Well, it's not nothing, it's everything. Everything I own. She threw out a fucking salt water fish tank. It's literally an object designed to be filled with salt water, but it was thrown out why exactly? Because salt water touched it? Seriously?"

"Look at this," I shouted as I pointed to a portion of the debris pile. "The Star Wars toys my mom was saving from when I was a kid. It's nothing but plastic. Those things could be cleaned with a bucket of soapy water! Why the fuck did this need to be thrown away?"

A rage was building, and if I didn't get myself under control soon that brick wall, which had been haunting me since the night of the storm, was going to smash me right in the face, and I couldn't have that. Not yet. People were counting on me. I took a deep breath and tried to focus on the positive. There would be a strongly worded conversation in the future about this, but not today. I escorted Bill into my house and started on the arduous system that is the FEMA process.

* * *

After an hour, I went back to the firehouse to check on John and Megan. I had another bit of personal business to attend to as well: my truck. GEICO had already chalked a claim number on the rear window, but before they could tow it away I had to remove my personal items. Everything of value was put into bags and stored in the gutted office. Tomorrow after work I planned to head over to Plaza Honda on Nostrand Avenue and rent a car, if they had any left.

On the passenger side dashboard were some Hustler and Penthouse magazines. They weren't mine; I'd admit it if they were. Besides, who gets magazines these days? The last time I physically held a porn publication was in my girlfriend's house just before the storm when I thumbed through her copy of *Fifty Shades of Gray* right next to the *Magic Mike* DVD. I have no moral objection to porn, but I do have a problem with paying for it. As far as I'm concerned it's covered in my cable bill. A mailing label on the bottom right corner, told me who the owner was. I put the magazines into one of my bags. With the electricity out they might come in handy sometime.

After a few more hours of pulling down sheetrock and removing debris, the office was starting to look pretty good. The Marines had done a terrific job in the main room and promised to come back tomorrow. John and Megan said goodbye, and I thought this was as good a time as any to head into Brooklyn and pick up some supplies. I rounded up a few guys and we loaded as many empty gas cans we could find into the back of Unit 9, though this time capped cans only. I had no desire to repeat the near disaster of a few nights prior.

We stopped at the local Walgreens at Flatbush and Utica Avenues to pick up the usual: cigarettes, chewing tobacco, soda and food. As we stood in line I felt a pair of eyes on me, watching my every move. I scanned the isles and found the source: Taylor Swift. Well…a life size cardboard cutout of Taylor Swift. There she was, in dark pants and a white shirt with the horizontal black stripes, calling to us to rescue her from this horrible place and whisk her away to our magical land of no running water or electricity.

"Excuse me miss," I said to the cashier, "how much for the cardboard cutout over there?"

She laughed, "It's not for sale."

"Can we have it anyway?" I pleaded.

"No, I can't do that until after the promotion is over," she replied, pointing to the display for her Red album which was already two weeks old.

"That's too bad; the guys would have really liked it."

One of the firefighters teased, "We live in a house with all guys and I want to do horrible things to that poster tonight."

I strutted over to the cutout and put my arm around her neck. Luckily the cashier had already rung up our goods and money was exchanged, because I leaned too heavily on Miss Swift and the whole display came apart. It was time for us to leave.

"Cashier lady," I said, "I'm really sorry. Keep the change!"

Everything was thrown into the back of the pickup as we drove out of the parking lot and onto Flatbush Avenue. I didn't mean to damage the display, but I left $15 in change to cover the cost of tape to put Taylor back together again. We stopped at the NYPD's Highway 2 command and explained our fuel arrangement. Once again my department came through for us. We departed with another 83 gallons of gasoline in fuel cans plus a full tank for Unit 9.

As we pulled into Camp Duff and unloaded the supplies, everyone got a good laugh about the Taylor Swift incident. I handed the keys for the pickup over to Brillo and wished him good luck. My girlfriend and I planned on a brief stay in a hotel to get cleaned up, and a good night's sleep before she drove me to work at 4:00 A.M. tomorrow morning. I wouldn't be back to the firehouse for almost 24 hours, but I told him to call me if there were any problems and I'd see what I could do. I felt bad leaving them, but she and I needed some time together as well, and I couldn't go into work looking and smelling the way I did.

"Oh, one more thing," I said to him and Kieran, "I found these in my truck while I was cleaning it out today. I thought you guys might want to put them to good use." I handed over the magazines.

"Nice! My colon isn't the only thing getting backed up these days, if you know what I mean."

"Have fun with the porn and try not to ruin the good socks," I teased…sort of. Clean socks were hard to find.

* * *

She picked me up at the firehouse around 7 o'clock that evening and we drove to a hotel near the airport. It had hot water, electricity, cable TV, and a clean comfortable bed. It was Heaven! We took a shower, opened a bottle of wine, and talked about everything that happened this week. I held her in my arms as she sobbed. My own stress and worries were set aside for the moment. I reassured her everything was going to be alright because we were going to get through this together. The crying stopped as she rolled on top of me and rested her chin on my chest. It felt good to commiserate, and what followed, before we fell asleep in each other's arms, was even better.

CHAPTER 13

THE FUEL CRISIS

Tuesday, November 6, 2012

"I'm home. Thank you so much for taking me away from all this for a while!" she wrote after dropping me off at work. It was 4:00 A.M. and the Conditions Team was doing 12-hour tours for the foreseeable future. The fuel shortage was crippling the city and Mayor Bloomberg has instituted a rationing system. This was also Election Day and by tomorrow morning we could have a new president.

My newest partner, Police Officer Vincent Garvey, drove us around Marine Park and Mill Basin for an up close look at the damage to those areas. We traded stories about the past week and he brought me up to speed about things in the precinct. The line at every gas station was around the block, some of them much longer. Our Sergeant could be a bit of a hard case but he knew what he was doing, especially in the day-to-day operations of gas stations it seemed. We went from one to the next, making sure there was no trouble and evaluating their status.

Erin, Marty's daughter, called me at work. I had previously complained about the lack of heat at Camp Duff and was looking for a solution. A nor'easter, dubbed Winter Storm Athena by the meteorologists at The Weather Channel, was expected to dump a foot of snow on us tomorrow and send temperatures plunging into the teens. Erin offered to ship down several propane heaters from her home town of Wilton, Connecticut, if I wanted them. I agreed, and though they cost me $650, it was money well spent. Knowing we were freezing at night and needed them as soon as possible, Erin drove all the way down that afternoon and dropped them off at the firehouse. I called Brillo to make sure someone picked up the heaters before they grew legs.

Around sundown I finished work and got a ride over to All Car Rental service on Nostrand Avenue. I asked for a truck, but all they had was a black, two-door Mazda M3 with an empty gas tank. "Beggars can't be choosers," I thought as I turned right off Kings Highway and onto Flatbush Avenue. Twenty minutes later I was parked in the lot outside Camp Duff where Mike Scannell and Kieran Carley were smoking a cigarette and talking.

"We gotta move out of Duff's house."

"What? Why?" I asked.

"I don't know, but I think he's getting pissed off. No one has helped him with the basement and the guys are making a real mess of the place."

I found Duffman and got to the bottom of things. Ten of us had been living in his home for almost a week and the place was a wreck. We promised him the basement would be our top priority since he had to return to work and couldn't do it himself, but it was only half done. There were a lot of little things too. One constant problem throughout the entire recovery was cleaning and household chores. Tim Dufficy and I are older men used to taking care of ourselves, but most of the others were barely out of college and still living at home.

We hypothesized that they were used to mom cleaning up after them and old habits die hard. When someone would make a sandwich, they would leave crumbs all over the place and the empty plate in the living room. Condiments would be left sitting on the counter and dirty utensils thrown in the sink. I cleaned up after them, as did Nick Ecock over the weekend, but after a while we gave up. The ensuing mess started to accumulate, so when Duff returned from work he was upset. I would be too. Tim Dufficy was very generous allowing us to stay in his home, but it was time to move on.

As we sat in the living room, huddled under blankets, watching the Presidential election coverage, suggestions were made about where our next home would be. I was tempted to volunteer my own place, but it was too far away from the firehouse to be effective and after witnessing what happened at Duffman's house, I bit my tongue. The firehouse was looking a lot better but wasn't fully gutted yet. Someone mentioned the Point Breeze Clubhouse where we sheltered during the storm. At present we were using it to store supplies, but it had the benefit of being close to the firehouse and no need for gutting due to its cinderblock walls.

It was decided. Tomorrow we would close down Camp Duff and move to the Point Breeze Clubhouse before the nor'easter arrived. For me this added a whole new bevy of logistical concerns, so I turned in early before the election results were announced. I lay in bed looking up at the ceiling and considered the changing needs of our evolving living situation. The light tower outside the firehouse, where we would draw power, required diesel fuel, not the gasoline we had stockpiled. Since we no longer had access to a refrigerator, food would have to be stored outside and secured. The propane heaters I just bought, which were perfect for a house, didn't put out enough heat to warm a place the size of the Clubhouse.

"Where can I find propane?" I thought as my eye lids grew heavy. Before I knew it my alarm went off at 3:00 A.M. and I was on the way to another day of work.

CHAPTER 14

NOR'EASTER

Wednesday, November 7, 2012

The nor'easter hit us hard, but we were ready. While I was at work the guys moved everything over to the Point Breeze Clubhouse. A dozen cots were set up on the stage and a curtain was strung up for privacy. Sleeping bags and donated blankets were found along with a some pillows. The few personal items we had, as well as individual firefighting gear, was stored under the cots, ready to go at a moment's notice. An extension cord ran from the ESU light tower in front of the firehouse all the way to the Clubhouse. Once again, Christmas lights provided enough illumination.

On the way home, I stopped at Lowes on Avenue U and bought eight 20-pound propane tanks for $54 each so we could run the heaters. As I drove along Rockaway Beach Boulevard, just past the Roxbury gate, I saw a man walking in the opposite direction without a coat or shoes. Before I could turn around he disappeared in the heavy snowfall. I stopped at the security booth to show ID to prove I was a resident, and I told them about the man on the road.

"Some FDNY guys caught him looting a house. They gave him a few options, and he chose to leave the property."

"Fair enough," I said. Running into looters was a real danger for those of us who stayed in Breezy Point and the Rockaways overnight. Once the sun went down, the entire peninsula was blacked out except a few corners with light towers on them. After a while the looters figured they would steal those too. Valued from $3,000 to $15,000 each, they were an expensive item to leave unattended.

When I arrived at the Clubhouse I noticed something very peculiar about the guys. Suddenly, they were all Pittsburg Steelers fans. I've been a huge Steelers fan since I went to college in Pennsylvania in 1996. My friend, John Gold, got me into watching football my sophomore year, and since he was a Pittsburg fan I became one too. Besides, I liked the way Bill Cowher always seemed to be one bad play away from going on a rampage. But this was New York, deep inside Giants and Jets territory.

"Where did you get all the Steelers swag?" I asked.

Brillo explained, "When the Steelers played the Giants on Sunday they left all their cold weather gear behind and donated it to us. It arrived this afternoon while you were gone."

"We got four boxes of stuff," Kieran added, "scarves, hats, gloves, windbreakers, and even a few bubble jackets."

Brillo threw me a black and gold bubble coat, "We saved this for you."

New Pittsburg Steelers fans Kevin Hernandez (left), Kieran Carley, Sebastian Danese, and Mike Scotko (right) huddle around a propane heater in the Point Breeze Clubhouse.

We warmed ourselves around the heaters while they discussed the day's events. I went to bed in my new Steelers bubble jacket on a cot in the far left corner. Brillo was in the next cot over, so close our blankets were touching. We were facing each other, alternating opening our eyes to see if the other one was asleep yet.

"Don't make this weird dude," I told him. "Just go to sleep."

* * *

The next few days were a blur. I was working 12-hour shifts keeping order at the gas stations across the bay in Brooklyn while the guys tended to their own homes and fixed up the firehouse. The Marines returned on Thursday to finish the gutting and debris removal. Marty's daughter, Erin, brought down chili in several crock pots which could be kept warm from the generator in the light tower. Hot food was a huge morale boost, as were the steady supply of cigarettes and chewing tobacco I brought home every night after work. Erin left for Connecticut and took with her all the Class A uniforms we managed to save. A dry cleaner volunteered to wash our uniforms at no cost and we were grateful to take him up on his generous offer.

Even as members' homes were pumped and gutted, dozens of jobs were handled. Fatigue worsened and one call seemed to blend with another until at some point a group discussion was required to remember details. I would come home from work every night half expecting the Clubhouse to be deserted. Our guys were exhausted, pushed to the verge of collapse, and no amount of pep talks or cigarettes was going to fix that. They needed to stand down for a night of recuperation.

Tomorrow, however, was the start of the weekend with thousands of residents and volunteers expected to flood the community. Earlier today, a man had shown up asking to borrow a folding table and some chairs which he set up under a blue pop-up tent in the parking lot behind the Point Breeze Fire Department. It was Kevin Adams, who along with fellow FDNY firefighter Phil Pillet and his long-time friend Erin Concoran-Daly, was about to launch a grass roots mold remediation service named Operation Breezy Point Gut and Pump (or "Gut 'n Pump" for short). Our part of the neighborhood was about to get a lot busier.

Any thoughts of rest would have to wait.

* * *

Throughout the Rockaways, the nerves of weary Hurricane Sandy survivors were pushed to their limits. Petty disagreements created tension between my girlfriend and her family which finally boiled over. She moved out of her parent's house where she had been staying since her own home was flooded and unlivable. I told Brillo I was leaving for the evening to help my girlfriend, but would stay in Breezy Point and was taking one of our few working radios with me in case of an emergency. We decided to stay at my house until other arrangements were figured out in the morning. It would be the first time I slept in my bed since the night before the hurricane.

She was upset. Right or wrong, no one likes to fight with their family. Her two small dogs, sensing their owner's emotional state, were nervous as well. The house was freezing cold and without power, so we looked for the box of candles I asked my sister to buy while preparing for the storm. Of course, my sister, in a perfect example of why I love her so much, bought twenty scented Yankee candles instead of the no frills brand. I set them up on the night stands on either side of the bed, and before long the aroma of vanilla, berry, and cinnamon filled the room. What we appreciated most was the little bit of heat they provided. The house was freezing cold!

We crawled under the blankets, and watched as the flickering candles cast dancing shadows across the ceiling. She had her face buried in my chest, sobbing. I held her tight, not knowing what to say. Our lives fell apart materially and came together romantically in the last two weeks. I clumsily fumbled through my emotions, trying to convince her that everything would be okay. Her dogs were cuddled at our feet.

"I love you," I said, for the first time. She didn't have to say anything in return. Deep down inside I already knew. She looked at me for a moment then threw her arms around my neck and kissed me. Her eyes were still watering, and I could feel the tears streaming down her cheeks onto mine. After a moment she broke our kiss and looked at me, her face inches from my own.

"I love you too!"

The dogs stared at us. One cocked its head to the left and made a funny face, then crawled on top of the pillow behind my head, and fell asleep.

We weren't far behind.

CHAPTER 15

SEMPER FIDELIS

Saturday, November 10, 2012

At 9:30 A.M. a ceremony was held at the Point Breeze Volunteer Fire Department for the 237th birthday of the United States Marine Corps. Ably lead by Major Craig Clarkson, the Marines of the 8th Engineer Support Battalion, 2nd Marine Logistics Group, II Marine Expeditionary Force had been a tremendous help over the last week. Sitting on the engine deck was a folding table with a red, white and blue frosted chocolate cake. A Ka-Bar knife was used to slice the cake into little squares and served on plastic plates. It was an honor to host them during their special day.

Marines from the 8th Engineer Support Battalion celebrate the Corps' birthday on the Point Breeze engine deck.

I was on patrol in Mill Basin during the ceremony when I received a phone call from a Sergeant at the Office of the Deputy Commissioner of Public Information office at Police Headquarters. They wanted me to do an interview with the New York Daily News and, therefore, sent me home at noon. I didn't argue and was looking forward to the next two days at the firehouse without the interference of working 12-hour shifts in Brooklyn. The guys had already taken one of the trucks to a member's house and were pumping it out, so I walked next door to see what Gut 'n Pump was all about. I had met Kevin Adams and John Norton the week before at Camp Duff, but this was my first time meeting the rest of the organizers.

Kevin introduced me to Erin Concoran-Daly, an energetic and approachable woman who makes everyone feel welcome. She and Kevin have been friends for more than two decades which is one of the reasons he found himself pumping and gutting homes in Breezy Point instead of skiing in Vermont that fall. Kevin had convinced Erin to stay in Breezy Point another week to help him organize the growing number of firefighters looking to volunteer to gut and pump houses in the neighborhood. They had already worked on dozens of homes, but now it was time for Kevin to make his ambition to organize the volunteers a reality.

One of the objectives was to better inform the homeowners what they should and should not do. Far too much conflicting information was being passed around. Earlier in the week Kevin found himself in the home of Tom Ahern, a family friend on Beach 222nd Street. He brought ten FDNY firefighters from his station with him.

"Hey Tom, you need any help gutting the place?"

"Nope, just gotta pump the basement out and that's it."

"You had water on the first floor though, right?"

Tom replied, "Yeah, but we let it dry out. It's okay now."

"Let me show you something," said Kevin as he decided to forgo subtlety and put his fist through the sheetrock wall. It was saturated and came apart easily in his hand. He reached inside and tore out a handful of soaking wet insulation and showed it to the elder Ahern. "Tom, you gotta gut the entire first floor. I know you don't want to, but the living room, kitchen, bathroom all need to be gutted. You can't just dry it out. The water which flooded your house was full of sewage, and the wet insulation behind it is going to cause poisonous mold to grow." Tom relented to Kevin's advice.

As the firefighters tore down chunks of wet sheetrock, he wondered how many other people would make the same mistake. Almost every home in Breezy Point had been flooded and needed to be gutted, but how many people were actually doing it instead of letting their homes air dry and hoping for the best? How many people could afford to? A lot of folks down here didn't even have flood insurance! Many residents were elderly retirees on a fixed income or blue-collar city workers who didn't have tens of thousands of dollars the professional mold remediation companies were charging.

That night Kevin spoke with Erin. Originally he intended on fixing John's and Erin's houses then going back home, but it was apparent so many other people needed help and he was in a position to make a significant contribution to the recovery. Kevin grew up in Breezy Point and knew a lot of families who needed support right now. It was time for a change of plans. He consulted Phil Pillet, a friend from the FDNY Incident Management Team (IMT) based at Floyd Bennett Field, and discussed the idea of creating a volunteer operation somewhere in Breezy Point. Phil agreed and began negotiations with the Co-op to secure a place to set up a base of operations. Kevin decided to cut through the red tape and asked the leaders at Point Breeze Volunteer Fire Department.

"Not a problem, but can you use the lot behind the Clubhouse instead? This one is a little too small and we need it to operate the trucks."

"You're sure it's okay?"

"Take as much room as you want. Let us know if you need anything. If anyone asks, tell them we said it was alright." We already commandeered the Clubhouse to store some supplies, and assumed the lot came with it as a package deal. Kevin seemed like a nice guy with a good heart, and if all he needed to fix up some homes was a place to rally his troops and store his equipment, then it was the least we could do. We lent him a table and a few folding chairs to set up under his blue pop-up tent. With those humble beginnings, and after a week of planning, Operation Breezy Point Gut 'n Pump was born.

"What's with the notebook?" I asked Erin. A few of us went next door to welcome our new neighbors and see if we could be of any help.

"Everyone that comes in today has to sign in, whether they're looking for help or to volunteer. We also keep a list of where the tools and generators are." She added, "Those are expensive."

"Yeah, tell me about it. We've lost a few already. How are you guys keeping this stuff safe at night?"

"We lock them in there." Erin nodded towards a decrepit white van sitting near the tent. I learned from Kevin later that night that Brian Norton owned the van but the brakes were locked up and Sandy's floodwaters finished off any hope of repair. They dragged it over to the parking lot, with one of Norton's tractors, to use as a makeshift storage container. It worked. The van looked like a derelict of no value to looters and the type of creepy vehicle children knew to stay away from. Aside from a new padlock, there was no hint of the tens of thousands of dollars in equipment sitting inside.

"Sounds like you guys are busy already. I saw you had a bunch of firefighters mulling around this morning." I asked, "How are things going so far?"

"Great! We have the guys from Kevin's firehouse plus some volunteers he knows from Burlington, Vermont. They're working on a few houses right now then they'll come back here when they're done for the next job."

"Sounds good. I'm gonna see if I can find my guys and check in with the other volunteers in the area. I'll stop by later." I took one last look around the parking lot and headed next door to the firehouse. On my way in from work this afternoon I saw several banners advertising organizations looking to gather volunteers and offering help. The Point Breeze volunteer firefighters had already pumped and gutted a number of homes, as did Kevin and his guys, and I was curious to see what the other volunteer groups were all about.

* * *

By the second weekend after the storm, four major volunteer organizations operated in Breezy Point. Habitat for Humanity and Operation Blessing are international faith-based volunteer-driven humanitarian organizations. Both had set up operations in the parking lot along the main road near Beach 208th Street. They have been helping provide disaster relief all over the world for decades and possess established infrastructure and logistics divisions. Camp Rockne, at the Reid Avenue North parking lot entrance, and Operation Breezy Point Gut and Pump, in the Beach 210th Street parking lot behind the Point Breeze Clubhouse, were grassroots volunteer groups. Both organizations were founded by members of the community and had, initially, modest assets with which to operate. All four groups shared the same mission: to help the residents repair and rebuild their battered community.

Camp Rockne, located near the entrance to Breezy Point at the Reid Avenue parking lot by the Security barracks.

The first step was pumping out water trapped in the basement of many houses. Although more than a week had passed since the storm, the water table was still high and the water was seeping back in through cracks in the foundation. Furthermore, as the city tested the water mains, turning them on and off without notice, broken pipes in homes across the neighborhood would start gushing, causing basements to flood again. Many homes had to be pumped several times, tying up already severely limited resources.

After pumping was complete the next step was appliance and debris removal. Homes with flooding in the first floor and/or basement usually had a large amount of flotsam swept in by the ocean in addition to wrecked personal items therein. Major appliances such as stoves, refrigerators, washers, and dryers needed to be disposed of—backbreaking work for the hardiest of volunteers. To further complicate matters, it wasn't as easy as leaving these items out back for the Department of Sanitation to pick up. Each appliance or bag of debris had to be taken dozens of yards to the ends of the block where sanitation trucks could pick them up lest the sidewalks become choked with garbage.

With the water pumped and appliances removed, it was time to gut all the sheetrock which had been saturated by the flood, plus an additional foot above the water line just to be sure. Any wet sheetrock left behind was a potential source of explosive mold growth which would result in long-term negative health effects. Big empty rooms were easy, but getting to the walls behind cabinets or in closets, such as kitchens and bathrooms, were a challenge. Piles of sheetrock needed to be packed into heavy duty garbage bags and taken to the same disposal areas as the appliances and debris before. Afterwards, the windows and doors would be left open to air the house out for a few days and let the saturated wood beams dry out.

The last step of the mold remediation process was spraying chemicals on the exposed wood to kill the mold spores already growing. In most cases the only remedy available was common bleach since the proper products were in high demand and either unavailable or prohibitively expensive. The necessary equipment for both chemical application and user safety was scarce. To do it right required trained professionals, but they were busy tending to their own booming businesses, so we did what we could with what we had. Results varied.

Every step required certain tools, equipment and disposable items, such as garbage bags and masks, which created a logistics nightmare. Rockaway Point was doing a great job warehousing supplies in the Catholic Club for the residents, but had little to spare for the volunteers—and rightfully so. Donations for mold remediation organizations had to be independently managed, though with no central location this would prove to be difficult at best. The lack of electricity or reliable phone service resulted in little communication, further exacerbating the issue. One group might have a windfall of garbage bags and no masks, while another had masks but no shovels, and so on and so forth.

There were also issues with the volunteers themselves who in most cases arrived with good intentions and little else. We deeply appreciated them volunteering their time and their willingness to work, however too many showed up with no equipment, food, or even the right clothing. Whenever possible we mixed those with rudimentary skills with volunteers who were more experienced, but it didn't always turn out that way. More often than not axes and sledgehammers were in the hands of people who never used them before, sometimes with disastrous results.

At most locations the homeowners were encouraged to take a walk over to the kitchen Bobby Eustace had set up in front of the Catholic Club and get a bite to eat or a cup of coffee. Watching strangers tear apart your house and pile cherished belongings into garbage bags is tough. Some broke down and cried while others kept getting in the way. Nobody blamed them. For most, home is a special place with its own history and the location of important family events. Some had stood for decades and bore witness to many milestones throughout the lives of the people who called it their own. After we were done, it would be but a memory. It was heartbreaking but necessary work.

* * *

Throughout the day I introduced myself to the organizers of the professional volunteer groups set up in Breezy Point. James Killoran is the Chief Executive Officer of Habitat for Humanity (Westchester) and has a long history of building homes even in the most primitive conditions. He set up his headquarters across from the Beach 208th Street parking lot near Christ Community Church. Next door to them was Operation Blessing who, like Habitat for Humanity, is a faith-based, international organization which specializes in disaster management. While they are perfectly capable of rebuilding homes, their greatest strength lay in their ability to stabilize otherwise chaotic, disaster-stricken areas. Both greeted me with open arms and immediately offered their services and support.

I told Dan, one of the leaders of Operation Blessing, about our material and equipment needs at the firehouse. He passed our information up their chain of command and was especially helpful lending us technical and logistical support later on. At one point, the president of Operation Blessing came to meet me. He asked me about my concerns. I told him that we had no aerial photographs despite the endless sorties of Blackhawk helicopters circling above. We needed to know the extent of the damage and debris that might block our routes if another fire broke out. The eastern side of the property at Graham Place was nearly impassable due to dozens of homes pushed off their foundations and smashed together. A fire at any of those homes would be a disaster.

A few days later we met again. Dan handed me a flash drive full of pictures and videos of Breezy Point from above. After our first meeting, the executive staff at Operation Blessing authorized the rental of a helicopter to take hundreds of photographs and hours of video of our neighborhood. We had been asking for this same information from FEMA for more than a week. Operation Blessing managed to get it to us in just a few days. Next he handed me the keys to a three-ton loader—a construction vehicle with a massive shovel in front. They had brought it up from Virginia the previous day. "If there's a fire and debris is in the way which you can't get through, I want you to use this tractor to smash right through it. Don't worry about the tractor, just make sure no one gets hurt and you put out that fire!"

A view of the Wedge where the fire occurred. This picture is one of 230 aerial photographs and videos provided by Operation Blessing.

Pardon my language, but Operation Blessing doesn't fuck around. If you ask them for something, they get it to you as soon as possible or have a damn good reason why it can't be done. They are the sixth largest international charity, and 99% of their funding goes towards humanitarian programs. For nearly a decade they've held the highest rating possible for fiscal responsibility among charity organizations—a title only 2% of all other worldwide charities have earned. But most importantly, they're genuinely good people. The president of their organization visited Breezy Point a number of times to make sure we were getting all the help we needed.

I shared my impressions with Kevin, Erin, and Phil that night while sitting around a bonfire built from bits of wood strewn about the parking lot, torn from the homes around us. Also with us were Jason Fernald from Long Island and Bob Gibbons from Pennsylvania. Both were between jobs and had come to the Rockaways after Sandy to volunteer when they ran into Kevin, Erin and Phil and decided to stay on full time. Jason was technologically savvy and a natural organizer, while Bob lent his mechanical expertise to the group and became the tool man.

* * *

The next day, members of the Point Breeze Volunteer Fire Department made our long-awaited return to the firehouse thanks to a final visit by the United States Marines. We moved our cots and personal belongings from the Clubhouse stage to our new sleeping quarters in the spacious main room in the firehouse. Firefighting equipment and tools were stored in the office, and other supplies were piled into the engine deck. The trucks were kept outside, ready to go in a moment's notice.

Before they left, the Marines gave us a parting gift. All of their gas-powered pumps, as well as several generators. This considerable act of generosity by The Corps enabled us and Gut 'n Pump next door, with whom we agreed to share supplies, to significantly expand our pumping operations. I immediately sought Kevin and Phil to share with them this good news.

"Wow, that's amazing. You give me two generators, I'm happy. I get two pumps and I'm happy. But now we get this," Kevin said as he pointed to the dozen machines on the engine deck. "We can really do a lot of good with this stuff."

"It's all yours buddy," I told him. "We're gonna keep one or two pumps to use for ourselves, but the rest is for you guys."

We loaded two sets of pumps and hoses onto the bed of Unit 9 and brought the rest to Gut 'n Pump. Our guys got settled in then headed over to a member's home that needed servicing. I stayed behind to welcome several volunteers who had shown up at our door. One was a firefighter from Engine Company 15 in Washington, D.C. named Rocco Baldino. The engine deck and office were a mess and he offered to clean them up. I happily took him up on his offer.

I headed over to Rockaway Point to see what kind of supplies they might be willing to part with before I made my shopping list for tonight. Despite the supply run made a few days ago, we were nearly out of food again. It was after 1:30P.M. when I pulled into the parking lot near the Catholic Club and saw something peculiar.

Standing in line were a dozen volunteers wearing orange and yellow reflective traffic vests carrying armfuls of supplies out of the Clubhouse and loading them into a black van. I watched as cases of water, batteries, food, clothing, and anything else which wasn't nailed down was pilfered from the warehouse. Finally I pulled my badge out and stopped one of the women carrying a box of flashlights and diapers.

"Excuse me ma'am, where are you going with this stuff?"

"They sent us down from Astoria and told us to get as much free stuff as we could before it runs out," she replied.

"What do you mean? Who sent you down?" I asked, trying to conceal my frustration.

She mentioned the name of a now defunct community group who had gotten a bad reputation for pulling stunts exactly like this. "They drove us down here and said there's lots of free stuff to be had in the Rockaways so we should grab as much as we can."

"This isn't a government cheese line. These are private donations for the victims of Hurricane Sandy. We barely have enough as it is," I shouted at her.

"I'm a victim," she replied. "Besides, who made you king?"

"You're a victim?" I roared, "What kind of problems did you suffer in Astoria in the middle of Queens?"

"We lost power for a few days. They told us there's a lot of free stuff here and I'm taking my share. Whatever I can't use I'm gonna sell to feed my kids."

"No you're not," I said as I ripped the box from her hands and walked back to the front door of the Catholic Club. She started to follow me, but turned back after a few steps. When I got to the door, one of her friends was stuffing rotisserie chickens into a large bag. Not one, or two, but all seven that someone had donated. She grabbed every last damn chicken like a selfish parasite, and I lost it.

"Put it back!" I commanded. She looked confused. My FDNY pullover conflicted with the NYPD badge hanging around my neck and she didn't know what to think. "Put it back or I swear to God I'll arrest you right now for grand larceny and looting!" It was a bluff, but the tone of my voice was convincing enough, and she knew this wasn't the time or place to push her luck. Her greasy paws rooted around the large shopping back and unloaded the chickens until she got to the very last one.

"Can I at least get one?" she pleaded.

"Take it and leave, and never come back. Better yet…" I walked her back to the van and wrote down the license plate number and the driver's information. I made them unload the entire van, hand over the traffic vests, and I escorted them off the property. I told the officers at the main gate about my encounter and they made a note of it. In the end, all they left with was one rotisserie chicken to split amongst themselves. I hope they choked on it. Disgusted, I got back into the pickup and drove back to the firehouse, totally forgetting the reason for going to Rockaway Point to begin with.

My mood was immediately improved upon walking into the engine deck. Rocco Baldino had not only cleaned up the office, but he organized all the equipment as well. Donated bunker gear was neatly stacked on tables while boots were paired and arranged according to size. Equipment was hung on the wall on exposed nails while tools and flashlights were arranged in buckets under them. In one afternoon, he had transformed our firehouse. He did such a good job we maintained his hard work until the office was rebuilt months later. Before his long trip back to Washington, D.C., I tried to convince him to stay another night, but he had work in the morning. I was sad to see him leave.

* * *

That night, my girlfriend and I escaped to a hotel further inland. No work tomorrow for either of us meant a relaxing night and sleeping in the next morning. We sat in the hotel bar and enjoyed a hot meal for the first time in days. Sunday night football was on and I was watching the Texans beat up on the Bears when her phone rang. The smile on her face changed immediately. This wasn't good news.

"We have to go," she said. "A bulldozer just smashed into my car in front of my parent's house and fled the scene."

"Jesus…can't we catch a fucking break?" It wasn't her fault but she was upset and worried about ruining our night. I held her hand in the elevator as we went back to the room to pick up my car keys. She was on the verge of tears.

We drove back to Rockaway and checked on her vehicle. While she inspected the damage, I went looking for the culprit. A witness saw a number painted across the back of the Bobcat which hit her car and it wasn't too long before I had the guy stopped and brought back to the scene. It was well after midnight when the police report was finally finished. The hotel bar was probably closed so we decided to stop for a drink locally before heading back to the hotel. Healy's Pub, the place where we first met, was open thanks to a red 40-kilowatt generator supplying power to the bar. I would have killed for a unit like that at the firehouse, but I couldn't argue with the logic of its location. This is Rockaway after all.

She and I were exhausted by the time we walked into our hotel room at nearly 3:00 A.M. The night hadn't gone according to plan, and our hopes of sleeping away the morning evaporated. At this rate we would be lucky to get seven hours of rest before checkout, although that was twice what I was used to these days. In addition to everything else, we had to worry about getting her car fixed. This was supposed to be our special night away to forget about all the stress and anxiety waiting for us at home.

It was dark as I walked out of the bathroom. She was lying on top of the sheets, a little tipsy, and wearing nothing but the moonlight.

"Well," I thought, "at least tonight isn't a total loss."

CHAPTER 16

BUILDING MOMENTUM

Tuesday, November 13, 2012

The Point Breeze Volunteer Fire Department and Gut 'n Pump serviced 75 homes thanks to an influx of volunteers over the weekend. Today, three eight-man crews were pumping and gutting houses in the area including Tim Dufficy's home. We had promised Tim it would get done a week ago while still living at Camp Duff, but by the time we left, the job was only half complete and we owed him for his hospitality. Before noon, my crew and I had the place so clean you could barely tell it was ever flooded. Tim was at work when I texted him the pictures of our handiwork and he appreciated the effort. I drove around the neighborhood checking on the other two crews who were doing an equally professional job on their assigned homes before leaving for work at 3:00 P.M.

"Hey man, you're a celebrity", said Police Officer Garvey, mocking me, when I arrived at the Special Operations office.

I looked at him quizzically, "What are you talking about?"

"You're all over the news, check out today's paper," he said as he slid over a copy of the New York Daily News. Sure enough, there I was in a photograph with Marty Ingram, Tim O'Brien Sr. and Tim Jr. sitting on the Clubhouse stage. It was a story about our ordeal that night, the rescues, and the power of our prayers. We had done a lot of interviews over the last two weeks but this was the first time seeing my picture in a print. I have to admit, it was pretty cool. Though I didn't know it at the time, this article, coupled with several others which would appear in the next few days, would have a major impact on the role I was able to play during the recovery in the coming months. Marty's decision to actively engage the media—a gamble each individual firehouse and organization dealt with in their own way—was starting to return some positive results.

* * *

We had done dozens of interviews over the last two weeks as members of the press scrambled all over the firehouse taking pictures and asking questions about the night of Sandy. For the most part, Marty deftly handled the narrative while Tim Dufficy, the Assistant Chief, and I provided a few additional details and reiterated our need for help. When Marty went on vacation and Dufficy returned to work our plans changed and I took the lead. In addition, my job had directed several reporters to me and asked if I would be willing to talk to them. They were happy with the positive press the NYPD was getting as a result of our actions, especially since everyone on Sand Flea that night—except for Tim Dufficy—was a current or retired uniform police officer.

After today's article, I suddenly found myself with inquiries from various media outlets. For me this was an opportunity to potentially solve some of our supply problems through requests for donations of specific items which were in short supply and to draw attention to the deficiencies plaguing the recovery, both material and administrative. Furthermore, we now had a means to call for desperately needed volunteers on the city, state, and national level depending on who we talked with. I consulted with Marty over the phone.

"The press is ringing my phone off the hook looking to know more about the fire that night, but I've told them pretty much everything I know."

Marty asked, "So what do you want to do?"

"They're always looking for a new story to tell and if they don't get one they'll go looking on their own and God knows what we'll see in the papers tomorrow. I was thinking we should shift focus away from the fire and tell them about Camp Duff and all the pumping and gutting we've been doing since then. We've also responded to a lot of calls. Let's change the message from surviving that night to still being here weeks later. We can let the world know we're not giving up."

"I like it," he said. "You're right. Clean the firehouse up. We want them to know we're beaten but not broken."

"I'm nervous," I admitted, "I don't want to come off as some glory-hounding attention whore, but we could really use the help. I'm already down a few thousand dollars of my own personal money and I can't keep this up."

"What's the problem with supplies now? Aren't there plenty of donations getting to you guys?" he asked.

"It's not that simple. Geography is killing us. Every day people are bringing stuff in from all over the country, but we're the last stop along the main road. By the time they get to us they've already stopped at Roxbury, Rockaway Point, and anyplace else with a sign in front of it. We get whatever everyone else didn't want. The Clubhouse is full of second-hand clothing. On the other hand, I don't want to send them away because they might not come back or we could seem ungrateful."

I continued, "We're also having a problem because of our name. People are calling up to see what we need and a few days later they call back to see if we got the package. Most of the time we don't get anything. They put 'Breezy Point Fire Department' on the address instead of 'Point Breeze' and in the confusion; the other two fire departments have mistakenly taken those donations as their own. I've had to go over there a few times to straighten it out, but I really can't blame them. People don't understand there are three volunteer departments down here and all of them could be the Breezy Point Fire Department. I write everything down to keep a record for the 501(c)(3) charity stuff we have to mail out to donors, and during follow up calls I keep finding out the donations we asked for are going to the wrong fire department!"

"We can't have that," said Marty. He was angry now. "When I get back I'll have a talk with the other Chiefs about it. Like you said, I can understand the confusion, but we're relying on those donations to get the firehouse back together."

"I'll make sure the papers get the name right in the future and hopefully this mess will go away," I told him. The Chief and I talked a little bit longer. We both agreed nothing was done maliciously, but the ensuing conversation with his counterparts would do little to smooth over already strained relations. Before the storm all three firehouses maintained a friendly rivalry, but since Sandy things had become less cordial as stress ate away at our nerves and we struggled for our survival. The stakes were higher than they had ever been. We were jealous of Rockaway Point's supplies and equipment, while they—still smarting from the loss of all their trucks—looked enviously at ours. Roxbury felt neglected by us both since they were detached from the main part of the community, while both Roxbury and Rockaway Point viewed our association with Gut 'n Pump and courting of the press as inappropriate.

It was stupid, but dangerously so. We are all neighbors and friends, especially the younger guys, but as you went further up the chain of command, relations started to sour as responsibilities to respective firehouses increased. Old men make for even older grudges and, with no effective unifying force, our problems were solved by impromptu conferences between the Chiefs and their consiglieres. I accompanied Marty to many of these meetings, and in his absence went in his place, but the politics of the "Old Guard" meant little to me. I didn't grow up in Breezy Point like most of my friends—I was a summer-only resident. When I turned eighteen, I left and didn't return until a decade later to live here full time. I had no rivalries or grudges with anyone. Hell, until a month ago I hadn't even dated a girl in Breezy Point since I was in my teens.

Before the call ended Marty asked how the guys were holding up and about morale. Most of us hadn't taken more than a half day break since the storm, and in a few cases we had guys like Brillo who hadn't gotten any rest at all. My occasional nights away at airport hotels with my girlfriend were the only thing keeping me from breaking down entirely, and I knew the longer I kept my brick wall at bay the worse it would be when it finally caught up with me. Fortunately for Marty, his wife insisted he take a vacation so he was gone a week for badly needed rest and recuperation, but you could tell he wished he was here with us.

* * *

I signed out of work just before midnight, exhausted and looking forward to my cot in the firehouse before another early day of gutting and pumping homes before returning to work. Coordinating volunteers and supplies around my work schedule was difficult and getting worse. Both my mind and body were exhausted. Pretty soon I would have to give up my work at the firehouse, and although our guys had lots of fighting spirit, I'm not sure how long they would last without me, Duffman, and Marty around on a regular basis to provide guidance and support. These thoughts troubled my mind as I crawled into my sleeping bag that night, and for the first time in days I slept uninterrupted through the night. Fatigue had finally overcome me. Enough was enough.

* * *

The next morning I awoke rested, but still worried about going in to work and leaving the guys behind. "What if they needed food or supplies?" I thought, "Should I leave them my credit card just in case?"

My phone had several missed called and texts, though the one that worried me the most was from roll call at work. I got myself cleaned up and returned their call, dreading the possibility of an assignment which might take me away for an extended period of time. As it turns out, the message awaiting me was quite the opposite. Apparently the Police Commissioner reads the same newspapers as everyone else, and when he was reading *The New York Daily News* yesterday he saw our story and was impressed. After a few phone calls I was connected with my commanding officer, Captain John Rowell.

"Sebastian, how are things out there in Breezy Point?"

"We're getting by, sir. There's a lot to do."

"That's great news. I got some even better news for you: as per the Commissioner's office you're assigned to Breezy Point for the immediate future. You start your tour today at that firehouse of yours, but check in with us every couple of days and let us know if you're okay and if you need anything. Take as much time as you need."

"Thank you so much, sir. I won't let you down," was all I could blurt out in my state of shock. This was a game-changing development, not just on a personal level, but for the firehouse as well. Without the constant worry about work I could fully concentrate on the issues closer to home. A great burden had been lifted from my mind. It was electrifying. I felt unshackled and ready to throw myself into this new assignment with everything I had left in me. Last night's worries were cast aside – the brick wall would have to wait for another day. I got a few of the guys together in Unit 9 and set out to gut a few homes of friends we had made promises to.

Pumping and gutting homes is backbreaking work, but every once in a while something interesting happens that breaks up the monotony. For example, volunteers working at Camp Rockne were smashing apart a cabinet at a house on Reid Avenue that needed to be thrown out when they found two gold bars and a pistol. They immediately took their find to Ridgewood Savings Bank near the Co-op offices for safekeeping. The bank manager did some math and estimated that each bar was worth $64,000. The pistol was a WWII relic, but still functional.

In another house on the other side of Breezy Point, Operation Gut n' Pump volunteers entered a home filled with trash. At first they thought the tides had swept an unusual amount of flotsam into the living room and kitchen, but upon closer inspection it became apparent it was the owner's property. She was a hoarder. Magazines, newspapers, flower pots…all sorts of random items were stacked from floor to ceiling. Most of it was covered in black mold, but the homeowner insisted nothing be thrown away. She asked the gutting be done around the biological hazards her treasures had become, and she was genuinely shocked when her request was refused.

I found myself in a young woman's home with Kieran Carley, Kevin Hernandez and Mike Scannell. While the homeowner was busy with an older woman from FEMA, we were tearing down sheetrock in her bedroom. After a couple dozen homes you stop noticing the personal stuff and treat each job with the same clinical detachment of an emergency room doctor. Well, most of the time anyway.

We had reached a part of the room where I had to get into a closet and start pre-cutting a line of sheetrock nearly four feet high. Kevin handed me a sledgehammer and I took a swing which resulted in some stuff falling off the shelf above me. When I looked down to see if anything was broken I did double-take. On the floor at our feet was a plastic blue vibrator. Not one of those smooth cigar shaped ones, but this grotesque dick-shaped thing with bumps and ridges and adjustable extensions jutting out from the base. Distracted, I stood up in the closet without thinking and hit my head on the same shelf, and three more dildos of various colors fell to the ground along with some other stuff we couldn't readily identify but had a similar purpose.

I'm not a prude, and we have always shown the deepest respect when gutting someone's house, but you can't drop a half dozen sex toys in front of a bunch of guys and not expect an impromptu game of light sabers to start up. By the color of the toy in my hand, I was Darth Vader. Sweet!

"Dude, don't touch it. You don't know where it's been," said Kevin, trying not to laugh and failing miserably.

I had bent down to pick another one up to put them away before the homeowner realized what happened. "I have a pretty good idea where it's been," which elicited another laugh from the group.

"This girl knows how to party."

I came to the young lady's defense, "This coming from the guys who've been sleeping next to unwashed men for the last two weeks and jerking off into dirty socks."

"True, but still, I can understand one, maybe two just in case you need a backup, but all these?"

Kevin observed, "Three of them are exactly the same. How fast is this chick burning them out?"

Scannell studied the one he was holding, "Where do you think this little piece goes? And why does it have rabbit ears?"

"Let's put these away before she comes in here," I said, but it was too late. Voices carry in houses with no interior walls and we weren't exactly quiet. The older FEMA woman voiced her discomfort, and the homeowner's face was beat red. She remembered, too late, to remove her intimate items before allowing a work crew into her bedroom. When I pulled her aside to smooth things over, she was a mix of angry and understandably embarrassed. It's not like we were expecting to find her personal items, but I apologized anyway and promised to be more professional. After a little self-deprecating humor, especially when I told her about the awkward situations our living conditions presented, she and I both started to laugh about it.

At some point we stopped being embarrassed about things that would have mortified us before the storm. For example, here I was in the home of an attractive young woman and it didn't even cross my mind that I hadn't showered in days and probably stank like gasoline and a rancid cesspool. Under any other circumstances I wouldn't even have considered stepping outside my house in that condition, but in post hurricane Breezy Point it didn't matter. I showed up to meetings with City officials looking this way because there was no other option, and frankly, after awhile, I didn't care.

Eastchester and Grasonville fire departments, from upstate New York and Maryland respectively, showed up at the firehouse early and ready to work. They accompanied several of our guys to homes which needed gutting and debris removal. I had to stay behind and work the firehouse phone which hadn't stopped ringing since it was reconnected. Tim Dufficy ran new CAT-5 cables and restored our internet connection too. The only thing missing now was a proper computer, so I enlisted the help of Ricky Savage and took a ride over to my house with my girlfriend. He sat on the Promenade in his pickup while she and I gathered a tower, monitor, printer and accessories. An hour later we had a fully-functional office set up in the main room of the firehouse.

In regard to gathering support through donations or in the form of volunteers, this was a giant leap forward. Previously all electronic communications were done by smart phone or on my laptop, or by members helping us from outside the community. The ability to efficiently communicate online, especially with the media, gave our long-term survival and rebuilding strategy greater scope. Another benefit of having a computer, especially the brand new one that I brought with its 32" flat-screen monitor, was the morale boost it gave for the guys. I made sure it was loaded with games and movies to enjoy during their down-time. Reconnecting them with social networks like Facebook and Instagram went a long way toward reducing the cumulative stress and anxiety they were suffering.

* * *

When the sun began to set and our members returned to base, my girlfriend and I packed up my rental car and headed toward Howard Beach to get dinner and check out a new apartment she found. We had another reason to celebrate: Marty had promoted me to Captain, which appropriately matched the level of leadership and responsibility I had taken on since the storm. Three weeks ago I was an inactive firefighter, and now the Chief was leaving me in charge when he or Tim Dufficy were not around. I was honored.

As my girlfriend and I drove down Rockaway Beach Boulevard, the radio was playing "Home" by American Idol winner, Phillip Phillips. I hadn't heard it before. For the most part I hadn't had a chance to watch TV or listen to the radio at all since the storm. She told me to listen to the lyrics carefully because it was the perfect song to describe was what going on in the Rockaways right now. She was singing along as we made our way down Rockaway Beach Boulevard and passed all the destruction Hurricane Sandy had left in its wake.

Hold on, to me as we go
As we roll down this unfamiliar road
And although this wave is stringing us along
Just know you're not alone
Cause I'm gonna make this place your home

Settle down, it'll all be clear
Don't pay no mind to the demons
They fill you with fear
The trouble it might drag you down
You get lost, you can always be found

Just know you're not alone
Cause I'm gonna make this place your home

"Wow," was all I could muster. I was too choked up to talk. She was right. In this one song, the entire ordeal of Hurricane Sandy and the struggle to survive and rebuild afterward was perfectly summarized. For me it still evokes an emotional response. To this day I can't hear that song without thinking of the devastation in Breezy Point and how we endured the many hardships after.

CHAPTER 17

REBUILDING BREEZY POINT

Friday, November 16, 2012

I was a wreck. My tooth was cracked from an errant fire hose whipping me in the face and it had become infected. My right hand was swollen as well, probably a result of open cuts exposed to filthy sewage tainted water as I worked the pumps in people's basements. I looked in the mirror and saw hollow eyes staring back at me. Every night I lay in bed, sure the fatigue that plagued me throughout the day would allow me some rest. On most nights, concerns about food, fuel and other supplies for the coming days would rob me of any such reprieve. I cleaned up myself the best I could, put on my lucky, though unwashed, FDNY pullover which stank of diesel fuel and fire, and headed back to Breezy Point.

Waiting at the firehouse were Chris Williams, Scott Heltsley, Joel Brinkley, Troy Devine, Rachel Henry, Brian Presgraves, Troy Murray and Chad Carroll from Southeast Canine Search and Rescue. They arrived yesterday afternoon after driving 13 hours all the way from Tennessee. Combined with our firefighters we were able to put more than thirty volunteers into action. Throughout the day our crews were able to pump and gut a dozen homes.

In the words of Chris Williams, "Most of us were firefighters either now or in the past, and it was amazing to see what you guys had been through and everything you had done. We couldn't understand how you were still going. To see you transform from firefighters one minute, then gutting out homes the next, was unbelievable. We always talk about things we can learn and how we can put it to use the next time. What we saw in Breezy Point taught us a lot."

✶ ✶ ✶

With the third weekend since Sandy at our doorstep, plans were made to ensure a smoother and more efficient operation than the weeks prior. During an OEM meeting, I had expressed to Chief Dalton of the FDNY—also a Breezy Point resident—my concerns about a lack of coordination between the volunteer groups in the community. He agreed it was an issue which needed to be addressed, so a meeting with all four of the major volunteer mold remediation services as well as the volunteer fire departments was called at nine o'clock that morning. It was a turning point for the recovery.

Contact information was exchanged and mailing lists were organized so we could keep each other up to date. Next, we addressed the issue of overlapping work orders which were becoming a serious problem. The residents would often sign up for help at all four organizations as an expedient way to get their homes serviced. It made sense from their point of view, but from our perspective it was an awful waste of our volunteers' time which we could ill afford. For example, Operation Breezy Point Gut 'n Pump would send a crew to a house on Reid Avenue only to find out Camp Rockne had gotten there first and finished the job. The transit times of work crews carrying all their equipment could take an hour, and that was time they could be spending on a house that still needed help. Homeowners who requested help from all four groups rarely called the other three to cancel once one had arrived.

As a solution we split Breezy Point into four zones. Sector 1 went to Camp Rockne and included everything east of Bedford Avenue from the ocean to the bay. Sector 2 was assigned to Habitat for Humanity which covered the homes between Ocean Avenue and Bedford Avenue, as well as all homes along the bayside west of Bedford Avenue. Habitat for Humanity also covered the entire Roxbury community. Operation Blessing took Sector 3 in the Wedge between Ocean Avenue and Tioga Walk. Lastly, Sector 4 was given to Operation Breezy Point Gut 'n Pump who were responsible for all houses between Tioga Walk and the western edge of the property at Beach 222nd Street. They also took the other side streets south of the Wedge. This system didn't entirely solve the problem, but it did drastically reduce the number of duplicate work orders.

Point Breeze Volunteer Fire Department, which had already serviced nearly a hundred homes, agreed to merge our mold remediation efforts with our neighbors at Operation Breezy Point Gut 'n Pump. In the future, we would send the vast majority of our volunteers and supplies over to them as well as provide internet and phone service. Also of great importance was our agreement to share our press contacts. As more and more media outlets arrived to cover our story, we made sure to bring them over to Gut 'n Pump as well.

Rockaway Point Volunteer Fire Department would continue to provide logistics support, information, and medical assistance to the community. I can't stress enough how important this was for the entire operation to continue. Warehousing donated supplies reserved for the residents took a great burden from us, and their medical service provided a capability we wouldn't have had otherwise. Their location in the center of Breezy Point was an ideal spot for meetings and the dissemination of information. They also coordinated with Bobby Eustace to provide hot food for the residents and volunteers.

An hour later, we had transformed the recovery effort from four loosely associated organizations to one big semi-coordinated operation. I proposed building a website and maintaining a database as a way of tracking completed work orders, and for residents to request future work orders online. We could also provide up to date information and instructions about mold removal, as well as local news and submitted articles. The website could also serve as a way for the organizations to talk to each other and track their progress. Everyone at the table thought it was a fantastic idea, although without electricity or internet service getting something like that off the ground would be tricky.

"The firehouse has electricity and internet. Duffman and I fixed it a few days ago," I said. All eyes turned in my direction, and with a few nods it was decided. The four volunteer mold remediation groups would retain their individual hierarchy and organization, and I would act as a coordinator among them, gauging their progress, sharing information, drumming up volunteer support, and generating new work orders online whenever possible. Without thinking, I had just taken on another huge chunk of responsibility for my already overworked mind to handle.

During the meeting I received several texts from Pat Dempsey, my old partner who had fought the fires alongside me the night of Sandy. He had taken the day off from work to gut and pump his house in the Wedge and was desperate for help. As it turned out, I was expecting a fair number of volunteers today. The West Elm Furniture Company arrived with forty employees ready to lend a hand. Among them was a summer resident, Meredith Erickson, who lived at the end of Newport Walk near the ocean. Her brother had come to Breezy Point a few days after the storm armed with household cleaning supplies expecting a long day of scrubbing crud off the walls of the family summer bungalow.

"When he got there he saw the back of the house was ripped off and so was the front," recalled Meredith in an interview after the storm. "The whole house had moved ten feet backwards into the house behind it. We're the last house on the block before the ocean, so it had gotten smashed by the waves. It was a traditional bungalow that we loved and it survived for thirty years. When my mom and dad bought the place, they painted it with boat paint so it would last through the bad weather."

She continued, "I waited a week or so before going down. When we got to the house, we saw the rooms we grew up and spent many summers in and all of our summer memories were destroyed. My grandmother passed away in 2010 and my dad a year later, so when we looked at the house and saw it all destroyed, it brought up a lot of emotions. I think for me that was the hardest, most heartbreaking thing. When I think about it now, my father making coffee and my grandmother sitting on the deck in the sun, it's hard to accept we can't ever go back to that place."

As the West Elm employees disembarked from their bus and assembled inside the firehouse we were faced with a wide variety of skill sets and personal gear. Most knew enough to wear proper boots, although a few failed to differentiate between work and designer footwear. The room filled up quickly. Our firefighters showed up in force once word got around that three dozen young ladies were in the firehouse. It was one of our best turnouts since the storm. Several FDNY firefighters and Gut 'n Pump volunteers from next door suddenly found excuses to drop by and lend a hand.

"It's almost all women," observed one firefighter behind me.

"I'm gonna split them up into teams," I explained, "and each team will have a few experienced workers mixed in to show them where to go and what to do. Who wants to help out?" There was no shortage of volunteers. After a half hour I had three large groups assembled and listening to a safety lecture. A few took advantage of my offer to organize the Clubhouse and avoid getting dirty, although sorting through that mess was no picnic either. Donated items, especially an overwhelming amount of used clothing, were stored in no discernible order which greatly reduced its usefulness.

"Help is on the way," I texted Pat as Brillo, Kieran, and Scannell and I lead a dozen volunteers to his house. Within hours, his basement was pumped of excess water, cleared of waterlogged couches and recliners, and the walls torn down. He is located in the middle of his block so every bit of debris had to be carried to the end of the walk for disposal. It was backbreaking work, but the women kept up without complaint, despite earlier predictions by some of the guys. We serviced six houses before it was time to head back to their bus.

Before they departed, Meredith asked us if we wouldn't mind stopping by her house on Newport Walk. It was a wreck. Two of the four walls were missing and the roof was poised to collapse, but we offered to go in anyway and recover some personal items for her. We found several flags, a Georgia O'Keefe painting which hung in her room growing up, and her grandmother's tea pot. "It was really sweet to be able to bring that back home," she told me. "Now we have something from the house to remember it by."

Her home was condemned and demolished. All that remains today is an empty sand lot. Since the house was not their primary residence her family isn't entitled to any FEMA money, and they didn't have flood insurance. When they rebuild it will be entirely at their own expense. These days Meredith and her family watch and wait to see what others around them are doing. The building process is an ever-changing puzzle of ordinances and rules, so they sit on the sidelines, alongside hundreds of other frustrated Breezy Point families, waiting. Her three-year-old son will miss yet another summer in the sand where his mother played at his age years before.

Firefighters Sebastian Danese (right), Kieran Carley, and Kevin Hernandez (background) inspect the damage to Meredith Erickson's bungalow.

* * *

At Operation Breezy Point Gut 'n Pump, Karen Donnelly was looking for FDNY Lieutenant John Nolan. Both were members of Friends of Firefighters, but hadn't met one another before today. Nancy Carbone, Executive Director of Friends of Firefighters, had asked Karen to help Lieutenant Nolan guide groups of firefighters, who were volunteering to gut homes on their day off, around Breezy Point to their assigned houses. She walked into the registration tent where Erin and Jason were taking work requests from residents.

"I'm looking for John Nolan."

"I'm Lieutenant Nolan," he replied.

She made her way toward him and introduced herself, "Nancy sent me here to find you."

John, believing she was there to ask for help, inquired, "What happened to your house?"

"It burned down."

Although momentarily stunned by her reply, Lieutenant Nolan put his arms around Karen and gave her a hug. She was so overwhelmed by his public display of sympathy that Karen was afraid she would fall apart and not be able to assist the Lieutenant. "He was the first person other than my family to give me a hug since the storm," said Karen afterwards. "To this day I tear up just thinking about it. It wasn't why I was there, but I needed that."

From that day forward, Lt. John Nolan and his counterpart, Lt. Chris Love, worked alongside Karen Donnelly. Her knowledge of the area helped Friends of Firefighters more effectively carry out their mission in Breezy Point to treat as many homes as possible. When she wasn't going door to door asking people if they needed help, Karen drove groups of volunteers from their base at Gut 'n Pump to one location after another, and, on occasion, into Rockaway and Gerritsen Beach in Brooklyn too.

"I would drive the guys to where they were supposed to go," said Karen. "Then I'd try to convince the homeowners to come back with me to Gut 'n Pump where Friends of Firefighters had set up a hospitality tent. We had cookies, coffee and all sorts of snacks for them. The idea was to take their mind off the harshness of what was happening at their home as it was being gutted. It was freezing cold most days, so we found a heater for them to stay warm. When the crew was done I'd take them back to their house. Sometimes they'd see their gutted home and start crying. All you could do was be there for them and let them work through it.

* * *

That night we said goodbye to the Gransonville and Eastchester volunteer firefighters as they prepared for their journey home. Southeast Canine Search and Rescue (SeK9SaR) was staying with us for a few nights, some in the firehouse and others in a newly deployed military tent at Gut 'n Pump. They bunked with Erin Concoran Daly; firefighter Kevin Neafsey, from FDNY Engine 45; and Bob Gibbons, the Gut 'n Pump tool man.

"We didn't expect to be as well taken care of as we were in New York," said Chris Williams. "You guys made sure we ate good and got anything we needed. To have us come up there and have you guys welcome us in, it's not what we're used to. From the beginning, you treated us like brothers and it isn't something we've experienced anywhere else. Most places we go, we're expected to be self-sufficient for 72 hours. We brought enough food and water with us to survive because we didn't know what to expect, but your hospitality was so overwhelming."

On the subject of hospitality, however, one of our brothers from Tennessee was missing. Troy Murray and Rachel Henry were at the Buckley residence with Brian "Twitch" Presgraves. The Buckley matriarch made a deal too good for Twitch to refuse, "If you can get into my flooded basement and retrieve a particular item, you can have all the alcohol you can carry from under there." Twitch, being a survivalist, knew he would find what Mrs. Buckley was looking for. What he didn't know was the Buckley's are, among other things, in the restaurant business. He was expecting one or two bottles of spirits to make this dangerous mission worth his while. What he found, however, was much different.

Troy and Rachel left Twitch to his own devices, but when he didn't return after dark they grew worried and told us the story. I hopped in Unit 9 with Chris and a few of our guys, and went looking for him, traveling west along Rockaway Point Boulevard toward the Buckley residence. The flashing lights of a police car were ahead, and there was Twitch pulling a borrowed wagon trying to convince the police, in his thick Tennessee accent, that he was not a looter.

I displayed my police credentials and said, "He's with us."

"This guy belongs with you?" asked the officer.

"Believe it or not, yeah, he's one of mine. I'll make sure the wagon gets back to the rightful owner. Thank you, officer."

We helped Twitch load the wagon, which had two big black plastic garbage bags in it, into the back of the pickup. In a minute we were back at the firehouse. Twitch hopped out and pulled down the tailgate. The wagon came next, and by the clanging of bottles I could guess what was inside. The garbage bags were torn open and out spilled fifty bottles of top-shelf liquor, generously donated by the Buckley family thanks to Twitch's bravery in their basement. The bounty was passed around as we pulled the wagon into the Gut 'n Pump parking lot to share the spoils. There was much rejoicing!

"When I saw the smiles on those guys faces," said Twitch in his humble, accented voice, "I felt like a hero for a whole minute!"

I remember taking a bottle of Johnnie Walker Blue Label for myself, and not much after. It was a good night.

* * *

The following afternoon a man arrived at Gut 'n Pump looking for Erin. He was six-and-a-half-feet tall with a long, salt and pepper beard and sun-kissed skin from too many days working out in the hot Florida sun. A church group collected donations to send him up to Breezy Point to help us out. One rumor was he used to be a mechanic at

Disney World. No one knew for sure. All we knew—all we really cared about—was that he was one of the most caring, hardest working and dedicated volunteers throughout the entire recovery. Most of us didn't even know his name. To us he was simply Road Dog.

The Road Dog

Road Dog was usually the first to rise, the last to bed, and non-stop in between. Despite his haggard appearance he had a big heart and nothing but good intentions. He was tough, but not afraid to share his feelings. When a reporter asked him why he came all the way from Florida to help in Breezy Point he broke down and cried on national television trying to make the reporter understand, in his way of thinking, the question was why anyone *wouldn't* try to help. I was standing next to Kevin Adams watching the interview at the firehouse.

"Jesus," said Kevin, "that's gonna get us at least another 200 volunteers this weekend." He was right.

Whatever his background, Road Dog could fix anything with an engine and was a big help to Bob Gibbons who maintained the gasoline-powered pumps and generators for Gut 'n Pump. At night, he stayed in one of the Gut 'n Pump tents and kept an eye on the tools and equipment, though he was a regular at the firehouse as well. He was able to fix some of our damaged equipment, and we fed him and kept him in clean clothes to return the favor. Road Dog was such a big help that I promised him, when he was ready to leave, I would personally buy him a ticket to anywhere in the country. When the time came, he chose to go to another storm-battered part of the country that needed help.

He's the perfect example of looks that can be deceiving.

CHAPTER 18

BREAKING POINTS

Sunday, November 18, 2012

John Ingram, Marty's brother and former Commissioner of the Point Breeze Volunteer Fire Department, was working alongside a professional public relations person named Jackie Pool. She told us her services were originally offered to Roxbury since they were the first stop along the main road, then Rockaway Point, but both politely declined her offer. By chance, Jackie found herself at our firehouse where she ran into John while he was checking in on us. He accepted her offer on the spot and she has been asking for donations and volunteers for our firehouse ever since. I had spoken with her over the phone several times, but this morning was our first meeting face to face. More than anyone else outside our ranks, she was responsible for directing the media and other volunteer organizations toward the firehouse during following weeks.

Jackie sympathized with our situation. She had endured her own trials and tribulations in life, losing a fiancé on September 11th and surviving ovarian cancer. Though not a member of the firehouse or a victim of Hurricane Sandy per se, we felt she could relate to what we were going through. Jackie was also a bit of a neat freak, which worked out okay for me since she compulsively cleaned up after the younger guys, which I had given up on weeks ago. Her network of media and volunteer contacts was invaluable. On the first day alone, a large sum of money was donated by her celebrity friends, to be distributed to the residents of Breezy Point and Roxbury.

She asked me if I knew anyone in particular who desperately needed the money. It was a loaded question since everyone in the neighborhood was in dire straits financially to one degree or another.

Fortunately my survey of the mold remediation groups included residents' names, ages, locations, the severity of damage to their homes, and the progress which had been made so far. We picked the oldest of our neighbors for whom Breezy Point was their only residence—the retirees on a fixed income who could barely afford to rebuild—and made sure the money found its way to them. We were off to a great start!

She also brought another volunteer with her named Clara who was a huge administrative help for me. The night before, while the rest of the firefighters were sleeping, I sat down in front of my laptop and built a website, RebuildingBreezyPoint.com. It had a database to manage the information collected from the pump and gut services so we could gauge our progress and plot it on a map. The database structure was done, but I didn't have time to input all the information I had collected. Clara volunteered to transcribe the written work orders into digital format. She sat through hours of mind numbing data entry, which freed me up to work on my other responsibilities.

As Clara and Jackie got down to business, I met with Bill from Eastchester Fire Department. He returned to the Breezy Point with a new American flag to replace the tattered one he observed waving above the firehouse days before. We didn't have enough time for a proper ceremony, but I made sure to pack away the storm-battered flag which flew at the firehouse the night of the hurricane. It hangs on the firehouse wall in a protective case, while the flag Bill and I hoisted still proudly waves atop the flag pole in front of our 9/11 monument.

Across town in front of Rockaway Point, Firefighter Bobby Eustace was having a difficult day. For weeks he and the FDNY firemen from the Bronx were feeding thousands of residents and volunteers in Breezy Point at their own expense. Today, not only was this a very busy weekend with unexpectedly high turnout of hungry people looking for a hot meal, but the New York City Department of Health decided to come by and check things out. Citing a lack of hair nets, rubber gloves, food thermometers, and other minor infractions, a summons was issued with a warning: Clean up your act or we'll be back to shut you down.

As word got around about the summons, many residents and volunteers became outraged. For weeks we toiled in Breezy Point and the Rockaways with little help from city, state and federal agencies who specialize in disaster relief. City agencies such as the FDNY, DSNY and NYPD made contributions to the recovery effort through coordination with OEM and FEMA. However, their greatest contributions were made within their own independent command structure by local, mid-level bosses. The further up the disaster relief chain of command, the more bureaucracy and red tape muddled the decision-making process.

For example, hundreds of trailers full of desperately needed equipment sat in Floyd Bennett Field only a few miles away but was unavailable because, as it was explained to us, bosses in offices hundreds of miles away hadn't decided when or how to distribute their contents yet. It was the port-a-potty issue all over again, but on a much larger scale. FEMA had assembled a massive base of operations with enough personnel, food and supplies to make a difference, but never deployed those resources in any meaningful way that we saw. In my entire experience at the forefront of the Hurricane Sandy recovery, I never personally witnessed anything come from that massive warehouse which we didn't take from it ourselves—usually by convincing some junior-level employee that it was a life or death scenario.

Those low-level czars who granted us a few gallons of gasoline or pounds of propane made more of a difference than anyone else in their crippled organization. To say it was frustrating is a gross understatement. A better way was needed, one which was flexible enough to adapt to individual situations and solve problems as they arose. On too many occasions, solutions, delayed by bureaucracy, were found long after the problem had been handled by desperate volunteers on the front lines using unconventional measures. Many people, myself included, spent a lot of our own time and money on issues and items which should have been handled by the appropriate agencies in the first place.

* * *

Friends of Firefighters, through close cooperation with Operation Breezy Point Gut 'n Pump, continued to pour resources into Breezy Point. Nancy Carbone was a regular visitor, checking in with Karen Donnelly and Lieutenants John Nolan and Chris Love to see if they needed anything. Consequently, if Marty Ingram was akin to a father figure during the storm, then Nancy and Karen definitely split time as the matriarchs. I went to them to talk about the problems I was facing or if I just needed to vent. I wasn't the only one, and they were always ready to listen.

"Firefighters from all over the country called to see if they could come to New York and help," said Karen Donnelly. "They came from Los Angles, San Francisco, New Orleans, Boston, Chicago, everywhere! Friends of Firefighters had guys go out and get bunk beds."

One day, Karen took several firefighters from California, who were living in a firehouse in Red Hook (Brooklyn), to Breezy Point. As they rode in a Friends of Firefighters van, the picturesque New York City skyline was in the rear view mirror. The firefighters were craning their necks to get a glimpse as they travelled farther away, while Karen was telling them which buildings were which. But they understood this wasn't a sight-seeing trip. She was able to take them down to the fire zone at the Wedge, however, and walked down the cracked sidewalk of Fulton Walk. Karen came to a stop halfway down the block and said, "This is where my house used to be."

While they were there, an older gentleman whose son is a FDNY firefighter, started to talk to Karen. He told her the red Department of Buildings sticker, which marked the house as condemned, was removed from their home, but it was a total mess inside. As fate would have it, she was with six California firefighters looking to help out. Karen gathered the guys and told them, "Come on, we're going to Roxbury to fix up this man's home." They gutted his entire house, removed the debris, and even took the time to sweep and mop the floors. By the time they were done the old man was so thankful they were in tears.

* * *

The rest of the day was a blur of activity as hundreds of homes were pumped and gutted by volunteers from all over the country who saw us on the news and came to help Breezy Point. After dark, we said goodbye to Jackie and Clara, who both did an amazing job turning our firehouse into a "fire-home." as they put it. We went next door to discuss dinner options with our neighbors at Gut 'n Pump, when a radio call for a house on fire on Highland Place behind the Co-op offices reached us. Within a minute, a dozen Point Breeze firefighters were ready for action as we scrambled aboard Sand Flea and Big Jack. As we raced eastbound on Rockaway Point Boulevard, we could see FDNY fire trucks coming toward us.

"He missed the turn!" shouted Tim Dufficy, our chauffer. "The rest are following him. They're heading in the wrong direction!"

"Someone get on the FDNY radio and advise them they're heading in the wrong fucking direction!" I said as the caravan of fire trucks passed us, headed westward.

A few of the guys read the unit numbers displayed on the sides of the FDNY apparatus as they drove by. We surmised they weren't from this area, and probably unfamiliar with Breezy Point. As a result, we pulled up to the hydrant closest to the fire's south side while Roxbury arrived and ran a line from the hydrant to the north. The initial report was a house on fire behind the Co-op office, though fortunately we found a large mound of burning debris instead. These piles, strewn all around the neighborhood, were made of discarded wood and sheetrock from gutted homes, as well as appliances and furniture. Some stood 10-feet tall and 20-feet wide. The Department of Sanitation was doing an excellent job cleaning up debris piles such as the flaming one in front of us, but as soon as one was cleaned up another would replace it.

These ready-made bonfires were filled with household garbage as well. Residents cleaning out their waterlogged kitchens and bathrooms, where most people keep their pressurized cleaning products or insect repellent, would often toss their garbage bags onto the trash heap as well. Fighting a fire mixed with contents under pressure is a lot like trying to hose down a box of flaming hand grenades. Captains Kevin Hernandez and Kevin O'Brien directed the pair of hoses we had been operating as they poured water onto the blaze, while I walked the perimeter of the fire looking for hazards.

"Is that a propane tank over there near the edge of the fire?" I asked, pointing to the north side of the fire where Roxbury was operating.

"I don't know," replied Brillo, "I see a hot water heater but I don't think that'll blow."

"We better try to pour some water on it," I advised him, "I'll see if I can raise Roxbury on the radio."

One of our hoses shifted focus onto the propane tank but the pressure was low and couldn't hit our mark. Fortunately, one of the Roxbury firefighters saw what we were doing, ran into the fire, and hurled the tank out of the flames. The canister was hosed down before it could explode, the force of the water pushing it further away. Clad entirely in bunker gear, the identity of that firefighter remains unknown, but he most likely saved his comrades from serious injury.

Minutes later the FDNY found us and requested we turn our active hoses over to them. It was an unusual request, mostly to do with a matter of pride, but it made perfect tactical sense in this case so we relented. Roxbury and Point Breeze were attached to the two closest working hydrants, so instead of wasting time having us disconnect and getting them set up, we handed over our nozzles. The fire was almost out anyway, and it gave us a chance to relax and talk to our friends in Roxbury and Rockaway Point who, still lacking working fire engines, showed up in their beach rescue vehicle to lend a hand. Within the hour we had collected and stowed our hoses for the trip back to the firehouse.

* * *

The following day was uneventful aside from the usual gutting and pumping, with one exception. For weeks we had been asking for all-terrain vehicles (ATVs) or their larger counterpart, gators, to help us move heavy equipment around the neighborhood. Since the storm we had been relying on John Norton's red ATV driven by Kevin Adams, but with the increasing amount of volunteers we needed at least one more. These lightweight but powerful vehicles could move generators and pumps around very quickly, acting as a force multiplier. They could be expensive, but FEMA had dozens of them zipping around the neighborhood. Unfortunately they couldn't spare one for our rag-tag operation.

That was about to change. After days of calling around to all the different agencies in our phone book, I finally got a working phone number for a Department of Environmental Protection (DEP) garage that was repairing gators damaged during the storm. Through a little subterfuge I discovered two gators were unclaimed and ready to be sent back into the general pool, but since FEMA promised they would replace them with new ones, no one was in a hurry to take the old ones back. It was exactly what we were looking for.

"I need to talk to whoever is in charge," I barked, using my command voice.

He replied cautiously, "This is Phil, what can I do for you?"

"Son, this is Assistant Chief Danese in Breezy Point. You know where that is Phil? A smart guy like you reads the newspapers I bet. It's where that big fire was. I understand you have two gators in your shop that should be sitting in my parking lot. What's the hold up?" I read out the vehicle numbers generously provided by the manager of the previous tour. I also promoted myself to Assistant Chief for a few minutes. It had a nice ring to it, and with Marty gone and Duffman back at work it wasn't far from the truth. One thing I learned about city service is that a little bit of moxie and having the word Chief in front of your name gets results. He never even asked what agency I was the Assistant Chief of.

"Give me the address and I'll send them out tonight, sir!"

"You're a good man, Phil, a good man. I expect to see them by 0800 hours tomorrow or I'll be calling back. You take care of yourself now. Have a good night!"

"No problem sir, you'll have them ASAP."

I hung up, not really expecting any results but figuring it didn't hurt to try. We went about our routine, breaking at the end of the day when the sun went down. We ate dinner with the guys next door at Gut 'n Pump and recapped the day's events. The NYPD had sent us a bunker trailer with 1,200 gallons of gasoline and diesel to top off the generators. I was talking with the driver when a flatbed pulled up with two green gators on the back.

"I'm looking for an Assistant Chief Danese. Is he around?"

"He's not here right now. I think he's on a supply run," I said. You never know. Phil could be looking to meet the suave, debonair Assistant Chief character I imagined myself as while we talked on the phone. Luckily they were just two deliverymen and after a few minutes of manhandling their cargo off the back of the flatbed, I was the proud owner of two beaten up but somewhat functional gators. We waited for the truck to pull away, then started up our new toys and took a victory lap over to Gut 'n Pump. We kept one at the firehouse and left one next door. I found gray spray paint, wrote "Road Dog" across the front of it, and handed Road Dog the keys.

We ran those gators into the ground, but I paid to fix them every time they broke down. Months later we brought them back to the Department of Environmental Protection in better condition than when we received them thanks to Road Dog's mechanical genius. They didn't even care. When we got them, those gators had already been written off and replaced. For us, they were a life saver. For the city, they were two broken down piles of junk destined for the scrap heap. The manager took them from us and unceremoniously drove them into a corner next to several other wrecked vehicles, only to be used for parts.

CHAPTER 19

CHANGING OF THE GUARD

Wednesday, November 21, 2012

A dozen Point Breeze firefighters stood in the baseball field, next to the firehouse, alongside Blackhawk helicopters from the National Guard. Governor Cuomo arrived a few minutes earlier and was whisked away by several unmarked sport utility vehicles for a meeting with the senior recovery leaders. Most were from city agencies and not the volunteer groups, but we had more than one friendly voice amongst the bureaucratic crowd. The summit was held in front of the Rockaway Point Volunteer Fire Department, in the same tent where Bobby Eustace served his meals. Friends of Firefighters, who hosted the visit, brought actor and former FDNY firefighter, Steve Buscemi, to thank the first responders.

I had the pleasure of meeting Steve several times already since Friends of Firefighters set up their operation alongside Gut 'n Pump in the parking lot behind us. He stopped by our firehouse to say hello to the guys on several occasions. When he found out we were living there to provide 24-hour coverage for the community, Steve started bringing pies and other deserts, baked by his wife the night before. Many of our members didn't know he was a former FDNY firefighter during the early 1980's. I was made aware of this by a firefighter friend of mine, while digging at Ground Zero after we ran into him while working the Bucket Brigade. Of course he has successfully moved on to acting, but he has never forgotten his brother firefighters and is an invaluable member of the Friends of Firefighters charity organization. It was thanks to Steve and the tireless efforts of Nancy Carbone, the Executive Director of Friends of Firefighters, that this visit was arranged.

Sebastian Danese, Steve Buscemi, Kevin Hernandez and Kieran Carley posing for a picture in front of Sand Flea.

While the Governor was serving hot meals and having lunch with selected members of the recovery effort, his aides were dispersed throughout Breezy Point evaluating our situation. I met with several members of his staff and suggested a meeting between all of the fire departments and mold remediation services, and a representative from the Governor's Office. Our message was clear. We needed help, politics be damned! A conference was scheduled for tonight at Fort Tilden, a U.S. Army Reserve base across from Roxbury. The Co-op had moved its offices there, as did several government agencies such as FEMA, OEM, and even the Department of Motor Vehicles and U.S. Post Office.

At the Governor's luncheon, our concerns were voiced to His Honor. Despite several assertions by invested agencies that everything was okay and on schedule, the truth was told, rather bluntly, by several guests who were fed up with the rhetoric. Complaints were made concerning the lack of tangible aid from FEMA and the Red Cross despite their endless assurances that help was on the way. The NYC OEM system was doing all it could, but, in the opinion of some, it was overwhelmed. The Mayor's Office, considering the interests of the city as a whole, was promoting an impression of a city fully recovered and ready for tourists for the upcoming holiday season.

Both sides had valid points. New York City relies on tourism, which is one of the reasons why it took so long to cancel the *New York City Marathon* scheduled days after the storm. Manhattan, though weather beaten, had been restored and was back to business. The outer boroughs, however, especially Staten Island, southern Brooklyn, and Queens, were still in dire need of help. While the rest of the city was preparing for Black Friday sales and the Rockefeller Christmas Tree Lighting, we were in our storm-ravaged communities without power, gas, or drinkable water. It was a tale of two cities. The contrast couldn't be made any clearer than at night, as first responders and volunteers shivered in the cold, standing around garbage can fires, looking across Jamaica Bay at a completely restored Manhattan skyline, mocking us.

Gut 'n Pump co-founder, Erin Concoran-Daly and New York Governor, Andrew Cuomo, during his visit to Breezy Point.

* * *

Among our visitors on this day was a National Guard Chaplain, Reverend John Wharton, who was intrigued by the story of our desperate prayers inside the Clubhouse the night of Hurricane Sandy. I told him about the water receding and the trucks starting against all odds, and how we all felt divine intervention had contributed to our good fortune. He wholeheartedly agreed and introduced us to his friend and painter, William West, who was with him taking pictures in Breezy Point.

"I photograph and recreate historical events," explained William in an interview after the storm, "I had been to Long Beach, Garden City, East Williston, and other places on Long Island. John asked me if I ever heard of Breezy Point—which I hadn't—so we headed out there. We talked to many people, and they told us the story of the local firefighters who stopped the fire. We went to Operation Blessing, Habitat for Humanity, and the Point Breeze firehouse. We tried to go to the other firehouse, but the Governor was there and we couldn't get in to talk to anyone."

We gave Reverend Wharton and William West a tour of our devastated community, and William took many photographs, including some of us in front of the firehouse and of Big Jack and Sand Flea. We exchanged phone numbers and after giving us a quick blessing to keep us safe, bid them farewell. Several weeks later they came back with two beautiful paintings of our fire trucks and of us in front of the firehouse. Both paintings still hang in the Chief's office today.

Later that night, the fire department and mold remediation leaders met with a member of the Governor's staff who patiently listened as we provided him with the latest information and the lessons we had learned during the previous weeks. Marty was on a much needed vacation that week, so I represented Point Breeze. One by one we went around the room, recounting our individual progress and material needs. When we were finished, the Governor's aide outlined a plan for the New York State OEM to take over for their exhausted New York City counterparts. A team of disaster management specialists was on its way to Breezy Point, and through them we could allocate whatever resources we needed, within reason. The meeting ended with a very positive outlook.

As we filed out of the room I overheard our Governor's liaison talking on his phone, "What we need is to start tracking the work that's already been done and what's still left to do."

"Excuse me," I interrupted. "Did you say you needed someone to keep track of all the work orders?"

"Yeah, that's one of the first things we're gonna have to do. We need to find out which houses need treatment and which ones have already been looked after. That's gonna take a couple of days, especially with the holiday weekend coming up."

"It's already done, more or less," I replied.

He looked at me quizzically, "What do you mean?"

"Well, last week I figured we needed to start keeping track of that stuff so I built a website and a database to do that. Almost every night I go to the different pump and gut services and take pictures of their log books. I then enter that information into the database to keep track of what we accomplished. If I see outstanding work orders for that same house for another service, I give them a heads up so they don't waste time sending a crew to that location. I have a pretty comprehensive list of what we've accomplished so far and what work orders are still outstanding."

"How did you set it up? Will it work with our GIS?" he asked. Geographic Information Systems (GIS) are used to plot addresses on digital maps, like the Global Positioning System (GPS) in your car and phone, but with the ability to handle a lot more data. I had only a vague understanding of how it worked and had to teach myself the system during the sleepless nights at the firehouse. I was lucky to have Clara, Jackie's friend, handling the data entry on the weekends while Chris, a volunteer from Operation Blessing, gave me a crash course to refresh my computer programming skills. Without them I would have been overwhelmed.

"I've been looking at that but haven't had the time to set it up, but yeah it'll work. It's just raw data." I explained, "For a few years before September 11th, I was programmer for Smith Barney on Wall Street. Two weeks after the storm hit we were able to restore the internet connection to the firehouse. Using my laptop I was able to build a website to track all that data and to provide information for the residents about what's happening here. I even set up a system where homeowners can register and request help online through the site without ever having to come down here in person. When your technology people get here I can explain the system in more detail. It shouldn't be too hard. I've been doing it at night in my free time."

"That's great work," he said. "Keep doing what you're doing. You're in charge of coordinating between the organizations and managing their progress until the State Incident Management Team (IMT) gets set up. Here's a phone number for their boss. Tell him what's going on and coordinate with him."

"What do you mean?" I asked.

"It sounds to me like you've already taken it upon yourself to coordinate things down here, so now you have the official blessing of the Governor's Office," he said as he walked down the hallway towards the exit. I couldn't tell if he was serious or not. My look over to Chief Dalton from the FDNY Marine Unit only got a shrug in return.

I called Marty and explained the situation to him. He laughed and gave me some good advice: "Try not to screw things up! I'll see you on Monday!"

I'm not an expert, therefore I won't attempt to speculate on what the Governor's visit to Breezy Point meant in the grand scheme of things politically. I can only talk with any authority, about the situation within my own community. That being said, I believe His Honor's trip to our beaten-up little town was a decisive point during the recovery. Whereas the Mayor's Office and all the city agencies were making their best possible effort, the arrival of the New York State disaster relief specialists and their assets created a surge of material and expertise which made an immediate and tangible difference. Not since the agreement to coordinate all the mold remediation efforts did any single event have such an impact, which rippled through the volunteer organizations. Our lives were not made much easier, but our hard work seemed to yield better results thanks to the organization and support from the New York State OEM/IMT personnel.

CHAPTER 20

THANKSGIVING

Thursday, November 22, 2012

The four-day Thanksgiving weekend combined with unusually warm weather brought a bumper crop of volunteers from all over the country. I had several work crews at the firehouse waiting for orders, and Gut 'n Pump next door looked like they were filled to capacity. Kevin Adams had mentioned that Erin Concoran-Daly had been too busy helping everyone else and hadn't finished cleaning her own home. I immediately sent a team of volunteers to her house, while the second team went to the home of Chris and John Paollilo, both of whom are retired NYPD officers living just outside the Wedge by the Sugar Bowl. Prior to Sandy, a row of houses along the Promenade separated their back deck and the Atlantic Ocean. A year and a half later they have a beachfront view. Empty sandlots mark the locations of nearly a dozen homes along the Promenade which have yet to be rebuilt.

Teri Dodge and her fiancé, Steve Peterson, drove down from Portland, Maine, to cook us a Thanksgiving dinner. They arrived last night with everything needed for tonight's feast including appetizers and sides. Even the Red Cross showed up and served us turkey sandwiches, corn, stuffing and mashed potatoes for lunch. Today marked the first time since the storm food wasn't going to be an issue for me to worry about, if only for one day.

One of the many items we requested from the Governor's liaison the night before—five port-a-potties—arrived at the firehouse. Of course nothing is perfect, and they came half full, but two guys could not have been happier to receive plastic booths full of human waste than me and Phil Pillet. It was absurd, but we took it as a good sign that the State OEM and IMT weren't blowing smoke up our asses when they told us we would get the material support we were desperate for. One port-a-potty was located near the firehouse and the other four were situated in the Gut 'n Pump parking lot. They needed to be emptied but we would figure that out later.

Jackie Pool, our public relations volunteer, was returning to Breezy Point with her friend Mike, an enlisted man in the U.S. Army from Fort Drum who volunteered some of his little remaining stateside time to help in Breezy Point before going back to Afghanistan. Words can't express how grateful and impressed we still are that this man, who had no personal stake in Breezy Point whatsoever, would spend his precious remaining days helping us—during a holiday no less. Volunteers like Mike are what inspired us to keep going.

That afternoon was a busy day with the media. Jackie set up interviews with NBC and Fox News to spread the word about the mold remediation efforts and to remind people we still needed their help. NYPD Inspector Roy Richter, who lost his home in the Wedge, arranged an interview with Al Jazeera Media Network. They were doing a special about life in Breezy Point during the Thanksgiving holiday, and Tim Dufficy and I were more than happy to help.

After the interview was completed, I went over to Christine and John's house to check on the progress our volunteers had made. The crew was just finishing up as I arrived. According to John, via Facebook, "My buddy Sebastian came through today as usual. He grabbed a group of volunteers and cleaned all the debris and wet insulation out from under our crawlspace to allow it all to dry out and let us treat for mold. It was a huge effort and I would like to say thanks. That group saved us tons of cash and moved work forward."

Next was Erin's home, to which I walked the volunteers who had just finished at John's house to bolster the detail already there. Within an hour we had the basement cleaned out and all debris removed. I sent several pictures to Erin, who was busy managing volunteers at the Gut 'n Pump tent. She was overjoyed. Like me, she was apprehensive about gutting her own home, but knowing the work was done was a relief. The rest of the day progressed much the same way.

I arrived at the firehouse parking lot around 4:00 P.M. to see how dinner was progressing. Teri and Steve, our betrothed cooks from Portland, didn't disappoint. A dozen deep-fried turkeys were almost ready to serve, as were an assortment of familiar side dishes one might find on any American table this holiday. I was sampling some of the turkey and mashed potatoes when Devon Collins came running up to me.

"My house is flooding!"

I looked at him, mouth full of turkey, hoping this was all some sort of practical joke. "Are you serious? You better not be fucking with me," I warned.

"The Co-op turned the water back on to test the water mains," he explained. "Houses all over Breezy Point are flooding from pipes in their basements that cracked when the foundations buckled."

"Get the gator. Let's check it out," I ordered, looking back at Teri and Steve. "Start serving dinner. We'll be back soon."

Devon and I drove to his house in the Wedge along the same route Sand Flea took the night of the storm. It was getting dark and cold, especially on the windy Promenade. We got to his house and you could hear the water splashing into his basement from a broken pipe jutting from the foundation. The valve to shut off the water from the outside of his house had been run over by a tractor and was broken. Devon had dry socks and sneakers on—a rare commodity in Breezy Point—so I went down into the basement and trudged through water up to my hips. I played with a series of levers and values until the water stopped gushing.

We went next door and could hear water running there as well, but we couldn't get into the home to shut it off. The same was true of the house next to that, and the one after. A lot of people were going to show up this weekend to homes filled with water again. I made a mental note to tell Kevin Adams to make sure the pumps were ready. Devon drove us back to the firehouse where I changed out of my soaking wet clothing and got something to eat.

Devon Collins (left) and Sebastian Danese (right) on the way to a call for help in the crew cab of Big Jack.

I was happy to see we had our friends from AmeriCorps joining us for dinner, as well as Gut 'n Pump, and some of the NYPD police officers who were assigned to Breezy Point. Word of our feast spread quickly through the community, and soon many residents joined in our revelry. The NBC News team was on hand to cover the event, and I felt it was the perfect time to do something I had been intending for a while now.

"Ladies and gentleman, can I have your attention," I shouted from the front of the room. "First, I want to thank Teri and Steve for driving all the way from Maine to serve us this fantastic Thanksgiving dinner. Let's give them a round of applause!" I handed each of them a Point Breeze Volunteer Fire Department patch and pin of which we had very few, but which were meant for occasions like this.

"Second, I'd like you to join me for a special event. We don't do this very often, but I think you'll agree with me when I say John Norton and Erin Concoran-Daly have been invaluable members of the community these last few weeks. They've become leaders, and now we'd like them to become something more," I proclaimed as I walked over to the table where Erin and John were sitting.

I withdrew two gold badges from my jacket pocket, one in each palm, and said, "Erin and John, if you'd do us the privilege I'd like to make you both honorary members of the Point Breeze Volunteer Fire Department!"

They both gratefully accepted my offer, and the crowd went fucking wild.

* * *

The next day we worked with renewed vigor. All of us were well-fed, well-rested, and in high spirits from the night before. The only problem was our hygiene. It had been at least a week since any of us had taken a shower, and as it was put so delicately to me by one of the AmeriCorps girls, "Things start getting nasty." I took her word for it. Shower trailers were promised but hadn't arrived yet, and with thirty or more people to clean up, I couldn't just show up at a friend's house. I called around to local businesses, but most were either closed for the holiday or didn't have the proper facilities. Someone suggested The Aviator Sports and Events Center in Floyd Bennett Field. After a brief phone call and they agreed to help us with our hygiene situation.

At 4:00 P.M., Tom Wutz, the Incident Commander for the New York State Incident Management Team, hosted our first meeting at Fort Tilden. His team was everything we hoped for—practical, efficient, understanding and competent. Above all else, they kept their promises. If they said something was going to be done, it was done. Every day we held meetings at the Catholic Club in Breezy Point at 8:00 A.M. and 4:00 P.M. to talk about our goals for that day, and recap our results. For the first time since the beginning of the storm, I felt like we had a real plan with the proper support.

After the IMT meeting that evening, several Point Breeze firefighters and twenty AmeriCorps members drove into Brooklyn and scrubbed ourselves clean at The Aviator. Next our caravan headed to the China Kettle, a Chinese restaurant on Avenue U. It's a favorite among 63rd Precinct cops and I made arrangements with the owner to host us for dinner. The volunteers had already completed two fast-paced, backbreaking days of work and we had two more to go before the weekend rush was over. Showers and a hot meal were exactly what they needed to keep their spirits up. We traded stories over dinner, the AmeriCorps people telling us where they had been before Breezy Point, while we shared our experience from the night of the storm.

✶ ✶ ✶

The next morning, while responding to a fire, the corroded electrical system in Big Jack caught fire and nearly consumed the truck. It confirmed what we already knew. The trucks were on borrowed time and it was only a matter of when, not if, they broke down for good. The electrical system in Big Jack had been acting up since the night of the storm, and Sand Flea's engine started to sound really bad. The pumps on both trucks were constantly breaking down, prompting Robert Johnson, our mechanical genius, to put in long hours fixing them.

Also in need of fixing were our bathrooms. Running water had been restored, and although undrinkable, we could at least wash clothes and use the flushable toilets in the firehouse for the first time since the storm hit. Despite the many warnings prohibiting the use of the toilets, many did so anyway, especially during the cold nights when a trip to the overflowing port-a-potty seemed unappealing. As a result we had a buildup of human waste that needed to be cleared before we could get the toilets in proper working order. This is why God invented probies.

Probationary firefighters (or "probies") are new members who haven't yet earned the privilege of full membership. Typically, an average probie is asked to perform menial tasks such as taking out the garbage or cleaning the trucks. During Hurricane Sandy, however, our probies had their trial by fire. Tom Morgan and Kevin Owens were assigned the unfortunate mission of digging through the accumulated pile of human waste until nothing but porcelain remained. Both took on the dirty job with good spirits. We granted them some protection in the form of white Tyvek suits, also known as "body-condoms." Their ensemble was completed with surgical masks, heavy duty rubber gloves, work boots, and donated hard hats. An hour later it was completed. The firehouse had taken another step toward normalcy.

Tom Morgan (left) and Kevin Owens (right) in their protective equipment as they prepare to clean our bathrooms.

CHAPTER 21

TURNING POINTS

Monday, November 26, 2012

Ten days had passed since Marty left for his vacation and it was great to see him when he returned. He needed the rest. The bags under his eyes had disappeared, and the color returned to his face. The Chief looked like a new man. A lot had happened in his absence, so I apprised him of the situation on our drive over to the 8:00 A.M. Office of Emergency Management meeting at the Breezy Point Catholic Club. It was his first time attending since the New York State IMT took over the recovery.

"You look terrible," he observed, laughing, "don't make me order you to take a break."

He was right of course. I wasn't sleeping very much and lost at least twenty pounds since the storm. Last night I slept in Howard Beach and even managed a shower this morning, but some things you just can't hide with a bar of soap. The sacrifice, however, was paying off, as he was about to see. We took our seats and recapped the progress made over the weekend. Only a few minor incidents happened over the weekend despite the record numbers of volunteers. Rockaway Point reported a shortage of cleaning supplies, which dovetailed nicely into the announcement by the mold remediation services that several hundred homes had been treated.

Despite our fatigue, operational tempo was at an all time high thanks to the support from the IMT. Fuel was no longer a concern as the fuel crisis passed and the NYPD had established a regular delivery schedule of fuel for our generators and vehicles. The Red Cross was becoming somewhat dependable, although they still only served one meal per day. Tomorrow would be Bobby Eustace's last day serving meals to the residents of Breezy Point, and he received a standing ovation from us. He and the firefighters from the Bronx had performed culinary miracles over the last three weeks. By my own personal conservative estimate, they had served at least 20,000 meals during that time.

The meeting concluded, but Marty and I remained behind so he could talk with the new IMT personnel, many of them volunteer firefighters in their hometowns. We got a bite to eat at the food tent in front of Rockaway Point, and headed back to the firehouse. I could tell something was on his mind, and it wasn't something good.

"Is everything okay?" I asked.

"Well, I have to be honest, I'm a little upset with you," he replied, "I've been getting a lot of shit from the other members of the firehouse about that stunt you pulled over Thanksgiving. You can't just go around making people honorary members of the firehouse. There's a process that usually take months. A committee makes that decision, not you. I went out on a limb and made you a Captain because of all the hard work you've done organizing this mess and taking charge when I'm not around. Don't make me regret that."

I look up to Marty, so it hurt that he was disappointed in me. In my fragile emotional and psychological state I was nearly brought to tears. "I'm sorry," was all I could muster. I thought about it for a minute, always thinking about morale, and asked, "If you don't mind, could you tell me who I pissed off so I can apologize to them?"

He rattled off some names, but I didn't recognize the majority of them. They weren't anyone that had been with us the night of the storm. Hell, they weren't anyone that had been with us since that time either. My stressed out mind snapped for a minute, "Wait…you mean to tell me some dickheads sitting in Florida sipping on Brandy Alexander's, who aren't here right now, are judging me from a thousand miles away? Do they know how far along the knife-edge we are here? Do they get the kind of stress we're under? The two people I inducted into the firehouse have done more to save this place in the last three weeks then they have in their entire lives! They're mad because I made two genuine heroes members of the department?"

I calmed myself down before my insubordination went too far. Marty saw the water building up in my eyes, getting dangerously close to actual tears. In my heart I felt I had done the right thing. He put his arm around me as we walked into the patio next to the firehouse where all the broken down equipment was stored. A couple of deep breaths later and my composure returned. The people who were complaining to him had no idea what was going on here. I had invested a lot of my own personal time and money to make sure life in the firehouse was as comfortable as possible for the guys staying here.

This was a *volunteer* firehouse. At any moment, our core of a dozen worn out men, barely in their twenties, could decide to get up and leave. My biggest fear was coming home from a night away to find a room full of empty cots and a note explaining how they had enough of sitting in filthy clothing with barely enough food, no heat, no entertainment, nothing. Even if we had all those things I still wouldn't judge them if their shattered mental and emotional states sent them running back to civilization which was right across Jamaica Bay. No one would blame them. It is to their eternal credit that they stayed when most would have run.

"Seabass," said Marty, snapping me out of my deep thoughts, "I completely agree with what you did. Erin and John have been very helpful, not only to us, but to the community. But please, don't give out any more badges until you consult me first."

"Okay, I won't. I'm sorry I fucked up."

He accepted my apology with a laugh. Marty rarely gets mad, and that was the end of the issue, aside from him teasing me about it these days. After my tirade, I think he understood just how much of a toll this was taking on me. Between trying to keep everyone happy, managing the database of treated houses, and taking care of logistics, I was getting burned out. I had lost thirty pounds since the beginning of the storm and was sleeping, at most, three or four hours each night. Whenever anyone needed anything the answer was, "Ask Seabass." All day people came up to me with problems, both professional and personal. Now I know how moms feel!

This is not to say I didn't care. I really did want to help, but after a while I started stressing out about it, worried if I was giving good advice or doing the right thing. Phil Pillet once told me I was at the magic age: old enough to seem like I know a thing or two, and young enough to be approachable. No one expected a twenty-year-old to have any answers, and someone in their fifties wasn't easy to talk with. I was 35 years old when Sandy struck, and that made me everyone's unofficial older sibling. I had one girl ask me where she could get her feminine needs looked after! How the fuck do I know? But I sure as hell found out. Thank you, Siri.

* * *

While Marty and I were talking, Nick Pappas walked over to Gut 'n Pump to join a work crew. He called me the week prior, looking to volunteer at the firehouse after reading our story online. Nick packed up his truck and started the long 14-hour drive from Streamwood, Illinois, where he is a professional firefighter. Traffic wasn't bad as he drove through the night, arriving at the parking lot in front of our firehouse just after 3:00 A.M. He decided not to wake us and slept in his car. Even at night he could see the extensive damage our community had suffered. "It reminded me of the time I spent down south after Hurricane Katrina," said Nick. "The condition of the houses there were similar to what I saw driving into Breezy Point."

At dawn, Nick walked next door to Gut 'n Pump and met with Erin who assigned him to a crew of FDNY firefighters from the Bronx who were volunteering on their day off. His crew set out to gut and remove debris from several homes throughout Breezy Point, and one of a retired firefighter in Rockaway. "Everyone I met was fantastic. The homeowners were so grateful and gracious despite losing everything. We were there to help them and they were offering us what little they had left."

"One thing that stands out the most were the family members who lost loved ones on September 11th," said Nick. "A lot of the mementos and pictures from that person were gone. The ceremonial axes and casket liners from the funerals are irreplaceable. It was very sad. Ten years after 9/11 and they have to re-live the loss all over again." His sentiment echoed our own. Being a community of first responders, Breezy Point suffered the loss of many family, friends, and neighbors on September 11th. Those who didn't pay the ultimate price still carry all kinds of scars from that day. It's an indelible part of who we are. Even on the night of Hurricane Sandy, as we prepared to deploy on the Promenade, the location we chose to make our stand was at the home of a 9/11 widow. Nick understood that, and respected it.

Nick Pappas, a firefighter from Streamwood, Illinois, during one of his many visits to the Point Breeze firehouse.

We had a lot of groups come to volunteer during the recovery, but few individuals traveled so far and stayed with us as long as Nick Pappas. He traded shifts with guys in his fire department in the Chicago suburbs in order to spend weeks with us each visit. His easy-going attitude allowed him to seamlessly fit in with us, and his professional expertise and work ethic earned our respect. It wasn't uncommon to find Nick sitting on the engine deck at night working on our damaged equipment, or taking the guys into Brooklyn in his truck to get supplies. We were, and still are, lucky to have him as a friend and colleague.

★ ★ ★

During the afternoon I had a special visitor—three-star Chief Joseph Fox of the NYPD came to the firehouse. I received a call from his secretary alerting me to his visit and she explained that the Chief had heard a lot of great things about the work we were doing in Breezy Point. He wanted to see for himself and find out if there was anything we needed. Under most circumstances I would be a little concerned about a visit from such a high-ranking officer, especially since I hadn't showered or shaved in a few days and was still wearing my dirty FDNY pullover. However, these were not most circumstances, and I had met Chief Fox on a few prior occasions.

The most accurate comparison, and compliment, would be to say he's a lot like my fire department chief, Marty Ingram. Despite the authority his rank affords him, Chief Fox is approachable and shows genuine concern for the well-being of the men under his command. Years ago, as a newly minted police officer, I sat in an auditorium at Fort Hamilton in Brooklyn for orientation. We had many speakers telling us what our job would be like enforcing the law on the streets of Brooklyn. One of them was Chief Fox, the Borough Commander of Brooklyn South, which included the Impact Response Team (IRT) where I was assigned at that time. He warned us, "It goes by quick!" and of course he was right.

It was lightly raining when the Chief arrived. I was working with several NYPD Emergency Service Unit personnel to deploy a shipping container in our parking lot so we could securely store our supplies. We had just unloaded it from their truck when we noticed a man in a charcoal raincoat with stars on the collar and an eight-point hat watching us. We dropped what we were doing and headed over to introduce ourselves, which was unnecessary, as the Chief seemed to remember each of us from one prior meeting or another.

Not wanting to keep him in the rain, I gave Chief Fox a quick tour of the Point Breeze Volunteer Fire Department and Gut 'n Pump next door. He was impressed, and was able to see a number of teams return to our base after a long day of gutting and pumping. They were tired, of course, but proud to have helped. Next to me, the Chief looked very pleased as well. It was comforting to know a high ranking member of the department understood I was performing my assignment, to assist the recovery in Breezy Point, to the best of my ability.

* * *

That evening, just after all the work crews made their way back to the Point Breeze firehouse and Gut 'n Pump parking lots, Erica Pitzi, from WPIX 11 News, arrived. We were expecting her earlier, but she ran into traffic on the Belt Parkway and missed most of the volunteers in action. I found Phil and Kevin and we discussed the situation. On one hand it was getting dark and there wasn't much to film, but on the other we couldn't turn her away because the media was crucial for getting volunteers. I came up with a plan.

"How about we use my house?"

Phil looked at me, "I thought your house was already gutted and pumped weeks ago by the guys at your firehouse."

"Yeah," I replied. "It was."

"Are you sure about this?" he asked, realizing what I intended.

"What else are we gonna do?"

Kevin chimed in, "I'll drive the tools over. You meet us there."

I rode with Erica and her cameraman in their van to Essex Walk where Kevin was already waiting with the ATV full of tools. Phil gave me one more "are-you-sure-about-this" look before the tools were handed out. I took an axe, as did Jason, while Kevin, Erin, and Phil took sledgehammers and crowbars. As fate would have it, we actually found a wall in the basement near the stairs that needed to be removed. As fate would also have it, my parents were just coming back from a walk on the Promenade. They came in from Florida for moral support.

This was not the time, although my dad was sporting a bitch'n "Keep Calm and Rebuild Breezy Point" sweatshirt. The cameraman loved it.

Phil got on his knees and pointed out the black mold growing on the sheetrock for the camera. He used a razor to cut a foot above the still visible water line, then pried the wall away from the wooden studs using a crowbar. The process took ten minutes, and I could finally say my house was completely gutted and pumped. It was better than gutting my perfectly dry living room. The tools were collected and shipped back to base courtesy of Kevin and his red ATV, while Phil, Jason, Erin and I walked to the firehouse so Erica could get to her office and start putting her story together.

Walking back to the firehouse I couldn't help but notice the amount of light towers which had deployed over the weekend. You could hear their diesel motors humming throughout the neighborhood. The NYPD had done a tremendous job keeping the volunteer firehouses and Gut 'n Pump supplied with fuel and provided field maintenance for the light tower generators. Without their support we wouldn't have been able to keep going. Cops were everywhere too. A week ago I wouldn't have felt safe walking around alone after dark, even with my off-duty pistol. Things were different now. Patrol cars made their way down the Promenade while uniformed officers did foot patrols crisscrossing the neighborhood. Plain clothes cops were keeping the peace along Rockaway Point Boulevard. They would occasionally stop by the firehouse looking for Road Dog, and at first I thought he was in some kind of trouble. Turns out he made friends with a lot of them during his nightly garbage runs to Riis Park in his gator. They were checking up on him to make sure he was okay.

When I got back to the firehouse, members of the Disaster Medical Assistance Team (DMAT) were there to prick us with needles—specifically the Tetanus shots we needed. I was thoroughly checked out, especially my infected tooth and hands. Several doctors were available to write prescriptions, although the general medical consensus was we were walking wounded. Each of us had medical issues which, under normal circumstances, would result a visit to the doctor, some medicine, and a few days rest. Unfortunately, those were not realistic options at that time. Instead, we chased down our pills with what we had available and lay down on our filthy cots for another night of Duck Dynasty re-runs on the TiVo.

Inside the Point Breeze Volunteer Fire Department. At maximum capacity we could sleep more than twenty volunteers on cots spread throughout the building. Jackie and Clara graciously provided us with the Christmas tree pictured above. It was an important reminder of home and better days ahead.

CHAPTER 22

FRIENDS FROM AFAR

Saturday, December 1, 2012

In Elizabethton, Tennessee, seven firefighters loaded their gear into a white Ford van and began the 12-hour drive to Breezy Point. The van was a rental, paid for by donations by the local residents and businesses. A week prior, Captain Steve Murray was browsing through Facebook when he came across a story about the recovery efforts by the firefighters at Point Breeze. He and I spoke on the phone the following day and plans were made for a visit to the firehouse. Six other members of his squad volunteered for the trip during their days off: Sergeant David Shouse, engineers Howard McAninch and Tony Edwards, and firefighters Jeremiah Tolley, Dalton Williams and Jerry Smith.

"It was an opportunity to help," said David Shouse. "We saw the letter that Steve had seen on Facebook about how all of ya'll had been helping other people. The opportunity to help our brother firefighters when they're hurting and needing help made us want to do something. It was a blessing to me that I was able to get my feet on the ground up there and actually do something that made a difference to somebody."

While they were making the 630-mile trip to New York, we were dealing with a minor catastrophe. The food trucks, which had supplemented our already meager nutritional resources since the departure of Bobby Eustace and the failure of the Red Cross to deliver on their promise to take over food services, were gone. Suddenly the firehouses had over 2,000 hungry residents and volunteers looking for food. We had some leftovers from Jay Marcus's catering the day before, as well as our own stockpile, but that was quickly consumed. Before long I was back in Brooklyn with Unit 9 accompanied by Kelly Johnson and Nick Ecock, shopping at B.J.'s Wholesale Club. A thousand dollars later, the bed of the pickup was overflowing with bulk food items. We raced back to Breezy Point and I put Ecock in charge of cooking on the charcoal grill. The food I purchased that morning was bolstered by our dwindling stockpile in the Clubhouse, and throughout the day we served an estimated 300 people.

Nick Ecock and Julie Martin from AmeriCorps cook and serve meals for nearly 300 people in front of the Point Breeze Volunteer Fire Department.

At approximately 4:00 P.M., a house fire was reported in Roxbury on Hillside Avenue. Roxbury volunteers were first on the scene and beat the fire back before it could spread. We ran hose to assist alongside FDNY units, but thankfully it was not needed. One of the residents, in an attempt to stave off the cold weather, tried to use his storm-damaged fireplace and ended up lighting his wall on fire instead. As we rolled up our hose and loaded it into the rig, a giant dark blue Hydro-Quebec utility truck lumbered around the parking lot, looking for a way to get around all the fire apparatus.

"He's gonna hit something," predicted Kevin O'Brien, who was proven correct a minute later as the bucket on the roof of the truck became snared by an electrical line. We yelled for the driver to stop, but it was too late. Sparks showered the parking lot as the power line was torn from the transformer above. Firefighters scrambled to get out of the way of the live wires falling around us. Seconds later, the breakers kicked in and the power was cut off. I marched over to a knot of Canadian workers with Hydro-Quebec uniforms.

"What the fuck guys!" I shouted. "What's with your driver?"

Suddenly our bi-lingual friends from the north, some of who I heard speak English in an OEM meeting the day before, feigned not understanding a word I was saying. They muttered amongst themselves in French, apparently arguing over what to do next. I pressed their boss for answers but he kept up his masquerade and shrugged his shoulders as if he didn't comprehend. They drove away after leaving red warning streamers on the slackened power line. I found out later it was their last day and they didn't have time to fix the damage. Someone eventually repaired the wires, but the streamers are still there even to this day, and that power line, next to the Sugar Shack, continues to sag precariously low across the Roxbury parking lot.

We packed up our equipment and headed back to the firehouse. The Elizabethton firefighters arrived after 8:30 P.M. and we found available cots in the firehouse main room. Most of them had never been to New York City and since it was too late for gutting and pumping tonight, I encouraged them to take a drive and explore the city. David had never been north of Washington, D.C., and wanted to try New York pizza so I gave him directions to Lenny and John's Pizza on Flatbush Avenue. On the way, they visited FDNY Engine 309 and Ladder 159, dubbed "The Friendly Firehouse," based in Marine Park. David later told me, "We spent a few hours with the guys who were on duty that night and they were great. They welcomed us with open arms. Two calls came in while we were there, so we saw them dispatch and it was very impressive."

The next day they went over to Gut 'n Pump looking for work. In the words of David Shouse, "In the overall scheme of things it was a very small impact, but we made a very big difference in the lives of a few people there. It felt great to do that. There was plenty of equipment and good people to point us in the right direction and make sure we got to where we needed to be." One of those places was the Breezy Point Medical Center which was badly damaged during the storm. A makeshift triage area was set up by Rockaway Point Volunteer Fire Department in the interim. David, Steven and the rest of the Tennessee crew thoroughly gutted the moldy sheetrock before noon and returned to Erin at Gut 'n Pump looking for more work.

Along the way they added a retired NYPD police officer, Bill, into their group, and Cathy, a summertime resident. It came to Steve's attention that Cathy's elderly parents were moved to a nursing home after the storm. She was trying to save their house but was refused aid from FEMA because it wasn't her home and she had no power-of-attorney over her parents' estate. Discouraged, she had given up hope and decided to help other people instead. Steve would have none of it. The next day, moldy sheetrock was torn from the wall studs, piled into heavy duty garbage bags, and dragged to the end of Neptune Walk where Cathy's parents lived.

The volunteers from Elizabethton, Tennessee, in front of the Point Breeze Volunteer Fire Department before their departure. From left to right, Steve Murray, David Shouse, Jeremiah Tolley, Howard McAninich, Tony Edwards, Jerry Smith and Dalton Williams.

That same day, Steve led a separate group over to FDNY Chief William Mundy's house. During their travels they met the Chief, who told them several trees had fallen on his house in Rockaway. The

Elizabethton men, wielding chainsaws they had brought with them, made short work of the trees. Chief Mundy gave Steve his phone number and told him if they ever needed anything, just pick up the phone. In the words of Steve, "He was so grateful. Such a gentleman! I believe he was an SCBA (Self Contained Breathing Apparatus) expert for the New York Fire Department. He really knew his business."

* * *

The next day, while Steve and David led separate work crews to a half-dozen homes, the Terry Farrell Firefighter's Fund arrived with a much needed donation: a Ford fire engine from Congers Volunteer Fire Department in upstate New York. It was a donation Jackie Pool negotiated on our behalf. The additional fire truck was a much needed piece of equipment, one which gave us the option of getting our own custom-built rigs fixed by the manufacturer. We are very grateful to the Congers firefighters and the Terry Farrell Firefighter's Fund for their generous gift.

Kevin, Brillo and Nick Pappas immediately got to work familiarizing themselves with our new equipment. There were challenges, of course, the biggest being hose adapters. The FDNY uses a different threading for its hoses than the national standard, so any time an apparatus from elsewhere arrives, an adapter needs to be installed. The truck also lacked off-road capability, but we would make do. Nick was especially enthralled with our new truck. It was old, but clean and in good working order. Its sleek lines and polished exterior gave it a classic look which he liked very much.

CHAPTER 23

NOLA TIL YA DIE

Tuesday, December 4, 2012

They arrived at dusk. A caravan of vehicles passed through the main gate and onward to the Point Breeze Volunteer Fire Department lot where spaces had already been reserved. Several trucks, a Saab, trailers, and a giant Winnebago were nearing the end of their 1,350-mile journey, escorted by an NYPD Highway Patrol unit for the last leg of their 20-hour drive. The fleur-de-lis was proudly displayed on the sides of some vehicles, while Louisiana license plates adorned the bumpers. The only thing missing was a jazz band playing "When the Saints Go Marching In" as they parked. NOLA Til Ya Die had arrived to help out in Breezy Point.

When news of a massive hurricane heading for New York City reached Jeff Winn, a retired Captain in the New Orleans Police Department (NOPD), he called Artie Mattor, a retired NYPD police officer in Breezy Point. Artie and Jeff met in Las Vegas a year prior and quickly became friends. It happens all the time. Police officers around the world, much like their colleagues in the fire department, see other officers as their brethren. Artie heeded Jeff's warning to evacuate before Sandy hit, but his house on Courtney Lane where he was enjoying retirement with his wife, Irene, was a wreck.

Jeff contacted his good friend and founder of NOLA Til Ya Die, Kathleen "Kassy" McCall, to inquire about a trip to New York City. The plan was to help the police officers and firefighters, some who had come to their aid during Hurricane Katrina seven years earlier, to gut and pump their damaged homes. "First responders don't have the ability to go home," said Jeff. "You gotta stay on the job. We saw a lot of cops and firefighters who would put in a day's work then go home and start ripping out sheetrock. They were exhausted. A man could get killed doing that. New York cops came and saved our butts during Hurricane Katrina. We wanted to pay them back for all they had done for us."

Money was raised and donated items collected throughout the weeks following the storm until finally, in the early morning hours of December 3rd they were ready to depart. Eleven of them, all private volunteers, many meeting for the first time that morning, gathered in a parking lot in New Orleans. Jeff and Kathleen were joined by current and former police officers Daniel Swear, Josh Colcough, Lynn Fletcher, Warren Braii, Henry Kuhn and Scott Monaco. General contractor Paul Bel and Bryan Civello provided their expertise to oversee the gutting, and consult with homeowners who undoubtedly would have questions about rebuilding their flooded houses—something both had become experts in after Hurricane Katrina. Nick DiGiorgio, a chef, joined with local bartender, George "Taco" Medina, to provide catering services during the trip. All had lived through Hurricane Katrina. On their way, they picked up New Orleans native Becky Banks Gray in Virginia, bringing the total number of volunteers to twelve.

On the ride in they realized just how widespread the effects of Hurricane Sandy were. The Rockaways, from the western tip of Breezy Point to the eastern border of Nassau County has roughly the same population as the city of New Orleans. "The geographical area was massive!" said Jeff, "New Orleans is a medium-sized American city, and you guys were one neighborhood that had more people than our entire city. The magnitude of Hurricane Sandy really started to sink in, especially when you consider how many first responders live in that area, which could be devastating on its own. It was one of the major reasons we felt we had picked the right place to come help out."

When they arrived in Breezy Point, I was in the Clubhouse gathering some canned goods from our dwindling supply. Food, as always, was an issue. My reaction to our influx of volunteers from the Big Easy was to count the additional mouths to feed that night and consider if a trip to the supermarket and the consequential charges to my credit card were really necessary. What started out as providing for a dozen worn out firefighters had grown into an additional 40 AmeriCorps workers and 17 others staying over with us tonight. In my mind, the dozen additional volunteers from New Orleans meant we would be cooking dinner for 80 or more people, and we didn't have enough food on hand.

NOLA Til Ya Die. From left to right: Josh Colcough, Jeff Winn, Paul Bel, Lynn Fletcher, George Medina, Becky Banks Gray, Daniel Swear, Kathleen McCall and Warren Braii.

I was getting ready to take a trip to B.J.'s Wholesale when Jeff Winn first approached me. "Hey brother," he said with a distinct southern drawl, "I just want you to know you don't need to worry about us. We have everything we need. You guys have been through Hell. We've been where you're at now. Just wanted to let you know we're here for you, not vise versa."

I explained the food situation, and he walked me over to where Nick and George were setting up a kitchen near the Winnebago in our parking lot. When Jeff assured me our meals for the next few days were covered, he wasn't kidding. I mentioned earlier that Nick was a chef, and not the kind of chef that works the deep fryer at McDonalds. He was an actual chef who competes in cooking contests all over the southern United States. Down there cooking gumbo ranks just under going to Sunday church, and with the help of Taco and Becky, they cooked the best gumbo I've had in my entire life. They did it in a parking lot in the freezing cold with no resources besides what they brought from home.

From the start, Jeff, a Marine and SWAT team commander, insisted the group be not only self-sufficient, but able to feed the people who they were coming to assist. During the weeks leading up to their departure thousands of pounds of food, equipment, and supplies were gathered. "We had to be 100% self contained," said Jeff, "We had to have everything we needed and shouldn't have to ask anyone for anything. The motivator and biggest teacher was Hurricane Katrina. After all the things that happened to us and the things we learned in that situation, we knew not to put any pressure on you guys or your infrastructure. If we showed up with twelve guys and had to lean on you for food, water, shelter, medical…that takes away from your assets. That's something we knew we couldn't do."

While NOLA Til Ya Die was settling in at the Clubhouse, I was arranging something special for Nick Pappas and the men from Elizabethton who had worked so hard over the last few days. Most of them had never been to New York City, and all of them are die-hard firefighters. They were able to see the FDNY in action, which gave them a tremendous thrill. Tonight, however, on a more somber note, the Elizabethton firefighters wanted to pay their respects to their fallen brothers and sisters at Ground Zero before leaving in the morning for Tennessee. Unfortunately, the site was still under construction and closed to visitors.

I gave Steve Murray a phone number to call when they got near Ground Zero. I assured him they would at least get a chance to peek from the outside. When they arrived, however, they were escorted past the security gate and brought into the memorial itself. Nick Pappas and the Tennessee firefighters were expecting to say a short prayer for their fallen comrades outside the fence. Instead they were treated to a solemn, guided tour by the security guards at the memorial who had heard of all the good they had done in Breezy Point. "It was breathtaking," said Nick Pappas. "It was a once in a lifetime experience, especially since it was just the eight of us."

"When you set up the World Trade Center Memorial tour," said Steve Murray, "that was above and beyond anything we ever expected. I can't put into words how I felt, and still feel about it."

The next day, the Elizabethton firefighters departed for Tennessee, which freed up enough cots to move our NOLA friends from the Clubhouse to the firehouse. I found bunk space for two new additions as well, Lee and Eddy, both retired firefighters from Miami. NOLA Til Ya Die added Nick Pappas, Lee and Eddy to their roster and set out to pump, gut, remove appliances and debris, and spray mold-killing chemicals at a dozen homes in Breezy Point. Jeff led a group to the home of a retired FDNY firefighter on Beach 207th Street, while Bryan led another team to assist Artie Mattor at his house on Courtney Lane. When they were finished, two more homes were serviced, one of a Homeland Security Agent in Roxbury and another on Arcadia Walk.

The quality and efficiency of their work reflected their arduous experience from Hurricane Katrina. A reporter assigned to cover their story asked me how the volunteers from Louisiana compared to those from other parts of the country. I told her, "To use a military analogy, the everyday volunteers who come here are a hardworking mix of conscripts and experts. The ones from New Orleans, because of their experience with Katrina, are like Special Forces. They've been through this before and know what they're doing. We don't have to show them anything—on the contrary—they're teaching us. We've learned things from them we should have been doing all along."

Back at the firehouse, Nick and George had developed their own following as they passed on lessons learned about dealing with FEMA. It wasn't unusual to see them distributing advice along with hot food to the residents who stopped by for something to eat. After years of negotiating the many dead-ends and pitfalls of government paperwork, both had become experts at navigating the bureaucracy. For the residents who lost everything, it was comforting to have such knowledgeable people on hand to give honest answers about the process. One of them told me, "We saw the same problems we had with FEMA and government agencies during Katrina that you guys were having right then, and it pissed me off that the system still hadn't been fixed."

The NOLA Til Ya Die food tent. Nick DiGiorgio, George Medina and Becky Banks Gray served hundreds of hot meals per day to the hungry workers and residents in Breezy Point.

That night I spent some time with Jeff and really got to know him. He showed me a video on his laptop which was a collection of pictures of him and his SWAT team members pulling people out of the water, living and dead, during Katrina. I cannot imagine how differently things would have gone if we had to endure those horrors. Could we have pumped and gutted so many homes? How many volunteers would have shied away when it was possible to find a bloated corpse in each home? How many of our own firefighters would have kept going under those conditions?

Jeff is a tough man, but you can see the humility, compassion and desire in his heart to help those who can't help themselves. There are qualities about him which cannot be taught that make him a natural leader. When he arrived at our firehouse he brought an attitude and demeanor of a leader who wanted to take charge but not to take over. As we talked I realized, for the first time since the hurricane, I could let my guard down and relax for a while. "We were uniquely qualified because of what we went through during Katrina," explained Jeff, "and if we could give back to the first responders and the city that helped us when we needed it, then I felt we would really make a difference. I think people were also looking for emotional support, and it might sound strange, but it was therapeutic for us too. After the way Hurricane Katrina went down, we felt like we didn't have that opportunity to come to terms with what happened to us. We wanted to be there for other people to lean on because we knew what they were going through. It was good for us too."

Lean we did. When NOLA Til Ya Die arrived, I was inches from my brick wall. All the responsibilities I took on were crushing me. Some days I would drop everything for a few hours, go next door, and join a work crew just to take out my frustration on some moldy sheetrock. When I was done I'd come back to the firehouse and spend the rest of the day solving one problem after another. I spent hours each day on the phone, on the computer, or in front of a camera begging for help and organizing volunteers. That week alone I appeared in four newspapers on three different continents asking for donations and manpower. I know it probably sounds like fun, but after you've done it 40 or 50 times the novelty wears off. Each time I had to drop what I was doing, put on my game face, and make sure I didn't say anything stupid. I only kept at it because it yielded results.

"I could see it in your eyes. You were burnt out," said Kathleen McCall. "It was very clear you guys were close and supporting each other, but everyone seemed like they had hit their limit and were about to crack. That probably dictated how some of us behaved. We knew how important it was to laugh and talk about something different for a while. The food you were eating was terrible, but you seemed genuinely happy because by that point anything edible was a gift. I remember seeing you cook a cup of Ramen Noodles and eat it on the equipment table like it was a meal at a five-star restaurant. When you told me you were paying for a lot of the food out of your own pocket, my heart just broke."

Thankfully I found in Jeff someone who could take care of the more taxing concerns, such as food and equipment, and give me the break I needed to keep going. I needed to unwind. The next day, after NOLA Til Ya Die serviced another three homes, George started cooking and I started drinking the last of the top-shelf booze which had rescued from the Buckley's house. The food was excellent, and soon people from all over Breezy Point joined our feast. We had the usual AmeriCorps people from next door, but this time they brought their comrades who were quartered in other areas of Breezy Point. Of course Gut 'n Pump was there, and many of the NYPD personnel assigned to Breezy Point stopped by at one point or another. Even Pat Dempsey, who fought the fires alongside me during the night of Sandy, showed up with a few of our mutual friends.

We had a record crowd in the firehouse—probably 100 people between the main room and the engine deck. The liquor helped loosen tongues at therapeutic levels as personal dramas from the storm were retold. Our frustrations were vented to people who understood what we had been through. There was a lot of ball-breaking and a few tears about all the things we had experienced since the storm. At some point a donated American flag bikini, a Roman candle and a gator combined to make an interesting trip down Rockaway Point Boulevard to salute our brothers and sisters at the other fire departments. We desperately needed a night like that and woke up the following day with a little less accumulated anxiety and stress.

Despite the party last night, everyone was up early and ready to work. Jeff and Bryan led their teams to the homes of retired NYPD police officers on Roosevelt Walk and Bedford Avenue. Contractor Paul Bel did some consulting at homes which had been treated and ready to rebuild, sharing his invaluable advice from his experience reconstructing shattered homes in New Orleans after Katrina. While this was going on, I went to the daily morning IMT meeting with Kevin and Erin to discuss the inevitable conclusion of Gut 'n Pump. Tomorrow a large number of our 40 AmeriCorps volunteers were leaving, and after NOLA Til Ya Die, we had no significant long-term volunteers lined up. It was that way by design. All of us had to get back to our regular jobs.

Kevin broke the news to the New York State IMT leaders that morning. We agreed that one last big weekend was possible, then both Camp Rockne and Gut 'n Pump would cease operations. Any future mold remediation and the eventual rebuilding would go through Habitat for Humanity and Operation Blessing. After the meeting, the Point Breeze Volunteer Fire Department kept busy throughout the day responding to alarms from smoke detectors, an electrical fire, and a water main break near the Wedge.

Robert Fogarty, founder of the Dear World project, was setting up his cameras in the Wedge at the end of Gotham Walk. I had talked to Robert the week before when he called and expressed an interest in photographing some residents of Breezy Point. His Dear World campaign raises awareness and sends positives messages in the midst of dire situations, written on the very people involved. For example, he asked us to each think of a short message we would like to convey to the world about Hurricane Sandy and Breezy Point. Timmy Brennan, an ironworker at the Freedom Tower in lower Manhattan where the World Trade Center once stood, wrote on his arms, "The reason why we fall is so we can get back up again."

The night of the hurricane, Timmy used his paddleboard to rescue a dozen neighbors who were forced from their flooded homes by the approaching fire. He and a few others fought their way through the floodwaters, escorting the elderly and infirm to St. Thomas Moore Church, taking turns carrying children in their arms. His own house, along with most of Gotham Walk, burned down to its foundation during the massive conflagration which followed. Similar dramas played out all around Breezy Point and the Rockaways that night as neighbors risked their lives to save each other.

Tim Brennan poses for Robert Fogarty in front of the ruins of his burned-down home in the Wedge.

When the light had faded from the cold December sky we were treated to another excellent buffet courtesy of Nick, Taco and Becky. Once again we were joined by 100 other volunteers, residents and police officers at the firehouse. As the night wore on a familiar face, Judy from AmeriCorps, stopped by looking to collect some magazines she had lent to the guys before leaving in the morning. She carried a suitcase with her which had "Check-in, Check-out" in black lettering across it. Over the last month she had provided an invaluable library service for those of us living in a world of limited electricity and only a few working computers. Books were available, but tonight Judy was here to retrieve entertainment of a more adult nature. A cache of pornographic magazines had been uncovered during the gutting of a home. The owner of the home, being a smart man, feigned shock, and insisted he had no idea where they came from. Privately, however, with a wink, he admitted the magazines had served him well throughout the years. Under the watchful eye of his angry wife, he donated his collection to the volunteers in lieu of throwing them away. We were all too happy to have them.

Tomorrow was the end of AmeriCorps deployment and we were sad to see them go. Judy stayed for a bit in recognition of all the hard work AmeriCorps had provided over the previous weeks. More people trickled in from the Clubhouse next door throughout the night to say goodbye. AmeriCorps had done a terrific job clearing debris in the Rockaways then pumping and gutting homes in Breezy Point. When their services were originally offered to me weeks prior, I was wary about housing and feeding so many additional people, but in the end they were more than worth it.

On their last day, after two more homes were gutted, cleaned, and sprayed with mold killing chemicals, we took NOLA Til Ya Die on a tour of Breezy Point. We started at The Bay House at the north end of the Reid Avenue parking lot—the spot where John Paolillo and I sat the afternoon of the hurricane and watched the waves push the dock back and forth. As we predicted, the dock where I had spent many an evening fishing for fluke and bluefish was reduced to a twisted heap of pilings. It still remains in that condition today, one of the many reminders that we have a long way to go before all of Sandy's damage is repaired.

Next we travelled to the southern end of Reid Avenue where the Promenade begins. As we walked westward toward the Wedge our group passed dozens of houses caved in on themselves, their cinderblock foundations yielded to the crushing waves of the Atlantic Ocean. We paused at the concrete pad and pile of debris that was the Sugar Bowl, where Tim O'Brien Jr. his father, and I stopped the night of the storm. The sweeping beachfront view was unobstructed by protective dunes or brush, resulting in total destruction by the same beautiful blue waters only a hundred yards away.

A slight drizzle set the mood as we entered the Wedge near the end of Fulton Walk. I had told and re-told the story of that night to so many media organizations and curious onlookers it had become automatic, but this time was different. Over the last few days, I had become very comfortable around our friends from New Orleans and let my guard down. My emotions, normally suppressed, were suddenly and uncontrollably out there for all to see. My voice cracked and throat ached as I told them about that night. Details I had forgotten sprung into my mind as if I was watching scenes from an old movie of my childhood. I was rambling, but Kathleen McCall pulled Nick Pappas aside before he could interrupt and said, "Let him keep going. He needs to do this. Trust me."

Sebastian Danese, George Medina, Jeff Winn, and Paul Bel at the Wedge where the fire occurred.

She was right. Kathleen, Jeff, Paul and all the other NOLA Til Ya Die volunteers had been through this themselves. Throughout the previous weeks we had so many wonderful groups come to Breezy Point to help us out. They sympathized with our situation and we are eternally grateful for their support. Our friends from New Orleans, however, could empathize with us. They had seen their community flooded and destroyed, and had been through the long recovery process afterwards. That made our bond with them unique amongst all the amazing men and women who had come to our aid after Hurricane Sandy.

"It was déjà-vu," said Jeff Winn, "because we had been through this already. And, because we had, we had a better idea of what to do and how to help. I can't tell you enough how much that experience means. You're able to instantly make a connection with people who are going through the same things. It means you're able to help them, not just with fixing their homes, but with working on the emotional and psychological problems also because you've been there before."

Kathleen McCall added, "Not in my wildest dreams did I ever think we'd be dealing with people who had been through what we had. For us it was positive…a good thing that left us with a feeling of great accomplishment. We found we had comrades and many new friends in Breezy Point."

* * *

That next morning, NOLA Til Ya Die departed Breezy Point for their long journey home. During their time with us, we laughed and cried alongside our friends from The Big Easy. It was a cathartic experience for all of us. Personally, their visit allowed me a respite from many of the worries which were weighing me down. I unwound, and although I was still a wreck, I could at least muster enough strength to see this to the end. They had carried us along the last leg of our race to fix as many homes as possible before the winter set in. Now it was time to cross the finish line.

CHAPTER 24

STANDING DOWN

Sunday December 9, 2012

The unusually warm weather finally turned cold just in time for Operation Breezy Point Gut 'n Pump to finish its last weekend. Kevin had publicly made the announcement days earlier, asking for one last push from the volunteers who had already given so much. They did not disappoint. Arriving by the busloads, people from all over the country helped us treat the last of the houses which requested assistance. We sat through the last IMT meeting at the Breezy Point Catholic Club as Tom Wutz, the Incident Commander, went over the numbers.

Since the storm, Operation Blessing, Habitat for Humanity, Camp Rockne, the Point Breeze Volunteer Fire Department, and Operation Breezy Point Gut 'n Pump treated 1,766 of a possible 2,878 structures within the Breezy Point and Roxbury community. Of the remaining 659 untreated structures, 337 had been burned down or swept away by the Atlantic Ocean and were untreatable. An additional 322 structures were refused treatment by their owners, usually because they had flood insurance and were able to be treated by professional services. Only 32 of the 322 structures surveyed by the Disaster Assistance Response Teams (DART) were unaccounted for. This number exactly matched the number of estate homes in Breezy Point. That is, houses in legal contest which the civil courts have not declared a rightful owner.

Each house treated by the volunteers saved the homeowners, on average, $20,000 when compared to estimates given by the professional services. I had flood insurance, and was billed $4,500 for three days of generator rental alone. For that price I could have bought a light tower and fueled it for a month. Using the figures listed above, the estimated savings to the residents of Breezy Point is somewhere in the area of $35 million. Furthermore, all the donated equipment was given to residents who still needed work done, passing on more savings. Finally, both

Operation Blessing and Habitat for Humanity continued to work in Breezy Point after the grassroots organizations were gone. Habitat for Humanity still maintains a strong presence in Breezy Point today.

Gut 'n Pump in December 2012. By this time the grassroots organization had grown from a single blue pop-up tent to three military tents with generators and heaters.

* * *

After five weeks of faithful service, the trucks of Point Breeze Volunteer Fire Department, Sand Flea and Big Jack, were sent back to K.M.E. in Pennsylvania for much needed repairs. In their place, we used the two donated fire engines from Congers and Mount Vernon, courtesy of the Terry Farrell Firefighters Fund. Neither truck had off-road capability, so we would have to stretch lines from paved roads by hand, same as the FDNY. If a fire broke out in the Wedge or by Graham Place, where dozens of homes were smashed into each other, our inability to respond quickly would lead to another massive fire. Thankfully, that did not happen.

Jackie called me with the news that fourteen members of the Point Breeze Volunteer Fire Department had been selected to attend the 12/12/12 Concert for Sandy Relief at Madison Square Garden. Five volunteers from Friends of Firefighters and Gut 'n Pump were chosen as well. It was her final contribution to our department. Although there are pitfalls when dealing with the media, she did a good job spreading the word about our plight, gathering donations and attracting volunteers. Having a public relations professional made a big difference and she has our gratitude and thanks for volunteering her time.

* * *

That night the Point Breeze firefighters joined the members of Gut 'n Pump for one last round of drinks in front of the bonfire. We had every reason in the world to celebrate. The volunteer mold remediation operation was a smashing success. What started as a bunch of waterlogged firefighters trying to help their neighbors escalated to the massive grassroots machine which grew by orders of magnitude before our very eyes. Everyone laughed as we told stories about a man showing up at our firehouse with a blue popup tent asking to borrow a table and some chairs. Tonight, three huge military tents, two massive generators, four port-a-potties, one ATV, two gators, and three large boxes of tools bore mute testament to Gut 'n Pump's explosive growth. In our wildest dreams we would never have thought Kevin, Erin and Phil's ambition to help the residents of Breezy Point would accomplish so much.

For our efforts, Kevin Adams and I agreed we had the right to start a barrel fire, ride an ATV, or pitch a tent anywhere in Breezy Point from this day forward. The consensus was we had earned it. There was also talk of a Gut 'n Pump float for the Mardi Gras parade this coming summer. We laughed as ideas were presented and critiqued. Secretly, however, all of us were wondering if there would be a parade at all next year. After the storm, some residents had talked about giving up on our beach community and moving elsewhere. Two back-to-back hurricanes, Irene and Sandy, and the damage they caused was enough to discourage some of our neighbors from living so close to the water.

We were facing tough times ahead. However, as I looked at those around me, as we warmed ourselves around our last bonfire together, I knew they were feeling the same way. Sandy didn't beat us. Houses can be rebuilt and infrastructure replaced. Most importantly, thanks to the bravery of those who stayed behind the night of Hurricane Sandy to help their neighbors, we would rebuild atop burned down and flooded houses, but not a graveyard. We were going to keep calm and carry on, because living among our neighbors in Rockaway and Breezy Point is worth the risk of Mother Nature's occasional wrath. Rebuilding would be difficult, but because of all that we accomplished during the previous weeks, the future of our community was no longer uncertain.

My girlfriend held my hand as we sat in a beach chair we had dragged from a nearby garbage pile. We had a reason to celebrate as well. Thanks to volunteers from Vermont and NOLA Til Ya Die there was hope that the repairs to her house weren't going to be as costly as we once feared. She sat on my lap with my arms around her as our feet were warmed by the fire, wondering what the future held for us. This time I was smart enough not to make her beg me to leave so we could have some time alone. We quietly said goodbye to the people who had been such a significant part of our lives for the last five weeks and headed to Howard Beach. For the first time since the storm I had nowhere to be in the morning, and we planned on taking full advantage of that.

CHAPTER 25

A NIGHT AT THE GARDEN

Wednesday, December 12, 2012

We were chauffeured through the city in a van generously donated by Friends of Firefighters. It was driven by Nancy Carbone, leader of that amazing organization, who went above and beyond all expectations after the storm. Security escorted us inside Madison Square Garden where we marveled at the stars who greeted us as we enjoyed refreshments backstage. In a reversal of roles, celebrities sought out us to shake our hands and take pictures with us. We met television and movie stars, famous athletes, musicians and artists from every genre and walk of life.

As the concert began we took our seats, surrounded by other first responders lucky enough to be invited. The music, of course, was amazing! When some of us went to get a bite to eat on the concourse I heard someone calling my name.

"Sebastian! Hey! Sebastian!"

I turned around and saw Steve Buscemi, who was so supportive during the recovery. Police officers have a saying for guys who go above and beyond for other cops; guys who you can count on to do the right thing. Cops say, "He's a real gentleman." For us it's the ultimate sign of respect you can give to a comrade. Steve is a real gentleman. We just had lunch two days prior in Chief Maynes' office, the Queens Borough Commander for the FDNY, with him, Kevin, Phil, Erin and Nancy. He's down to earth and never forgot his brothers on the front lines. Even so, I was shocked, and more than a little flattered, that he remembered me. He gave me a hug, shook all of our hands, then left to find Kevin, Phil, Bob and Jason with whom he was seated.

When we returned to our seats Marty told us they might put a camera on us and to look sharp. Not long after Christoph Waltz, Jamie

Foxx and Quentin Tarantino introduced us and we received a standing ovation from the crowd at The Garden. Near the end of the show we were asked to follow one of the concert coordinators backstage along with a lot of the other first responders. More celebrities were answering phones and taking pictures along the way. We were joined by the Greybeards, a volunteer group of retirees who moved mountains to help the Rockaways. All of us were herded throughout a maze of hallways until we were behind the stage. Rumors had circulated about a few of us going out there, but as it happened, all of us went.

Chief Marty Ingram (right), Mike Scotko, Tim Dufficy, Rick Savage, and Sebastian Danese during our standing ovation at the 12/12/12 Concert for Hurricane Sandy Relief

* * *

Forty-four days after Sandy, fourteen firefighters who fought alongside each other the night of the storm, stood beside one another once again, on stage at Madison Square Garden. Paul McCartney was in front of us, finishing "Live and Let Die" to a sold out crowd. A salvo of fireworks erupted as we joined him with Alicia Keys to close out the show, appropriately, to her rendition of "Empire State of Mind." Blake Lively gave me, Brillo and Kieran a kiss on the cheek and escorted us out. Joe Drennan dropped all pretense of decorum and gave Paul McCartney a bear hug.

Marty and Pat Dempsey shook hands with Paul. Just before going on stage, Marty learned Paul McCartney's father, James, was a volunteer firefighter in London during World War II. James McCartney missed the birth of his son while dousing flames caused by German bombs during The Blitz in June, 1942. As Marty shook Paul's hand, he presented him a Chief's coin from the Point Breeze Volunteer Fire Department and said, "I'm sure your father would appreciate this. Take it, with our thanks, on behalf of all the Sandy survivors." Paul was stunned, and threw his arms around Marty and Pat as they all sang together to close out the show.

We were honored guests on the most famous stage in the world at the biggest concert in history. One out of four families in the United States tuned in. More than a quarter of a million contributors from 90 countries donated $50 million in disaster relief.

It was surreal culmination of our extraordinary ordeal.

EPILOGUE

NO HOLLYWOOD ENDING

Present Day

The bulldozers I watched with morbid fascination on the first day of writing this book have long since disappeared from Essex Walk. None of the houses torn from my block have been replaced; one third of my walk is occupied by empty sand lots. Promises made during the heady days of Hurricane Sandy died alongside the media coverage, as the press left to cover other disasters in different parts of the world. Some of my neighbors wanted to rebuild but couldn't endure the haggling over permits and incessant delays by their insurance companies. Many residents called it quits when the system made victims of them a second time. I don't blame them.

I feel it would be a great disservice to the men and women who sacrificed so much during Sandy to give this book a Hollywood ending, so you won't find one here. I think it's important for readers, especially the first responders who may have to someday experience what we went through, to understand that's not the way the world works. This is not a John Wayne movie. In reality the hero and the lady at his side do not ride off into the sunset and live happily ever after. That's something storytellers concocted to give the audience closure so they can feel confident that it all works out in the end.

The truth is, the volunteers and residents who stayed in Breezy Point throughout Hurricane Sandy and the recovery were shell-shocked and continue to struggle to this day. The invisible injuries—wounds that leave no physical mark, but scar the heart and soul—took their toll. Nerves were shattered. Anxiety and depression set in for some. The smart ones got professional help and the young ones bounced back quickly, but too many others turned to vices in order to get by. Relationships were tested; some fell apart. Mine was no exception.

Our mission to protect and rebuild Breezy Point didn't end on stage at Madison Square Garden, although it heralded the closure of that phase of the recovery. The firehouse stayed ready and manned 24 hours a day for the next several months. The FDNY usually deploys their Incident Management Teams for fifteen days before exhaustion and stress start to noticeably erode their ability to function effectively. The longest deployment of an IMT since the adoption of the system after September 11th is 35 days, from November 24th to December 28th during Hurricane Sandy. Many of our members, myself included, spent double or triple that amount of time helping hold things together at the firehouse. As we wore out, it wasn't uncommon to find a member crying to himself or looking off into the distance with a thousand yard stare. There is no shame in that; everyone breaks down eventually. We are only human, and this wouldn't be a very interesting story if we weren't. How you build yourself back up afterwards is what matters most. The members of Point Breeze were there for each other, as we had been during the storm, and are now stronger than ever.

Despite the mounting challenges we faced, all of the volunteer fire departments in Breezy Point held their respective Christmas parties for the local children that year. At the Point Breeze Volunteer Fire Department we were fortunate to have a former volunteer firefighter, Cliff Falman, call me and offer to be a liaison between us and the tourism board for the island of Aruba where he spends much of his time. Thanks to Cliff's hard work, Aruba donated a truckload of toys for our party. We even received a guest appearance from one of the American Idol contestants to sing Christmas carols. On Christmas day, Nicholas Ecock, Road Dog and I celebrated the holiday in the firehouse eating food leftover from the kid's Christmas party two days before, ready to answer calls for help within our community.

Our neighbors in the next lot over closed up shop, as did Camp Rockne at Reid Avenue, in mid-December. The men and women of AmeriCorps who were living in the Point Breeze Clubhouse had also left to go back home after a nearly two-month deployment. The volunteers at Operation Blessing left in February 2013, having contributed a staggering amount of supplies, equipment, and technical support. James Killoran, leader of Habitat for Humanity (Westchester), is still in Breezy Point rebuilding houses. If you have time, he's always looking for volunteers.

The day after Christmas, Road Dog stumbled upon a blue-gray finback whale which had beached itself on the bayside near Camp Duff. We used the pumps donated to us by the United States Marine Corps months earlier to spray seawater on the stranded animal for two days. Sadly, our attempts to alter its fate were in vain. Once again, Breezy Point was front page news as the city held watched with curiosity; anxious to see if we could pull off another miracle. Unfortunately, the hapless finback whale succumbed to the crushing forces of its own weight on the third day. It's buried in an unmarked grave in the dunes past the lighthouse along the bay.

Nick Ecock and other Point Breeze Volunteer Fire Department firefighters pour seawater on the stranded whale.

Chief Marty Ingram, having reached his term limit as leader of the Point Breeze Volunteer Fire Department, was succeeded by John 'Tiny' Fahy in 2013. Marty received several awards for his leadership during

Hurricane Sandy, including being made an honorary FDNY Battalion Chief and the New York State Fire Chief of the Year. Supported by his officers Mike Scotko, Kevin O'Brien, Kevin Hernandez and Mike Scannell, Chief Fahy faithfully continues to reconstitute the fire department and oversaw much of its reconstruction. We are ready, now more than ever, to handle whatever the future may bring.

Captain Michael Valentine, Lieutenants James Morton and Brandon Reilly, and Firefighters Mike Kahlau and Brian Doyle from Rockaway Point Volunteer Fire Department were honored to receive the "Higgins & Langley Memorial Award in Swiftwater Rescue" for their sortie into the storm the night of Hurricane Sandy. The award recognizes teamwork and preparedness during extreme conditions—criteria they certainly met. They are credited with saving 25 lives during their mission.

All of the Rockaway Point, Roxbury, and Point Breeze volunteer firefighters who fought the fire that night were given the "Firemark Award" from Liberty Mutual. The citation reads: "Recognizing an outstanding act of valor done selflessly and without due regard for personal safety." Together, the three volunteer firehouses rescued almost 100 stranded residents of Breezy Point and Roxbury and fought one of the largest residential fires in New York City history without the loss of a single human life.

FDNY firefighters Kevin Adams and Bobby Eustace were assigned to the New York City Fire Department's elite Incident Management Team with Phil Pillet. Erin Concoran-Daly returned to her job as a prosecutor in Florida, while Jason Fernald and Bob Gibbons resumed their lives in New York and Pennsylvania, respectively. In April, 2013, Jason and Bob were reunited with Kevin, Erin and Phil in Washington, D.C. as they received the "Champions of Change" award at the White House.

Road Dog stayed in Breezy Point for a few months doing odd jobs, but left to find work elsewhere. He was nearly killed when the tent he was living in was caught by a gust of wind, sailed into a nearby house, and was tangled in the power lines. I like to imagine he's out there somewhere helping other people the way he did for us. If your town needs help, and if you can find him, look for a gentle giant riding a motorcycle with a NOLA Til Ya Die sticker on his helmet.

Nick Pappas continues to travel from Chicago to Breezy Point whenever he has time off and was made an honorary Point Breeze firefighter for his invaluable service and dedication. He helped rebuild the firehouse after Sandy, participated in some of our charity events, and has responded to many runs within the community. You can find Nick marching alongside us in the Rockaway St. Patrick's Day parade in March, as well as at Breezy Point and Roxbury Mardi Gras over Labor Day weekend.

Kathleen McCall and Paul Bel from NOLA Til Ya Die returned in January to organize another trip and give advice to residents looking to rebuild. Some of us stay in touch with our brothers (and sisters) in New Orleans. Together we continue to rebuild our storm-shattered neighborhoods. I've talked to Jeff and Kathleen about the future of NOLA Til Ya Die, and agreed if another disaster like Hurricane Sandy or Katrina strikes somewhere in the United States I'll be willing to join them to help the unfortunate victims with whom we can empathize.

Friends of Firefighters, ably lead by Nancy Carbone at its helm, is still providing support for the brave men and women of the FDNY. She still has the invaluable assistance of Karen Donnelly, and Lieutenants John Nolan and Chris Love. "When I tell my friends in the Bronx about what happened in Breezy Point they don't believe me," said Karen, "Thousands of volunteers showed up, and kept showing up. They did some pretty dirty jobs, like crawling under houses to rip out moldy insulation that had been festering for weeks. It was truly amazing!"

* * *

I returned to work at the 63rd Precinct in mid-December and rejoined my friends on the Conditions Team. There was no official department recognition for the off-duty police officers from Breezy Point who risked so much to keep their community safe, and that is okay with me. That was never our motivation. I'm eternally grateful to the NYPD and the powers that be who assigned me to Breezy Point to oversee the recovery. Without their generous support, most of my accomplishments during the storm would not have been possible. I quietly slipped back into my command and picked up where I had left off the weekend before Hurricane Sandy. In the words of my Sergeant, "My little vacation on the beach was over and now it was time to get back to work."

It felt good to resume my professional routine and 2013 was my best year in the police department yet. However, in all other aspects of my life I had a very tough time. I was emotionally, psychologically and physically exhausted. In addition, I had spent more than $10,000 of my own money keeping things going at the firehouse which could have been used fixing my home. Finally, while walking across Flatbush Avenue to get breakfast with my girlfriend, I was struck by a drunk driver who was on his way to the Kings Plaza Mall. Thankfully I was not seriously injured, but I took it as a sign to slow down. I had pushed my luck too far.

I resigned my commission as Captain of the Point Breeze Volunteer Fire Department in March 2013 and took a hiatus from the firehouse. It took me a long time to completely decompress after the months of intensity during the post-hurricane recovery. That brick wall which I had been pushing further and further down the road finally caught up with me and closed in from all sides. Unfortunately, like many others in communities who suffered Hurricane Sandy's wrath, the stress of rebuilding and moving on afterward strained my relationship with my girlfriend. While we were able to repair my home and hers, I lost someone infinitely more important in the process.

You see, this story is not just about hope and heroes, bravery and sacrifice. This is also a warning about the consequences and after-effects of living through an event like Hurricane Sandy. In my eagerness to help, I allowed the accumulated stress, anxiety, attention and fame which followed in the storm's wake to get to me. I kept taking on more responsibility, well past the point when I should have known enough was enough. My intentions were good, so I tried to be tough and I bottled it all up, not realizing I was poisoning myself in the process. Consequently I wasn't as good of a friend, boyfriend, brother, son, or co-worker as I should have been for a long time after the storm had passed. I was a hero to strangers, but an asshole to those closest to me.

My whole life I believed real men don't cry or talk about their feelings. That's bullshit. Real men do what they have to do for their families and loved ones, even if that means opening up and talking your way through the emotional intricacies of the traumatic event you experienced. It's okay to be sad, scared and worried about the future. That doesn't make you weak or crazy; it makes you human. A lot of time went by before I realized that, and when I did it was too late. By then, when I had finally hit rock bottom, my relationship—forged in the fires and floods of Hurricane Sandy with the woman I thought I would spend the rest of my life with—was over. Whenever I think of her these days, I prefer to remember the brave, passionate girl who stood by my side and loved me unconditionally as we faced the storm together. Wherever she is, whatever she's doing, I hope she finds the happiness she deserves.

I am not sharing this for sympathy or pity. I'm putting my feelings out there for other first responders and their families who might read this book and find themselves in a similar situation. It's a lesson Jeff Winn was trying to teach me because he had been through the same after Hurricane Katrina. He recognized what I was going through and real empathy developed between us, but I wasn't ready to listen to him. He was trying to tell me that ignoring the traumatic emotional and psychological consequences of the disaster you are dealing with does not make any more sense than ignoring the disaster itself and it will cost you in the long run. I learned that the hard way, and so did Jeff during Hurricane Katrina. We both hope others won't have to.

* * *

The Battle for Breezy Point continues, although it's simmered down to a cold war between the residents who lost everything, the various government agencies who go back and forth about how to proceed next, and the insurance companies who continuously refuse to honor their commitments. In the interim, our neighborhood is littered with empty sand lots where houses once stood. Though the fire zone in the Wedge has made significant progress, far too many homes are still conspicuously absent.

Thankfully, all three volunteer firehouses have been repaired, with alterations that reflect our experience with Sandy. Regularly scheduled drills are carried out, incorporating the lessons learned during the hurricane. Many of the members are seasoned veterans, ready to accept whatever challenge fate decides to confront us with next. All are welcome to come by for a visit and see what we do. You would be surprised at the familiar faces. We are your next door neighbors, that guy who fixes your hot water heater, and the kid that bags groceries at the local store. We are paramedics, police officers, firefighters, soldiers, garbage men and regular people from all walks of life. We stayed during Hurricane Irene, we didn't back down during Hurricane Sandy, and we'll continue to be there for the people of Breezy Point every time you need us.

We're your local volunteer fire department.

You can count on us, whatever the cost.

We got your back.

Photo Credits

Sebastian Danese
Pg 18, 22, 41, 44, 84, 93, 150, 159, 200, 213, 226, 246

The Point Breeze Volunteer Fire Department
Pg 24, 81

Operation Breezy Point Gut 'n Pump
Pg 188, 201

Todd Maisel, The New York Daily News
Pg 67, front cover, back cover

Robert Fogarty, Dear World
Pg 240

Operation Blessing
Pg 163

The Robin Hood Foundation, 12/12/12
Pg 250

Kathleen A McCall, NOLA Til Ya Die, LLC
Pg 233, 236, 242

Lance Corporal Scott Whiting, USMC
Pg 140

Stacie Mark
Pg 108

Rocky Baldino
Pg 155

Meredith Erickson
Pg 184

The Road Dog
Pg 255

David Shouse
Pg 223, 228

Dana Daniels
Pg 210

Nick Pappas
Pg 219

Volunteer Fire Departments

A portion of the proceeds from this book will be donated to the three firehouse listed below. If you would like to make a charitable contribution, please consider the following volunteer fire departments and organizations.

Point Breeze Volunteer Fire Department
1 Fireman's Plaza
Breezy Point, NY 11697
(718) 634-7967
www.facebook.com/PointBreezeVFD

Rockaway Point Volunteer Fire Department
20426 Rockaway Point Boulevard
Breezy Point, NY 11697
(718) 474-2593
www.facebook.com/RPVFD

Roxbury Volunteer Fire Department
42 State Road
Breezy Point, NY 11697
(718) 474-9382
www.facebook.com/Breezypoint.RVF

Volunteer Organizations

Operation Blessing
P.O. Box 2636
Virginia Beach, VA 23450
(800) 730-2537
www.ob.org

Habitat for Humanity (Westchester)
524 Main Street
New Rochelle, NY 10801
(914) 636-8335
www.habitatwc.org

Friends of Firefighters
199 Van Brunt Street
Brooklyn, NY 11231
(718) 643-0980
www.friendsoffirefighters.org

NOLA Til Ya Die
P.O. Box 791672
New Orleans, LA 70179
(504) 345-9504
www.nolatilyadie.com

Made in the USA
Coppell, TX
08 May 2023